Cycle of Life

by

Peter "Pirata" Illetschko

Thank you,
To all the authors, who inspire us to read.
To my family, who taught me the joy of travel.
To Mestre Acordeón, for the audacity.

DEAR FELLOW
BICYCLE NOMAD!
YOU WILL RECOGNIZE MANY
THINGS IN THIS HERE LITTLE ADVENTURE
STORY! I HOPE YOU WILL ENJOY!

KEEP ON RIDING!

PETER

TUCSON 02/2020

Chapters

Part I

Part II

Part I

Don't Turn Around

Date: Early October 2013
Location: Somewhere in Baja California

The road in front of me floats straight to the horizon. The air above it ripples in the afternoon heat. All I see around me is brush, cacti, and eroded rocks. For days now, the landscape has been unchanged. It offers as little hope as the dead cows and skeletons next to the road.

This is an empty place. You can feel it in the stillness of the air.

Only one companion follows the traveler here: the buzzard. With his ugly beak and rotten smell, he reminds me of the countless Karl May books I read as a kid growing up in Austria; of cowboys lost in Llano Estacado and Bedouins kneeling next to their dying camels in the dunes of Arabia.

When I see the shadows of the carrion birds circling on the ground around me I shake my fists at the bleached sky and yell, only half in jest, "Not today, Motherfuckers. Today you won't recycle me. My organs are for science."

They make you wonder if you are slowing down. Are they waiting for you to draw your last breath? But when I stop to drink, and look for my group, I realize that I have been going faster than I thought. I am alone, and, as far as I can tell, the only person alive in a ten-mile radius of pure, harsh empty. The thought leaves me ecstatic. I want to measure myself against this uncaring brutality.

I am on a bicycle, and I am headed to Brazil.

After the short break, I step back into my pedals and sing my traveling song *Reise nach Afrika* (Journey to Africa), a folksy 70s tune about a bicycle journey to Africa by Austrian artist Arik Brauer.

Fohr weg min Radl
Drah mi ned um
I fohr weg min Radl
Und drah mi nimma um

This translates roughly to, "I ride away on my bicycle, without turning around." To any nomad this, of course, carries many meanings. To me personally, the words epitomize both a yearning for the open road and the need to be unattached from one's past. If you are seeking what's ahead of you, you can't keep turning around to look at what you left behind.

Well, behind me lies California and ahead of me await more than a thousand miles of desert - all the way to La Paz at the bottom tip of Baja California. Heat will be the only certainty for the next six weeks. The lack of water around me could not make this any clearer.

Baja California is not home to a rolling sand dune desert like the Sahara where an unaided human is obviously dead in a couple of days. This desert gives you the illusion that you might be able to make it if you had to. Don't believe it; you better carry everything you need. Google or Facebook won't work either. On a bicycle it takes days to reach the next village. This is the home of tarantulas, scorpions, and snakes.

I don't remember how many days it has been since we left Tijuana, days that started to meld into one another almost immediately after the border-crossing from the United States. No schedule, no plan, and little variation in the simple yet attractive scenery tricked my mind, stretching time into a continuum of tranquil

#suffering

Rightfully, you ask how does a hitherto constant nomad, who has, after fifteen years, four continents and too many countries to count, finally settled down in a city he actually likes, even with a job his mom approves of - decide to sit his rickety behind on a bicycle and ride halfway around the world with ten lunatic martial artists he has never met before?

Well, not very carefully. I can tell you that much.

Shift

Date: August 2013

Location: Slightly Rainy Seattle, Old Rainier Brewery

It turns out that the first day of my new life was August 2ⁿᵈ, 2013. Throughout the previous five years in Seattle, I had, like a well-balanced little cog in the machine, kept on going to my Release Manager job at Microsoft even though it had become stale like day old kale.

Now, working at Microsoft is awesome, even if you are chasing a carrot on a blinged-out rodent treadmill, and especially, if you are a driven kind of guy. You want action? Go to the *War Room*, the meeting of the major stakeholders during the final months of a software release. As opposed to Stanley Kubrik's film *Dr. Strangelove* nobody at Microsoft will deny fighting in the War Room. Fighting will happen. F-bombs will drop.

One fine day in that blighted room in late July, Harry, Director of Development for a 2000-person team that was building the Windows Phone, ripped someone a new one, "I don't give a shit how you do it. But you better fucking build me the fucking system to test these fucking phones *before* I am supposed to god-damn ship them."

Harry was the only guy in a room full of geniuses, I counted 9 Microsoft Partners, who didn't use a laptop and still knew everything about every issue that came up. I was glad that it wasn't me sitting pretty in his crosshairs.

So he turned around and said, "German guy, I mean, Austrian, I hope you have better news for me."

I said, "Get into my chopper, Harry."

Harry, "How many bugs are you bringing? Are you going to break my fucking build again?"

"No Harry, I have two code defects for you. They may as well have been tested by god."

He stared at me with his blue steel for three seconds. Three seconds is a long time in a room full of hotshots waiting for someone else to be the bigger fool.

But I held his gaze. I simply had to, because the truth was, I was bringing 5000 linguistic defects, any of which could break his *fucking* build because one of the less detailed oriented languages went over a character limit. Of course, if I had revealed that to Harry, he would have told me to go fuck myself and Microsoft's attempt to kill the i-droid-phones would have shipped in one country instead of fifty.

Harry and I did the high noon thing a bit longer and then he decided to fry bigger fish. The build didn't break.

As strange as it may sound, this job still became routine for me. We all know the feeling of running on auto pilot. Don't feel bad Microsoft, it's not you, it's me.

What kept me sane during that time? Capoeira, the Brazilian martial art, developed by Afro-Brazilians during the Portuguese occupation of South America. Capoeira's history carries instructive lessons for all of humanity, but when I started, I only cared about the physicality of it. By that I mean that Capoeira is really hard.

Every night I trained for hours trying to transform my body from a slow and steady Austrian mountain creature into an explosive dance-fighting machine (LOL, anyone?). Every night I got to blow off corporate steam.

And though it seems obvious, I want to very clearly state from the outset that a white boy from Vienna, Austria, working at Microsoft no less, has not even close to an inkling of an idea what it means to be a slave, a person of color, or a woman. Let's get that appropriation thing out of the way, right away, shall we. This does not mean that I should not engage in activities which further equality amongst all of us over-imaginative bipeds.

No matter my privileged roots, constantly having meetings in which you are walking a tightrope between being a rock star or being fired on the spot wears you out. This particular time it was tough because everybody at Microsoft knew that not having a horse in the cell phone race was like being Apple in the 1990s - it sucks so bad that you start making advertisements depicting your competition as Nazis while your hero is a sexy Arian in short shorts. Which can really only make sense in these fantastical US of A.

Nobody at Microsoft was looking forward to that, and so we tworked our little tushies off like there was no brave, new, button-free phone world out there already.

After spending the summer months fending off more or less geographically mal-adapted, yet somehow well-meaning insults, I mean, inquiries from Harry in the War Room you can imagine I was excited to get a chance to blow of some corporate steam for four days straight when my Capoeira group participated in a local Capoeira event on the first weekend of August. For you who have not yet witnessed a Capoeira Batizado: just imagine a bunch of people doing some kind of super-athletic yoga, fight-dance combo workout. In tight, white pants.

There you go.

Towards the end of the event, I took my first ever workshop with Mestre Acordeon, fabled grand-master martial artist, sage of life and philosophy, and Capoeira pioneer in the USA. I could spend pages describing this real life *Most Interesting Man Alive*, and the glory and history of the mythic origins of our art, but this is a travel book. Travel books have pictures, which apparently say more than a thousand words.

This one does the job nicely.

Here he carries an Atabaqué, the drum traditionally used in Capoeira. I don't think he does it on purpose, the Zeus thing.

After sharing his wisdom, I mean, kicking our ass for two hours, Mestre Acordeon gave a talk.

He said, "Maybe you have heard about my little project already, but some of my friends and I will ride our bicycles all the way from California to Brazil. We will leave Berkeley in four weeks."

I was one of the ones who had heard of this foolhardy idea, and, in all honesty, had been completely infatuated with it. It was my perfect corporate parachute: no stocks or gold plated Bentleys for me, please. Give me suffering and a cultural immersion program any day of the week instead. I even knew a Capoeira buddy (Bebum) from Utah who was going with Mestre.

"The project is called B2B – Berkeley to Bahia - We will ride over 12,000 miles all the way to Salvador de Bahia, my home and that of Capoeira", Mestre said with a cheeky smile.

People listening looked like they were in shock and awe at the idea of this somewhat paunchy Santa Claus riding his bicycle to Brazil. It is one thing to dance-fight your way to glory, but riding bike for a year puts you in another, rather singular, category of *Humans are Awesome*.

Berkeley to Bahia, such a romantic sounding name, one that, like the Orient Express, invokes extreme wanderlust and dreams of exotic lands. It's just that, you know, when you are on a bicycle instead of in a swanky mid-century train, you are in for bucket showers instead of buckets of oysters.

Mestre continued," We want to discover the impact of Capoeira on the Americas. We will shoot a documentary, produce a music CD, and write a book about our adventure. The proceeds from this multi-media project are dedicated to Projéto Kirimuré, our children's charity in Salvador, Bahia."

To me, the foolhardy idea started to sound more intelligent by the minute.

Then Mestre Acordeon smiled, paused, and said, "And if you want to join us for some time, ride with us for a few weeks in California… just get your bike and come along."

- Shift -

My mind went blank.

Then I have this very distinct memory of thinking: *Mestre just invited me to ride to Brazil with him.*

Pop went the travel weasel with the vengeance of a caged tiger on a yoghurt diet. You know when someone talks about an out of body experience? My outer body was stellar -- floating next to Alpha Centauri.

Yes, I am going to Brazil. I don't have a bike. Capoeira! I can't leave my job because we are about to ship Windows Blue. He didn't say go all the way. Fuck, my parents are coming to visit. What about my car? What about my apartment? What about her?

I must have walked over to Mestre while I was thinking all that negative crap because next thing I knew I was shaking his hand and saying, "Salve Mestre, my name is Pirata, I train with Professor Fenix here in Seattle. Thank you for the workshop."

As he shook my hand I blurted out "Did you mean that about coming along to ride with you for a bit?"

Mestre kept holding on to my hand. And gave me the look. The look he uses to gaze into your soul. That was the first time I felt the magic. Goosebumps stuff. I have no idea what I thought during these longest seconds of my life.

Then Mestre said, "Write me a letter."

I walked out of there on cloud nine, called up my roomie and said, "Yo, Andy, I am going to ride bike to Brazil."

Andy said, "The Fuck?"

"Yeah, man, I'm gonna do it."

"You mean motorcycle? Alone?"

"It's a Capoeira thing."

"Oh!"

"And no, on a bicycle."

I had one month to get ready. One month to tell my parents I wouldn't be in Seattle for their coming visit, arrange something for work and my Puget Sound apartment, sell my OJ truck, and get rid of all my stuff. One month to prepare for a one year, 12,000-mile bicycle journey through malaria swamps, over freezing mountains, and past drug lords and various Amazonian critters.

Piece of cake.

Application Letters Are Never Easy
Date: August 4th 2013, four weeks to B2B
Location: Seattle

I was working at the top software shop in the world, and before that at the biggest chipmaker. I think of these jobs as historical accidents – as if fate had dyslexia: one day I was in Los Angeles making orchid arrangements and building stages for Barry Manilow et. al., the next I was building Windows Phones in Seattle. Also, you should know that Barry Manilow fairly impolitely hollered at me while I was up on a ladder above the stage fastening pink chiffon in gorgeous wave patterns for him to float through later that night.

Sorry to burst that Mandy bubble.

Over the years, I had made lives on four continents after arriving on each with nothing more to my name than a sort of blind trust that this new world would bring me whatever it was that I was looking for.

Throughout, I wrote many application letters. But writing one to Mestre Acordeon was the toughest one yet. I never wanted anything as badly as this. For crying out loud, when I am at my happiest I sing a song about riding my bicycle to another continent.

After Mestre Acordeon shook my hand I did not sleep a wink. I wrote and re-wrote the thing a million times, called a friend, and finally sent it off at 7.00 a.m. the next day. I thought that I wouldn't hear back for days.

I know you want to read it.

Dear Mestre Acordeon,

Thank you for inviting me to write this letter regarding the possibility of joining you on the bicycle trip to Bahia. I am humbled, honored, and excited that you are thinking of including me. My mind and heart are full of inspiration for what a wonderful, life-changing opportunity this could be. I want to share with you the ways I think I could contribute to the success of your journey and the fulfillment of its mission.

Even though I am a relatively new student of capoeira, I have a long history of international travel motivated by intellectual and spiritual curiosity and organized around social service projects. (And, I will confess, I may have also fallen in love and followed a woman - or two)

I left my home country of Austria when I was 19, and have since lived in Finland, Australia, and Japan, as well as several places in the United States, including Hawaii and California. I have also traveled extensively across Europe and Southeast Asia. I've roughed it, camped it, hitched it, couch-surfed it, and just made it up and figured it out as I went along. I've been in plenty of difficult situations, and always kept my head and made great friends along the way. I blogged about my travel

adventures and other themes that are important to me here:
www.mindgloaming.blogspot.com

In Burma, I worked on charitable projects, including an organization founded by my uncle that builds nurseries for toddlers and schools and boarding houses for girls aged 6-18. My time in Burma changed my life, and I have continued volunteering ever since. I work with Simon Khin at Northwest Communities of Burma here in Seattle, a refugee organization that helps Burmese refugees settle into their new homes and get acclimated to American culture. More recently, I began offering basic capoeira classes to refugee youths.

I have a comfortable life as a software project manager working for Microsoft in Seattle. But comfort has never been my interest and I have fallen in love with Capoeira! Even though I really have very little knowledge, experience, and skill in the art, I know that it is for me and I am for it. I have been considering leaving my job in order to travel for Capoeira for some time – to visit groups in the USA and then go to Brazil and South America for a longer period. I would feel incredibly blessed and impossibly lucky if I were able to join you as a student and helper on your epic journey, whether for a month or for a year.

Here in Seattle, I am with Professor Fenix. I look up to Mestre Curisco, who has been a great source of inspiration to the Capoeira community in Seattle. Professor Fenix encourages us to travel to Batizados, especially to Mestre Jamaika's events in Utah, who also knows me well. I profit so much from traveling to Capoeira events and this year I have been lucky to visit seven so far.

I am organized, reliable, resourceful, hard-working, and honest. I have excellent project management, social media, and language skills. I also am really good at making fire. I am a very poor capoerista, but I hope to improve. Please consider taking me along. I can cover my own expenses, or contribute my share, and I will commit to helping you every day, in any way I can, in exchange for the opportunity to travel with and learn from you.

Sincerely,
Peter "Pirata" Illetschko

Thirty minutes later my inbox yelled at me. I felt like the President had dropped me a note.

Dear Pirata,
Thank you for writing to me. You have had a great opportunity to travel and to experience life in many places. The number of the people among the B2B travel group is growing beyond my expectations. I appreciated your interest but I can not tell you: come along. Other people in the group have the right to express their opinion. I'm passing your e-mail to them to contact you.
Take care and bons jogos.
Acordeon

After the first sentence I opened craigslist to look for a bike. Then I realized Mestre was saying yes and no in the same paragraph without actually saying yes or no.

Because I knew Mestre Acordeon didn't really have to ask anyone for permission for anything I was impressed by this, for Capoeira Mestres, rather democratic bend. I didn't like it, but I had to wait for the group's word. Later, I realized his response had been quintessential. He always strives to help you take initiative for your own life.

Two weeks passed. Not a peep out of Mestre Acordeon's United Capoeira Association.

I was too scared to follow up. It's not like Mestre is a coder at Microsoft who I can yell at if he is late on a deliverable. I finally asked my Capoeira teacher, Professor Fenix what he thought.

He shrugged and said, "I don't know."

Two hours later, probably not really coincidentally, Bebum, my Capoeira friend from Utah who was going on the B2B trip, called, "Yo Pirata, you got your bike yet?"

I said, "No man, I haven't heard back from these guys."

Bebum, his Capoeira name means *drunken, often falling down dude* said, "How long has it been since you wrote to Mestre?"

"Two weeks. I guess it was too good to be true."

"Ok Pirata, here is what you gonna do. Tonight, I'll send you a list with 200 items of stuff that you need for the trip that these guys at UCA put together. Go buy a bike, get everything ready, and come to the big event in San Francisco. When everyone gets in line behind Mestre to ride, you get in line, too. And when we all ride, you ride. And you ride until Mestre tells you to go home."

"..."

I was baffled.

After a pause, Bebum asked, "You there, bro?"

I said, "Yeah, I'm here. And you are fucking crazy. I don't know them. They don't know me. Are you nuts? White people don't do this shit. We make plans. We have schedules. And we sure as hell don't ride for a year with someone we've never met before."

"Bro... it's gonna be ok."

I may have yelled, "I want my laminated folder."

Then I thought about it for thirty seconds and realized that this was Capoeira in its essence.

And, I couldn't believe my own ears, but I heard myself say, "I'm gonna do it."

But before I could shift my life, I had to set some of it in order.

I called a few friends to seek out their opinion and left mom for last. While my friends were supportive, I was pretty sure she would be rather less so. Understandable, since six months ago, my parents had bought plane tickets to Seattle for the day that I was now planning to leave San Francisco on a bicycle. Epic timing, yes.

Also, let me state here for the entire world to read, before any fanciful notions of reality, of truthiness even, can mar your understanding of what's what.

All of it, everything, in its entirety, is my mother's fault. Yes, that's right. It's her fault that I left home twenty years ago, that I've lived on five continents and crossed two on a bike, and that I keep moving like a migratory windup bird.

Not because we don't like each other, that couldn't be further from the truth, but rather because she modeled this life for me. My mom is in her 60s, volunteers for Save Tibet and the Development Aid Club in Vienna. She learns a new hobby, like Tai Chi or patch-working every three years, and travels so much that the running joke in my family is that she needs a re-entry visa... to Austria.

Though, I know exactly what to blame my mother for, I am not yet sure which part of me is my old man's fault. I am sure in due course of writing this book it will come to me.

My parents value experience and knowledge. I thank them for it every day of my life, like you thank yours for the things you enjoy about yourself.

"Illetschko," she answered the phone.

"Likewise," I said.

"Awwww, Juuuuunior. So nice of you to call."

"Hi, how is it going over there - in about to be horribly cold, dark, and foggy fall-time Vienna," I was crazy nervous about this call, which I knew she could tell, even from 10,000 miles away.

"Very funny, son of mine. But there is hope for an Indian summer when your dad and I visit you in a couple of weeks in Seattle. What's up?"

Really mom, did you have to hit the nail on the head right away?

"Uhm, about that, I have to tell you something…."

As I then told her about my idea to ride bike to Brazil, she barely remained civil, "What about your job? Your car? Your apartment? I thought you liked this girl? Do you know how dangerous it is? You should talk to our friend in Uruguay about it. What about your father's birthday?"

Five minutes of listening and apologizing for my inherently ungrateful and altogether inadequate nature later my mother was at, "So there is nothing that I can say that will change your mind?"

Never in my long years of being away from home did my mother revert to parental blackmail (thank you, mom). She never asked me to get married, give her grandchildren or move back to Austria. But right then her voice carried that note. I knew, I really hurt her. That feeling sucked.

Mom said, "Talk to your dad."

Ugh, it was like I was sixteen again, and failing English, Math, Chemistry, Physics, and probably French – at the same time. Considering my last job and the language this book is written in, I will politely refrain from commenting on my teachers, or Austria's educational system. Let's just say I'm with Elon Musk in his opinion of schools vs. books.

My dad came on the line and breathed, "*Servas.*"

That my parents wanted to travel to me on his birthday was a big deal. He hates celebrating it. I had no idea what to say to him. So I started singing the first lines of Reise nach Afrika:

> "*I find an oidn Autorafn, und an Lederfleck*
> *Moch ma neiche Hergottschlapfn für an bsondern Zweck*
> *I kauf a Kilo Würfelzucker und an Kilo Speck*
> *Dann bind I ma die Schlapfn um, und foahr min Radl weg...*"
>> I grab an old car tire and a leather patch
>> Make myself new jesus sandals for a special cause
>> I buy a kilo sugar and a kilo bacon
>> Put on my sandals and ride off on my bike

My dad giggled and said, "Well, if you think that you have to do this."

"I do, pops."

He put my mom back on the phone, and I sure wished he had suppressed that giggle. If she was a fire breathing dragon before, now hell froze over. In my world life becomes difficult when things get cold and quiet. The call was over soon after that.

2 weeks before B2B at a Karen Wrist Tying ceremony in Seattle with Ko Simon. I had just told him what I was planning.

Coinkidink – Or Selective Recognition
Date: August 14th 2013, two weeks before B2B
Location: Seattle

The next two weeks were a hurricane of cashing good Karma checks. I talked to my roomie, he wanted to take over the lease. I told my idea to a friend of mine, he wanted to buy my Bronco. Because I didn't know if Mestre would let me ride I could not quit my job, so I asked for four weeks' vacation and got them because, "I can't stop you," my boss said.

I responded, "Wait? What?" (*I'm out*)

Then I gave away most of what I owned. Two bags remained. Just the right amount, if you ask me.

Except for the nagging guilt about my parents, things seemed to fall in place like I was meant to ride. It was destiny.

But I needed a bike. Five years earlier I had surfed a couch in Bangkok. A French couple who rode around the world on recumbent bicycles had surfed the same couch. For all you none-crazy people out there who may not know about recumbent bikes let me describe it: it is a suicide device disguised as a transportation tool. On it, you don't sit upright. You lay on your back in an L-shaped elongated seat, on top of full-sized wheels, with your pedaling feet pointed forward and your hands all T-Rex on the handle bar at your chest. The Frenchies swore that these were the best touring bikes in the world because your wrists, neck, and back don't suffer, and because you see much more.

They forgot to mention how inconvenient it might be to lose balance all the fucking time.

Not knowing that last pertinent detail, Pirata was definitely getting himself this bike. Just the right kind of smart, different, and flat out weird that tickles his fancy.[1] Two days later, I bought my fleet-footed steed on Craigslist. Didn't even negotiate. She was meant for me. The fact that I couldn't ride the POS without falling over every ten feet didn't faze me. I just had to practice a little to get used to the balance points. I was going to Brazil.

Hah!

On my arrival in Berkeley, on Friday before Labor Day Weekend, the event was in full swing. I didn't know anyone at UCA and pretended to belong.

A guy named Diego said to me, "Hey, I am Diego."

I said, "Hi, I am Pirata, I am going to Brazil."

Diego said, "Weird, me too. But I never met you before."

Most of my conversations went that way, totally faking it till I was making it. Like when you go to your first ever job interview with a made-up resume to short circuit the impossible experience requirement since you just came out of school.

I also talked to Mestre Acordeon for a few minutes. He was his usual affable self.

I said, "Hello Mestre, good to see you."

Mestre said, "Pirata, good to see you. So are you ready?"

I said, "Ready as I'll ever be Mestre."

"That's great", he said, with a big Santa Claus smile on his face.

If you think that it is completely nuts to commit to a one-year adventure without knowing the first thing about the people that you are going with, you are right.

This was the biggest Capoeira event of my life with at least fifty Mestres and other *formados* (very experienced Capoeiristas) and two hundred Capoeiristas. It was one huge, sambalicious three day Brazilian party. Unfortunately, I was too busy freaking out over the future to enjoy the present because I was still preparing and running around to make last minute purchases, which meant I could not take any of workshops. That was probably a good thing. While I did mention in my letter to Mestre Acordeon that I was a horrible Capoeirista, seeing it for real might have changed his mind about bringing me along.

Mariano, another one of the riders, checked my gear. He seemed a little stunned by the recumbent thing.

Mariano asked, "So have you done any bike touring before?"

"As a kid," I told him.

"How about camping?"

I was mystified. Who plans a year-long expedition without having camped before?

But I answered politely, "Oh, I go all the time."

---

[1] Oh, found something that's my pops' fault. Growing up we used to have a Maccaw. My parents rescued the obviously illegally imported bird from some asshole pet shop for a lot of money. Pedro usually perched on my dad's shoulder but also had a swing next to my dad's work desk and another one next to our dining table. Yes, bird ate Wienerschnitzel for lunch. No evolutionary irony there at all: four humans and a bird eating a pig. He used to say, "*Eine Nuß,*" when he wanted a nut. Highfalutin architects would come over to discuss huge building projects and my old man would greet them at the door in a full-length Indian Lungi and a fucking talking bird on his shoulder. I still don't know how he kept us roofed and fed.

I found out later that some of the riders had neither ridden a bicycle nor camped before. Ever.

Makes you shake your head in wonder. Then again, I was on a recumbent.

We Have Lift-Off, Kind Of
Date: September 2nd 2013
Location: Berkeley, California

On Monday, Labor Day, Sept. 2ᵈ 2013, we left Berkeley for Brazil. I was appropriately hyped as well as scared out of my mind, and not just because I had no idea about the plan.

The only thing that I knew was that the group was to take the BART metro train from Berkeley to the Pacific Coast at Daly City and then ride bicycle for about thirty miles south to Half Moon Bay campground along the gorgeous Pacific coast.

In my, more German, world we would have left at the crack of dawn, but this was a Brazilian affair. And so, after a day of farewell festivities - dancing, hugging, singing, crying - Mestre Acordeon sat himself on his bike at 3 p.m. and without much ado gunned it across San Pablo Ave to disappear down a side street. Berkeley Police Department had closed the four-lane street. The police barricade indicated that there was at least some planning involved in the affair. The thirty or so riders who made up the temporarily bloated California B2B contingent scrambled to follow as quickly as they could.

Everyone, that is, except me. Apparently, you don't do anything quickly on a recumbent bike. In that moment, I realized how utterly screwed I was. You see, on my kind of awesome bike you can't just start riding on a sidewalk and pop over the curb like you would on a normal bike. You have to stop first, get off, walk your bike over the curb, and then get back on and start riding again.

Dear reader, yes, I do understand, it was a little late to realize this.

As I walked my bike out on the street, people started to mill about in typical post event fashion. I got on my bike, leaned back into my back support chair thing, put one foot on one pedal, pushed off, raised the other foot, and started pedaling - too slowly.

And in front of fifty Mestres, two hundred Capoeiristas, their families and the prettiest Brazilian Samba girls Pirata fell, also without much ado, flat on his face.

I couldn't get my foot down fast enough to stop my fall because on my kind of awesome bike you are immobilized, you remember, on your back like a pregnant whale. I hit the ground hard, a stabbing pain exploded in my wrist and my hip wasn't too happy either. Then I was stuck under my bike's frame and had to awkwardly wiggle out from underneath. I hoped that nobody paid attention.

They did.

I heard them ask, "Who is that guy?"

A crimson tide rose in my face, I pretended to clown around and got on my bike again. This time I put the other foot on the pedal, pushed off, raised the second foot, pushed off… and, too slow again, fell over again. This time to the other side.

This was quickly turning into the worst moment of my life. I awkwardly wiggled out from underneath my bike again.

Have you ever seen a 200 pound 6'1" guy wiggle? Not a pretty sight.

Two kind Capoeira Mestres came over and asked, "Can we help you?"

I desperately waved them off and huffed, "No, I need to do this by myself."

"You sure you are going to Brazil on this bike?"

Not much I could say to that other than try again. I may have hoped for an earthquake along the San Andreas fault. Sorry San Francisco, but I wanted to disappear into the ground beneath your feet.

Someone asked, "What's with the pirate flag?"

I tried again, and fell again.

"Is that even a bike?"

Finally, on the fourth try I managed to gather enough speed, mostly because the side street that Mestre had taken an eternity ago, which I had reached by falling over four times, was slightly downhill.

If nobody knew my name five minutes ago, you can be sure right then everybody knew who the fuck Pirata was. Without a shadow of a doubt it couldn't get any worse than this.

Oh wait.

All the other riders were gone. I rode down the small residential street and stopped to ask some people who were making like Brazilians and barbequing by the side of the road," You guys seen a group of cyclists going by?"

"What cyclists?"

I said, "You know, thirty of them, huge bags on front and back of bikes. Crazy Santa Claus looking dude leading the pack. Can't miss them."

"Nope, they didn't come past here."

The fuck? I was about three blocks straight down the street that Mestre took. Either these guys were messing with the gringo or I was already going the wrong way. *Nice job Pirata, proving to Mestre Acordeon right away what a good idea it is to have you along.*

I did know that they were headed for the Metro, so I asked which way the BART station was. Of course, I was just about halfway in between two of them. Since I didn't know which one the group went to, I picked the one further away from Daly City, and rode as fast as the wind, which, on my recumbent, resembled the fantastic gale force of a gentle summer breeze.

When I arrived at the station nobody was there. Instead there was a sinking feeling the size of a black hole in my stomach. I knew for sure that these guys didn't manage to load thirty bikes on a train in five minutes, so they must have had gone to the other station. Not perfect, but OK. I figured if I just got on the next train I would either see them at the next station, or be just ahead or just behind of them. Either way, we would all be together again in Daly City.

I got on the train, got to the next station. Nobody was there. I kept going to Daly City, thinking they were ahead of me. I got off the train at 4.30 and saw exactly nobody. Instead of thirty B2B riders I saw tumbleweeds rolling across the tracks.

By now I would understand if you thought it was about time my highly acute sense of selective recognition should have made me consider going home.

Two minutes later Bebum called me. *Finally!*

"Yo Pirata, where you at?"

I answered, "In Daly City, you?"

Bebum said, "At a Metro Station in town somewhere. Are those guys with you?"

I think that was when the Bebum/Pirata combo really started to hit its stride. A drunken, often falling down guy and a pirate on a journey to nowhere in a dazed haze of misguided adventuring.

Ignoring this important fact, I figured that the group had to be between the two of us and told him to come to Daly City.

Bebum arrived half an hour later. Alone. A harmonica should have started a sad Ennio Morricone tune when he stepped off the train.

You can imagine we did not feel entirely good about this situation and decided that there was no way Mestre Acordeon's group was going to try to reach Half Moon Bay that day, now that it was getting dark. We thought they all went back to their moms and girlfriends and had one last good dinner and cozy night in a real bed.

Later, we found out that the main group had, in fact, kept going by a different route. They never made it to Half Moon Bay, suffered broken chains, and flats galore. Maybe it was a blessing that Bebum and I got lost because the lurking Teutonic in me might have gotten tripped out by the chaos. Who would want to go ride failed states like Honduras with a ragtag bunch that can't even make it past the Tender Loin? Of course the next two days would prove that Bebum and I were indeed a perfect fit for B2B.

Since we didn't know anyone in San Francisco, there would be no girlfriends, no families, no warm beds or tasty dinners for us. And we were certainly not going back to our Capoeira hosts, tails between our legs. Instead, we checked our maps, realized we were two miles from a beach, and decided to go sleep there.

The beach in Daly City is a two-tiered cliff, each about a hundred feet tall. A broad flat expanse of low trees and shrubs lies between the two cliffs. We arrived at dusk and did not have much time to find a spot to camp. Dragging our fully loaded bikes down the steep sandy path was just ridiculously difficult. I took it as another good lesson (because I really needed one more) why not to ride a recumbent around the world. After we struggled down the first cliff, we pulled our bikes along further sandy, and now winding paths through stunted trees leaning with the constant pacific winds. After some time, Bebum spotted a small tree cave next to the path.

"Let's toss our stuff in here," he said.

I had a bad feeling about this, "I don't know bro."

"Nobody's gonna see, we can hike down to the beach, sleep there, come back in the morning, and roll."

"Na Bebum, I don't know. You want to leave all our gear here?"

"It's OK, nobody can even see it."

At the time, I didn't realize that this was the same modus operandi that made Bebum tell me to toss out my life and ride bicycle with a bunch of strangers for a year. I turned the little voice of caution in my head off. I wanted to go to the beach, too, and I didn't want to lug my stupid recumbent around this joint for another mile.

We grabbed our overnight gear, tent and sleeping bag, some *Chapul Cricket Energy Bars*, and hiked down to the beach. Even though this was a horrible situation for us to be in, we were happy, enjoying the peaceful night next to the crashing waves.

When we woke up, a typical San Francisco dark gray morning greeted us with fog so thick you can wrap it around yourself like a wet blanket. We quickly got going because we thought if Mestre did make it to Half Moon Bay the night before, we would have to ride to the second day's goal at Pigeon Point Lighthouse.

On the quick hike up the cliff, Bebum's old, never repaired snowboarding knee injury bothered him quite a bit. It was a good thing we were going to ride bicycle a lot as it is a good therapy for a bad knee.

Yeah, we felt lonely, we felt left behind by the main group, we felt disorganized, and, yeah, we had our bike shorts in a bunch. But we were on an adventure of the first order. Bunched up bike shorts are a necessary part of any serious adventuring.

Yet the closer we got to our bicycles, the more that bad feeling returned, until it rang like a hypersonic alarm bell. Funny, how these things work sometimes.

We came upon the tree cave. Everything was gone. Bebum's bike and trailer with everything he owned. The pannier that I had left behind with my tools, my clothes, and my wallet. Yes, I had forgotten that my wallet was in the bag I had left. Keel this pirate. That's what you get when you have 200 items distributed in four bags. It was going take a few months to figure out efficient storage systems. At least I had kept my passport separate out of old travel habits.

Bebum had kept his cash on him, because the last time he had slept in Golden Gate Park he had 1500 USD stolen out of his bag. I wished he had shared that little piece of pertinent info with me the night before.

There was one thing that the thieves didn't take - my recumbent bike. You could see they tried to take it, but gave up when they realized it's not rideable.

Remembering the previous day's exercise in self-mortification I may have screamed "TAKE MY FUCKING BIKE" inside my head. I felt conflicting emotions of empathy and anger for the thief.

I guess they were smarter than yours truly and didn't bother with it. Note to all future bicycle vagabonds: you don't need a lock with a recumbent bike. It functions as its own security device.

Bebum and I went into beast mode. But following bike tracks, running up and down various cliff paths, calling the police, and canceling my credit cards led to no trace of our stuff. The bike, the gear, the wallet, the Greencard, the clothes, the tools remained gone.

What was left was an 80-year-old hippie on his morning walk who offered to take us poor saps to his house to regroup.

Hippie Daniel and his peace-sign-shirted wife Cherie let us shower and fed us. They commiserated about the evils of the world, and lent us their interwebs. We canned a carton of pears with them. Cherie's 92-year-old mom came over, full of chutzpah and admiration for the two crazies who were (trying) to ride to Brazil. She brought us home-made bread and told her daughter to offer us gherkin made from an ancient Austrian kosher recipe. Made me feel like we might actually make it out of the pickle we were in.

In the afternoon, I found a cheap whip (Bebum speak for rig, a.k.a. bike) on Craigslist and incredibly, in this megalopolis of eight million people, the person selling it was located ten minutes away. We went in Daniel's pickup to pick the bike up. After, he dropped us off at the beach and we finally got to ride.

Three hours later, we linked up with Mestre and the rest of the group at Half Moon Bay campground. Mestre was a little surprised when Bebum told him, "Look, I got a new bike. Didn't like the old one any way."

Should You Desire the Life of a Nomad
Date: Early September 2013
Location: Pacific Coast Highway 1

You will be lonely. You will leave your family and friends behind. You will exchange feeling at home for feeling foreign. This will broaden your horizon and let you learn much about humanity, your homeland, and yourself. You will grow, a lot. And you will fall on your face, often.

Sometimes, you will find yourself at a crossroad with distinct choices that will change the course of your existence. Stay in Austria or go to Australia. Return to Austria or move to Japan with fifty bucks and a one-way ticket in your pocket. Stay in your job at Microsoft or ride your bike to Brazil.

Nobody knows how things would have turned out for me had I made a different choice in any of those cases.

What is certain, however, is that choosing between two continents has a lot more impact on someone's life then choosing between living in Hollywood or in Santa Monica, or between driving a Honda or a Toyota.

Imagine a continuum of decision making. On the left are secure, picket fence choices, on the right Fountains of Youth and outer stellar bodies. A decision to the left leaves you in roughly the same circumstance. A decision to the right is a *Life Paradigm Shifter*, an event horizon of your existence. You don't know what's on the other side. All bets are off.

If there were a test for this, you might find me to the right - of the right edge. The part that says *rolling stone*, or DRD4, shorthand for a gene cluster that drives novelty seeking behavior. DRD4 apparently encodes your dopamine receptors for riding with Marco Polo on the Silk Road instead of playing Marco Polo with your cousins in the neighborhood pool.

Many dream of these event horizons. The grass seems so much juicier on the other side. But to actually be foolish enough to fling yourself through a black hole takes a special level of irresponsibility. I seem to have an abundance of that requirement.

Should you care to take a stroll along the Shore of Singularities then at some point you may wonder about the life you left behind. What if you had never taken off in the first place? Would you be the same person? What if you never saw the Bazar of Zanzibar? Would you dream differently? What if you had listened to that voice in your head that said you couldn't do it? Would you have loved the same?

Would you never know?

#ViaErgoSum

California Dreaming
Date: September 2013
Location: Big Sur, California

But you don't need to shift your paradigm just for the sake of doing so. There are much better reasons than blaming a gene cluster.

Change has an effect on us. It keeps us young. It keeps us from growing set in our ways. We all realize this better as the years of our lives creep by. One day, we wake up and wonder how we went from thirty to fifty in a heartbeat and all we did was work fifty hours a week for fifty weeks a year. Suddenly, we feel inflexible. Suddenly, we feel old.

At that point, we may not have had the chance to add a lot of new activities or experiences to our lives but at least we feel good about being on top of everything that we do. Not knowing something reminds us of being kids, of being stupid, when all the tall people ran the show. In due course of that thing called growing up we have eliminated all those pesky sources of shame. Can't do rhythm? Stop trying to waltz. Can't remember what fromage is? Stop learning French. Just focus on the stuff we can do, and all is good in the ego hood.

But every once in a while we come across that one spry granny who rocks out to hip-hop and reads a new book every week. She amazes us. She might even do Acro Yoga, or fly to Buenos Aires to learn Tango, though she's gotta dance with cats half her age.

The rest of us think we look like idiots trying to dance some sexy Latin hip swinging affair with our stiff white boy office hips, or it takes us months to remember that word for cheese in French.

But what if the requirement for staying young like that spry Granny is not excellence, but simply the willingness to keep changing, to keep trying new things, to keep feeling stupid? Just like we did when we had no other choice, because what were we going to do when we learned walking? We certainly didn't say, "Fuck it, I am tired of falling on my face. I don't need this walking thing. I don't want to change, crawling around works just fine."

No, of course we tried to get up one more time. And we tried to learn from the experience. It seems that same logic applies, always. We must humble ourselves in front of the altar of learning until the day we die, or we are the walking dead long before the fat lady sings.

This is like smiling on the outside when you feel like shit on the inside. You take the action in order to influence how you feel.

Change is like that. You change to feel and stay young.

You best believe I was doing a lot of changing while I was California dreaming along the coast. *Cantigas de Capoeira*, one of Mestre Acordeon's CDs, set me a good rhythm as I struggled up Big Sur along Highway 1. It was only appropriate to listen to the man's music whose vision and courage would lead ten Capoeiristas across the Americas.

The first few days of riding were incredibly tough. None of us had practiced, all our behinds hurt like hell. But I learned quickly that riding with a seventy-year-old means you can't ever be tired, because you know how much harder it is for him. And as if that wasn't enough motivation, his wife, Mestra Suelly, first USA born female Capoeira Master, herself in her late fifties, also rode.

The craggy and sparsely vegetated Big Sur Mountains represented the first uphill challenges of the journey and scared the crap out of us. It was a good thing that I had plenty of motivation, because that's about all I had. No clothes, no tools, no patch kit for flats, and no money or credit cards.

But at least that meant I rode light. And as opposed to Bebum, I still had my bike, though it was so difficult to balance that I might as well have been riding on a tightrope. Under a circus tent. The inevitable fall was relatively short, which was good since, to Mestre Beiramar's endless amusement, I fell over at least five times a day. He got into the habit of filming me when I was starting or stopping, I should say, falling.

Mestre Beiramar, "Hey, Pirata! Are you about to take off?"

"Yeah, whatever Mestre."

He yelled, "Pirata, wait, don't ride yet, let me set up."

If I had wanted to rough it right away after leaving my comfy office existence, I could not have planned it any better.

"Nãooo, Pirata, now you gonna have to pay some pushups."

At least, though I was in dire straits, they were good looking dire straits. The Pacific Coast Highway takes your breath away with its curves and vistas leading you through nature so pretty you remember Thoreau's Walking while riding:

> *I wish to speak a word for Nature, for absolute Freedom and Wildness, as contrasted with a Freedom and Culture merely civil, — to regard man as an inhabitant, or a part and parcel of Nature, rather than a member of society.*
>
> — "Walking"

Thirty years ago, my family took a road trip along the California coast line between San Francisco and Los Angeles, á la the movie *Vacation*, including ridiculous wood-paneled station wagon. The experience was imprinted on my seven-year-old mind.

Back then we saw cyclists touring up and down the coast and we talked about how amazing (and crazy) it looked. To return to the Pacific Coast Highway all these years later to ride my bicycle was magical. I was on a daily high and not just because of the ounce and a half of medical grade MaryJane that Bebum and I had brought, which, yes, we had kept on us the first night out. I guess it was more important than the green card.

Seeing Mestre Acordeon's stiff back surmount one hill after the other pushed us. Every day, I was riding with Capoeira greats Mestre Acordeon, Mestra Suelly, Mestre Efraim, and Mestre Mago. Mestre Beiramar, Yolanda, and Penguin filmed it all for the documentary. I broke bread with and camped next to guys like Professor Mniska and Instrutor Parafuso from UCA, awesome humans and Capoeiristas. I also got to know the rest of the B2B crew, those of us who planned to ride all the way to Salvador, Bahia.

Imagine thirty bike riders with tons of gear strapped to their bikes and weird broomsticks (*Berimbaus*) sticking out the back, stop in front of your house and start a *roda*, the circle of people in which two people play Capoeira. Then they stand in that circle and clap along to the Berimbau rhythm and sing Capoeira songs about slavery, Africa, and Capoeira. Because of the caliber of Mestres present, the songs and the play of the Berimbau was powerful. You felt the *Axé*, the energy, vibrating.

If you come upon a roda for the first time your impression would be somewhat like what happened to me when I started Capoeira in Seattle:

> I approached the circle of people carefully, wondering what the commotion was about. Everyone was in tight white pants and a white t-shirt with colorful ropes as belts. They sang loud call and response tribal songs in a foreign language, while clapping their hands. Three people on one side of the circle played instruments.
>
> A guy with fullback shoulders (Contramestre Fenix) held a bow with a round thing attached to its bottom in one hand and banged out a twangy banjo sound with a skinny stick in his other hand. Next to him a carrot-topped woman played a monotonous staccato on a tall African drum. The third instrument was a tambourine.
>
> As I stood behind two people in the circle they made a little room for me and fullback shoulders motioned for me to join with a friendly

smile. Two people inside the circle were throwing kicks at each other's heads They kept missing by millimeters; I don't know how they weren't on the way to the hospital already. Everybody else sang, clapped, jumped up and down, and swayed to the music as if all of this was - Completely. Fucking. Normal.

Then Fenix slowed down the rhythm with his bow thing and the two in the middle of the circle adjusted their cadence. Instead of throwing kicks they were now engaged in some kind of athletic dance yoga. They kept returning to one particular move, which looked like a really long backward lounge (explaining the bootyliscious perkiness around me), except they had the wrong arm up in front of their face. Out of that move they did cartwheels on one hand, dropped into back bends, spun on their heads, and leaped over each other.

People kept smiling at me encouragingly, which was good, because I thought I was tripping balls. My only hope was that they would not make me go play, as they called it.

Of course that was in vain.

We did impromptu rodas all up and down California: on the beach, on street corners, in parking lots, on lawns in front of office buildings, and at gas stations. The Mestres played a lot and beat the crap out of each other. Mestre Mago's *Bensão* (straight push kick) was crazy fast, and you never knew which way Mestre Beiramar was going to sway. These rodas were different and much more aggressive than the ones we did at Capoeira Events where they played showy and open *jogos* (games), as the contest between two Capoeiristas is called.

It was like I got to roll with the 90's Bulls for a month and watch Michael Jordan and Scottie Pippen go at it every day in practice. Mystical Mestre Acordeon, the Phil Jackson of Capoeira, reigned over it all with his immaculate Berimbau.

If you are a Capoeirista you know Mestre Acordeon. You listened to one of his nine Capoeira CDs while you train. You watched grainy old VHS tapes of his legendary games. If you have been lucky enough to attend one of his workshops you have experienced his intensity and unrelenting desire to make you better. You bring one of his books for him to sign. In the world of Capoeira, he is a legend.

But not only Capoeira recognizes his contributions to society. Yes, Capoeira is a UNESCO Cultural World Heritage, but Mestre Acordeon has his own "Mestre Acordeon Day" in Berkeley. It's on October 18th, in case you want to drop by the *Casa de Cultura* (Mestre Acordeon's academia) and pay your respects. Representatives from Berkeley City Hall sent us off on Labor Day, and when we left Bogota months later we had a letter from the Brazilian Ambassador in our pockets urging people to help us in any way possible.

Mestre Acordeon forms a direct line to the most recognized Master of modern Capoeira. He received his Capoeira Apelido (alias) from Mestre Bimba, the Mestre who had successfully pushed for the legalization of Capoeira in the 1920s. Through decades of his own work, Mestre Acordeon took the art to the next level. He enabled its spread around the world by bringing it to the West Coast and by tirelessly traveling in its name. Capoeira before Mestre Acordeon was a rough, inherently conservative expression of a violent past. Capoeira after Mestre Acordeon was global, it was community, it was one (tough) love.

Through him, a sharing of culture and history started to trickle out of Brazil. Mestre Acordeon is the driving force behind this diaspora because he was the first one to go, because he invited people to join him, and because he has that Zeus charisma thing going on. Now, decades later, there are thousands of Capoeira teachers living around the world. They all followed Mestre Acordeon.

This is why fifty Mestres from all over the world came to pay their respect in Berkeley when we left. It is why ten of them rode with him for a month in California. Why they walked their bikes next to him when he could not ride anymore and why they carried his bags at the end of a long day when his back was killing him. Because one last time, their Mestre, all our Mestre, was showing them what it meant to do the unthinkable. What it meant to lead.

Mestre Bimba died embittered in Goiânia, far away from the soft shores of his beloved Bahia, even though he was the one person most responsible for the legalization of Capoeira in Brazil forty years after slavery was abolished there. Mestre Pastinha, who canonized Capoeira Angola, died as a blind and poor man. And only in death did we recognize and honor them as the greats that they are. It's seems a little bit like Austria, where you also have to be dead, or emigrated, in order to be accepted as a great person who contributed much to society. Unless you are a downhill racer, of course, but even then it's also better to be dead. Let us learn from that and honor today's Mestres before they are gone. Hopefully nobody will forget Mestre Acordeon, or his address. If you do, you are not a Capoeira, instead you are arrogance, envy, and stinginess.

Today, we desperately cling to a past that comes to us only through oral traditions, through living receptacles like Mestre Acordeon. We see glimpses of these traditions in Capoeira songs and quotes such as this one:

> I am not a Mestre of Capoeira - Mestre Acordeon, Mestre Waldemar,
> they are Mestres de Capoeira. I am just the Mestre of my students.
> Mestre Xuxo

Riders - Following the Dreams of a Youngster
Date: September 2013
Location: California Highway Number 1

The riders were a mixed bag of nuts. Any CEO worth her salt will tell you that a diverse workforce is often highly functioning and creative, but that cultural conflict points can capsize your ship before you can ask "What are you sinking about?"

Our motivations to join B2B were far from uniform. Some were running away from something, others toward a better future. A couple of us wanted to prove to themselves that they could do this, because then they could do anything.

Yet, what was Mestre Acordeon's motivation? *To follow the dreams of a youngster*, as he so eloquently put it, with the smirk of a boy who just pulled a fast one. I think he probably just wanted to get away from it all for a little bit.

The quickest way to describe Mestre is to say he looks like Santa Claus - minus the paunch, plus some arcane, lethal knowledge. Mestre has a shock of curly white hair, a fantastic white beard that he loves to stroke thoughtfully, and hands the size of toilet covers. When you are in the roda with him, get ready to be slapped around by those. I can not yet report on where his seemingly endless supply of testosterone to maintain his muscle tone stems from. Probably Vulcan. When not in the roda, Mestre is usually smiling and always has a kind, encouraging word for you… until you piss him off and make him go Bad Santa.

Mestre eats, sleeps, drinks, and rides Capoeira. When he goes rock climbing in Yosemite, he thinks of how to apply the learnings in the roda. When he hears a Cumbia tune in Colombia, he wants to make a Capoeira song out of it.

It is a testament to the complexity of humanity that this dedicated focus produced a modern day renaissance man who leads a martial art globally, mentors people everywhere, plays too many instruments to count, sings Bossa Nova like a boss, beats your ass anytime he likes, writes books, and creates Samba Shows in Vegas.

The most important aspect of his personality is an absolute desire to deliver the best he can. It is contagious and difficult to deal with at the same time.

His wife, Mestra Suelly is nearly sixty, about five feet two, and can not possibly weigh more than a 120 pounds, without a gram of fat on her. And make no mistake she will also beat your ass, with a kind smile. She was born in Colorado, and before Capoeira she was in a dance troupe in New York. I want to describe her as a highly functioning granny, except she routinely shows twenty-somethings what's what in the roda. She has thousands of kids and grandkids; we call them Capoeiristas. Her grey hair sometimes turns brunette, but her laugh wrinkles are always present. Mestra is the first female Mestre of the United States. She is a trailblazer in a male dominated, originally extremely chauvinistic art, that still struggles to adjust to the realities of equality. It's not easy being a woman in a world of fighters, it's downright amazing to break down these walls and remain graceful. Mestra does not like being singled out, or being called a role model for women all around the world. Instead she prefers to point to the power of her community. We all know that in this one regard she is full of humble shit. And we love her even more for it.

Then there was the couple, Elisa (Tuchegas) and Diego (Tarantula). They were riding out of love for Capoeira, Projéto Kirimuré, and their Mestres. Tuchegas' parents are Brazilian; she grew up in Berkeley and fulminantly combines kindness and badassery. She is tiny, her black hair is starting to turn straight white, apparently perfectly paralleling her growing wisdom. Also, she seems to be physically indestructible. Her passions are Capoeira, teaching pre-schoolers, and Frida Kahlo. Diego's parents are from Mexico, he bailed Watsonville California, where he grew up, after high-school for the big city lights of San Francisco. Diego is the most rhythmic Capoeirista I have ever seen. Because he is so in tune he usually *rasteras* (leg swipe) you before you knew you were going to kick. He says he used to be the fat kid, but I don't believe him, because in the roda he is usually already waiting for me wherever I wanted to go. Still, there is no way he could ever keep up with Tuchegas on a mountain day.

Their son Keith (Balão), second generation Chinese, grew up in the East Bay of San Francisco. He is funny, straightforward, and has the voice of an angel. Before joining B2B he earned his foodie bacon in an IT role. Of course Balão is not actually Tuchegas's and Diego's son, but since he was usually attached to them we thought of him that way. Do not underestimate Balão in the roda, just because you know that Balão means balloon. Though he is short and round, he moves smooth like butter. His physical strength and intimidation factor remind of that toad character in Kung Fu Hustle. You don't see that shit coming, but suddenly you are attached to some kind of force that is propelling you away from your reality. Balão brought a miniature guitar, and many a night serenaded the camp to sleep with his always completely depressing yet amazing choice of songs. We all carry our demons with us.

Mariano (Galán), self-proclaimed Chile-fornian, was the one *Graduado* (graduate) of us, having just received his Instrutor (Instructor) belt. He is six feet tall, way too handsome for his own good and usually wears a hat or beanie. In a previous life he posed for that David statue in Florence, that's how ripped he is. Galán loves silly humor and can charm an ogre into giving up his wife. Of course he would never be caught in public with an ogre's wife. At 27 years he is proficient in Capoeira and Wing Chun, a UC Davis Biology graduate, and owner of a Gyrotonic studio (East Bay Gyro). I think of him as my favorite overachiever. After Mestre and Mestra he was second in command. I know, it is fuzzy math, but they relied on him because Mariano has a gift for managing people. Also, his legs are made of some kind of alloy.

It is of course impossible to leave out Amber (Peninha). As her capoeira name suggests she is tiny, even tinier than Mestra or Tuchegas. Maybe it's just my (tall) point of view, but it seems that short yet powerful women congregate around Capoeira and B2B. It's either an empowerment or a Napoleonic thing. The daughter of a Mexican-American mom discovered her love for South America when her stepdad worked for the State Department in Lima. Amber did not ride bike but drove her Toyota truck in the role of sometimes support vehicle. She found Capoeira after her fiancé's traumatic shooting death on the night streets of Oakland. UCA's Capoeira family became her therapy. In the real world she was an architect. At first, Amber had a unique ability to not see ten bikes parked by the side of the road, and though the name Peninha may be physically appropriate, her character shines larger than life.

Tora, the 47-year-old Japanese meteorologist cum computer developer was another international addition to the crew. He could edit one photo for hours and read camera manuals while riding bicycle, despite having front-flipped over his handlebars multiple times. It would be fair to blame Tora's cat-like reflexes for his survival. He spoke a smidgen of English, and less Spanish or Portuguese.

In Mexico City, four Capoeiristas - Banano, Tartaruga (Juanjo), Ken, and Indi from the group Longe Do Mar joined us. These four sequestrados[2] of permanent status sometimes get lumped into a single mass of chill chilango awesomeness, but of course, they were as diverse as the rest of us.

And then there were Bebum and Pirata. The two wildcards. The odd ones out. Round pegs for square holes. More about those fools later.

These are the people that would go all the way to Brazil but in California the B2B peloton was much larger, roughly 25 people, many of whom had taken a month vacation to ride their bicycles with Mestre Acordeon in California.

So, now that you know who was riding, you also know that it was obviously nuts to go on this trip with a bunch of strangers. No two people were of the same background in a group that planned to live in each other's shirts for a year.

Our saving grace was that we did not organize ourselves along the lines of what is known as the least bad of all political systems. Though Mestre likes to promote democratic decision models, when important decisions were to be made, he was a benevolent dictator and this anti-democratic bent kept us functioning somewhat cohesively.

---

[2] Sequestrada is what Mestre called Rose, who joined us to ride for a day in California. From that point on all random hangers-on, as well as explicit if momentary B2B additions carried the moniker *Sequestrado* - Kidnap Victim. Except that being kidnapped by Mestre's B2B One Love train was hella cool.

Tora Pirata Parafuso Joaninha Maré Mestra Suelly Diego Tuchegas Bebum Mariano Balão Mestre Acordeon in Baja California

While approaching Santa Barbara from the north our mixed bag of nuts passed a multitude of California coast dream spots. The days merged into a continuum of freedom. We forgot dates and times and adjusted to the celestial rhythms. We were on a never-ending endorphin joyride.

Though we became closer to nature, most of us still used our tents compulsively. Camping in a tent is what city folk do. The only one who hardly ever used his was Bebum. Whenever there was a beach, he slept on it. I soon followed suit.

Going to sleep with the stars, awaking to luna's bright light, and rising with the sun connects you to something old inside you. The chill of the morning air crystalizes the joy of an easy sense of belonging. Maybe this was the reason why Bebum seems meant not to own anything in this life. Whenever he does, he gets in trouble.

But the sleeping on beaches was not the only thing that Bebum taught me, or the rest of the group. He also added an ethic of sharing, probably in response to some unsavory experiences made courtesy of the Utah State Correctional System. However little money he and I had, whatever we cooked or ate, if anyone showed up, Bebum offered them a bite. Of course, since Bebum spent most of his money on his replacement bike it was usually my stuff being offered, but why nitpick. Mestre loved it (except for the second hand sharing) and joined in. When I told my dad about our little mobile Kibbutz, he drily remarked, "Bebum brought Marxism to B2B."

Some people will respond with, "Seems like it's usually the province of those with nothing else to add to the pot."

Except in this case it added something large, if intangible: group cohesion. Simply put, there is a reason why humans congregate around food. Births, deaths, birthdays, weddings, meeting strangers, sealing business deals, celebrating a figment of our imagination all have one thing in common: Food. It gives us life and it brings us together.

Bebum and Pirata
Date: September 2013
Location: California

In Capeoira people receive their *apelido*, their nickname, according to certain character traits or physical attributes. The apelidos used to be much meaner, picking on your weakness, forcing you to face it. Today you will not find as many *pigs*, *fat noses*, or *stinkies* around. Modern day Capoeiristas are a little more sensitive about their image and weaknesses. It's all Borboletas and Piratas now. The thing about Capoeira nick names is that you need to accept and wear your name with pride. You own it, or it owns you.

Bebum and Pirata never had any issues with accepting their names. Bebum, the drunken guy who falls down a lot, literally and figuratively. And a Pirate, who seems to have a code of honor, but it's a very particular, none-conformist one. All I can say is that if you are going to ride into the big unknown, maybe one or two rough around the edges guys are good to bring along.

Our relationship grew through Capoeira because our groups collaborated and I had taken my first ever class with Mestre Jamaica in Utah, who was Bebum's Capoeira teacher. I was lucky to continue interacting with them over the next couple of years. Without Bebum's phone call I would have stayed in Seattle and hated myself for the rest of my life once I saw people joining B2B like it was Forest Gump running instead of Mestre Acordeon riding. Even though I had already lived all over the world, exhibiting plenty of nomadic testicular fortitude, I still needed the push from Bebum in order to join B2B. I was following the dogmas of our society *These guys don't know you, you don't know them. You can't give up your job for something crazy like that. Etc., etc.* and needed a wild card to break me out. This constitutes a huge debt. Our miserable first night only further cemented our friendship.

After Bebum spent his first, and last, thousand dollars it soon became clear that he wasn't going to get any more money from back home. It boggles my mind to this day that he showed up to a year-long journey with a thousand dollars and no real resources other than the expectation to make it to Brazil somehow.

I started buying food and taking care of other costs for Bebum. Since money meant little to me in comparison to having the opportunity to ride with B2B I was happy to support him. On the night of our departure Bebum's Capoeira teacher, Mestre Jamaica had asked us two to stick together. I planned on sticking together.

When the going gets tough in the future, and it will, as it always does, I will try to remember Mestre Efraim's words, "Pirata, what you did was extraordinary. Anyone would have used what happened on the first night as an excuse to go home. But you didn't. No matter what happened, you and Bebum never stopped. Remember that when life gets tough, in your work, your relationship, or in the roda. Remember that you have the balls to do anything."

I just love sitting in a hot tub with a Brazilian in his speedos talking about my balls. Jokes aside though, those words meant a lot to me. Mestre Efraim's back might be broken, but his heart beats strong and knows how to heal.

Despite our history Bebum and I did not know each other very well at the beginning of B2B. We had only met a few times before and we both don't let you into our sanctuary too easily. Bebum finds out about you by not talking, I do the opposite. For the sake of our sanity I had to re-learn how not to talk, otherwise I'd have run my mouth all day long and his head would have exploded.

However much or little we talked, Pirata and Bebum were a force to be reckoned with, for better and worse. We lived a primordial existence in which only today mattered - how hard we rode, how much food we could carry, and how long we could go without water. Deep into Baja California we smoked, drank, and rode like bats from hell.

I had always thought that Professor Fenix gave me the *apelido* Pirata because it rolled of the tongue easy with Peter. There was nothing outwardly Pirata about me when I was working at Microsoft and starting Capoeira. But to the B2B crew *Pirata* made perfect sense. Capoeira is like that, full of strange inherent wisdom that often does not reveal itself until much later. And so I found new ways to explain my existence.

After a Roda a Capoeirista asked me, *"Porque Pirata?"* (Why Pirata?)

"Como?" (What?)

"Porque seu apelido é Pirata?" (Why is your nick name Pirata?)

"Porque eu quero tesouro." (It's because I like treasure)

It was her turn to ask, *"Como?"*

I said, *"Sabes Piratas? Piratas siempre querem tesouros, ouro, diamantes… coisas caras."* (You know Pirates, we like gold and diamonds… expensive things.)

"Oh!"

I said, *"Em Inglês existe palavra que tem o mesmo significa como tesouro."* (In English there is another word for treasure)

"Qual?" (What?)

"Booty!"

"Bootieee?"

Indeed. Though, pursuing piratical ways was not all we did.

One lovely coast-cruising day I asked Bebum, "You ever read Eckhart Tolle's Power of Now?"

Bebum said, "I love that book. Changed my life when I was in prison. It's in the app that I gave you,"

I said, "Oh, really? That's cool man. But I can't listen to audio books other than the language books. My brain is too dyslexic to track when someone reads to me."

Bebum imitated my Austrian accent and said, "Olla, Jo soy Austriaco."

I may have lol'd since I knew how funny it was for the locals to see a gringo cycling by with his headset on, muttering under his breath, "*Buenos Dias, mi nombre e Pirata. Donde eres el banco/barco?*"

(Throughout this book I try to document my actual linguistic inability with some honesty)

Though I do not like listening to music when I am riding, I did go through an hour of language lessons with those Spanish, and later Portuguese, audio books each morning while riding.

Bebum said, "I hate reading. The only way you gonna get me into a book is to listen to it."

"Hmmm," I said. (This is called learning silence)

In his magic sesame app of literary joy Bebum also had a ton of *make the world a better place*, starting with yourself, hippie books.

He continued, "Those books saved my life. They helped me realize why I was in trouble."

"I thought you were raised Mormon? Not that that won't fuck you up enough by itself."

"Hah, my parents split early, I was in and out of a bunch of schools. Never learned a thing, I still can't write for shit. They even put me on the short bus. So I just learned how to fight because people called me stupid all the time."

"Sounds normal for kids with your background."

"Yeah, but most people look at me and think, Bebum is always broke, doing this sharing thing just so that everyone shares with him. But I made a choice in prison not to care about money."

"Why?"

"When school sucked so bad I dropped out and started working for my brother, we made tons of money. We had a corporate cleaning business and I started doing landscaping and other things on the side."

"Hmmm" (silence, I embrace you)

"But all I did was work, tryna make as much money as I could. I wanted to be a millionaire. Thought that's how I prove my value. I had a huge truck, a big house, smoked as much as I wanted, and nobody told me what to do."

I did not share the stories of my weird, yet comparatively picket fence childhood.

Bebum continued, "But I was so unhappy. Getting into more and more of the bad shit, had troubles with the police. I just couldn't handle authority trying to fuck with me all the time."

I asked, "Bro, you ok?"

"Yeah man, why?"

"That's the longest sentence you've ever said to me. You must really love me."

"Don't try to hug me bro."

We rode and worked on our egos. A booty-seeking pirate and a falling-down drunkard doing self-improvement and enlightenment. It's a brave, new, bro-losophic world out there.

All of us carry unseen depths and offer various fears and gifts to our fellow humans. Our actions are dictated by the entirety of our being and are therefore equally complex.

I still wish to be better at remembering this truth for others when I give into my impatient arrogant ways.

Legalize
Date: Mid-September 2013
Location: Campground North of Santa Barbara

So what do you get when you put a couple of hippies on a bicycle, and then take all their shit except a bunch of Chapul Cricket Bars (backed by Marc Cuban via Shark Tank) and an ounce and a half of medical grade sweet sticky stank?

One, in the State of California quite legal, hell of a good time. Except on federal campgrounds. Those, apparently, are federal lands.

Right.

One balmy California beach night, Bebum, Joaninha, and I rolled a fatty outside the common area of a campground. We wanted to celebrate this day of perfection. Tons of Capoeiristas, a few people, and kids milled about. That a girl with the Capoeira name of June bug (Joaninha) was with us proves we did not knowingly engage in an illicit activity. We walked outside the campgrounds to smoke on these fantastic sand dunes under the stars and went to sleep shortly after.

The next morning, we were getting ready for some Capoeira when Instrutor Parafuso gathered a crowd and said, "Everybody's gotta leave now," which was a problem since we meant to return to the campsite later that day.

Balão asked, "What you mean?"

Parafuso said, "I guess some of us smoked pot last night, some kids saw it, told their parents, the parents complained, and they are kicking us out."

Ice in my gut. Here was my return ticket to my Microsoft desk.

"That's crazy," said someone.

Parafuso said, "I know, I tried to explain it to them, but they are nuts. Camp grounds seem to be federal land so we need to leave."

Ten minutes later Mestre Acordeon held a meeting. Before he could start too deep into what happened I asked, "Mestre, may I say something please?"

Mestre stared at me, "Ok, Pirata."

I grabbed ahold of my two pieces of brass, which at that point felt more like a doughy, sweaty mass and said, "I want to apologize to you and everyone else. It is true we rolled a joint next to the common area yesterday, though we smoked it outside. I am sorry."

Mestre said, "Thanks Pirata. Once and for all. I don't like smoking. Of anything. But I won't forbid it. Just don't do it around me. Let's pack up and leave. I wanted to ride earlier anyway."

I was surprised by this non-reaction. Most Brazilians dislike drugs of any kind. In Brazil there is no difference between marihuana and crack, it all comes from the same violent hands and the good herb isn't organically grown by your friendly neighborhood hippie. I don't know if that's the reason Brazilians love drinking themselves into oblivion, but OMG if you smoked a joint.

Here is some pertinent back ground info: Growing up in Austria there were two overriding activities in my life. Sports and reading. Everything else - school, friends, hobbies, musical instruments, later on girls... all of it took a backseat.

I had a library card for my neighborhood center of learning when I was five and tramped back and forth at least once a week to pick up a new stack of books. Often I could barely schlepp all the hardcovers about animals, dinosaurs, and galaxies home.

I did more sports than you can shake a stick at. You name it, I played it. When I was seventeen I trained basketball ten sessions a week, lifted in the gym and played pick-up games on the Donauinsel courts with my friends the rest of the time. Pick up beach volley? Heck yes. Riding road bikes up and down Donauinsel with my old man? Mhm. Hiking and climbing? Yes, please. You'll get bored if I keep going.

I didn't drink, smoke cigarettes, and sure as hell didn't use drugs.

I remember saying to my friends, "Anyone who smokes pot is weak and tries to hide from reality. I don't want anything to do with those kinds of people."

This did not change until I was 23 and living in Australia. In Australia I tried ecstasy for the first time. I liked it but it didn't make me want to do it all the time. I experimented with most things from that point on.

How did this happen to a nerdy little in your face sporty punk?

The truth is drugs weren't the first things I experimented with. Long before I dropped that half a Molly in OZ, I expanded my horizons by leaving Austria. Drugs came to be a mind expansion that, to me, was a logical extension of expanding my life.

But, let us also not ignore the fact that travel life can be lonesome. There is a reason why people experiment when they hit the road. It is easier to connect when you are high. Also, a random traveler you met on a beach in Phuket won't react as much to your drug habit as your best friend from primary school.

Hopefully, I learned many things about myself and others over these past twenty years. Whatever their weight, I can say that experience and knowledge, as such value-free entities, are what I live for. The totality of who I am today is an aggregation of these experiences; the gorgeous and the sad ones, the dangerous and the peaceful ones, the mind expansions and the suicidal come-downs.

I have spent the last ten years of my life more or less stoned. I think of it as a step up from all the soda, coffee, and alcohol many of us pour down our throats on the daily.

The 130 pounds of sugar that the average US citizen consumes per year hit the same reward centers in our brain as marijuana or cocaine. Those dopamine receptors spike when our mother holds us for the first time, when we make love to our partner, when we hug our father for the last time. Nature is an ironic, fail-safe creating asshole - some are more successfully adapted to her than others. We usually call those who are the best-adapted overweight.

Programmed by a harsh and unforgiving environment we crave fatty and sugary foods. Those kept us alive, instead of running out of energy, chasing a deer across the plains of the Fertile Crescent. Un/fortunately, nobody in most developed countries needs to chase deer anymore. Hence, the number one causes of death in those areas of the world are diseases of affluence.

The weed had the nice side effect of chilling my over-driving brain and so I could fit better into the patterns required by those around me, even though it meant caring about games of thrones and kids named East West instead of global warming and spending trillions of dollars on dropping bombs on brown people. It also made me a much more bearable date.

I am left with the thought that the good herb is nothing less or more than Soma for the people. I am surprised it took The Man so long to legalize.

And so, the hippie pirate and the drunken guy left the whack federal lands with, what was then, only one ounce of weed, to ride to a Capoeira event in town.

We may have lit one up on the way out.

Capoeira events are always high-octane affairs, and with the Mestres on B2B we could not help but pick up a lot of Capoeira wisdom. This is because you can't put a bunch of Capoeira Mestres in a room together without them running their mouths for hours.

Sometimes you'll hear real nuggets of wisdom. That day Mestre Mago launched into one of his typical jokester stories.

In Portuguese he said, "I like to travel to other countries and see how different things are. What people eat, how they talk. What's legal, what isn't. For example, marihuana, in my country it's not legal, but here it is."

He mimics a Brazilian comedian's voice and knows you can say anything if you are a funny guy, "Still, we got kicked out of a campground because of pot today. That surprised me. I am glad they didn't see where we went two weeks ago. We visited an amazing place. We saw marihuana plants the size of Christmas trees. There was so much weed, they would have had to kick us off the planet and not just out of a campground!"

The interesting thing about Mestre Mago's statement was his purpose. Doing it in that setting is not expected, but he masterfully got ahead of a potential story. A true Capoeirista always finds the cracks in the logic.

However I kept my dopamine levels elevated I was always on edge because I didn't know if I was going to be allowed to continue riding. It was like a four-week interview with a sorcerer, because who knows the parameters of success with a sorcerer, or a Capoeira Mestre?

With 20/20 hindsight it is amazing to think that a guy who fell of his bike four times before even leaving Berkeley, who had all his shit stolen on the first night, and then got everyone kicked out of a campground for, cough_cough, smoking pot, was NOT politely asked to GTFO.

Instead, just a few days south of San Francisco, Mestra Suelly said, "You are definitely coming to Brazil with us."

The occasion was having to schlepp our bikes 150 feet up a steep incline because Mestre had taken a cul-de-sac coastal road. This is also known as a *Mestre Shortcut*, one that more often than not leads to a place called *Nowhere*. Ask Mestre Curisco and Contramestre Jaba about that sometimes. I still think Mestre does it on purpose, just to make us get those extra training units in.

It was not to be the last Mestre Shortcut, but it was the first opportunity to prove myself as a member of B2B. That my size and strength were required, sort of like that big guy in *Of Mice and Men* did not bother me in the least. If Mestra, Joaninha, and Tora needed help dragging their bikes up some slippery slope I was ready.

After all, I was on every Capoeirista's dream journey. California is the home of Capoeira Batuque, UCA, Capoeira Brasil, and tons of other schools. Some of the first Capoeira groups in the USA reside in California. You find open Rodas everywhere.

And I could not play. My left hip flexor was acting like a rusty jackknife from the cold up north. I could barely raise my leg above my hips for a kick. My wrists refused to carry any weight because I kept falling on them. All of us, including Mestra Suelly would be bothered by painful wrists till Costa Rica, where a Capoeirista Physical Therapist told us to spread the cartilage, sinews, and muscles in order to heal (it worked).

Other than being injured, I was frustrated because, on top of sucking at Capoeira, I was confused. I felt like I had thrown myself from a small, if comfortable, pond into a big Capoeira ocean, though little did I know that California was kind of like a medium sized lake compared to Brazil.

I was confused because I went from my own group's Capoeira Contemporânea to riding with the heir to Mestre Bimba's Capoeira Regional, a distinctly different style. My group's jinga (backwards lunge) is different, upper body less exposed, head tucked in between raised shoulders. Our *batteria* (instruments) is organized differently. It's like going from Wing Chun to Karate.

At some point I realized I was in a 24/7 Batizado environment.

When you go to another group's Batizado event you often feel like a beginner. The styles, sequences, and moves tend to be quite different. I have seen instructors look like newbies trying to figure out the timing of a move because they hadn't practiced it before. This resistance training is why it's so important to travel in Capoeira. It checks our ability in the real world. It teaches us versatility and humility. Also, we can go home and beat our friend's ass with a new move.

This is great for a weekend, but for a month straight... not so much. I let it confuse me.

And so I learned to *learn by watching* - not something we (I) like to do. Usually, we are told to play, play, play because the roda is where your game develops. But there is a lot of value in watching other people play. Good and bad players, Mestres and first cords. Watch them with your Capoeira eyes. Without arrogance, envy, or stinginess.

I won't learn anything by playing Mestre Beiramar other than that I can easily bore the shit out of him. Nothing that he wouldn't rather have someone else teach me. But I sure can learn a lot by watching him.

Capoeira is one of the most complex things anyone can attempt. Your journey will make you into an Olympic gymnast, a world class musician, and an intrepid anthropologist. This is why it takes thirty years to become a Mestre of Capoeira.

I remained confused until I talked to Mestre Acordeon about it in Baja California.

He said, in that scratchy-comfy gramper voice of his, "Well... you can't be confused."

Only, what Bebum had been telling me for months. Yet, weirdly, probably more to me than to Mestre, that's all I needed. From that moment on I just played.

How we must have appeared to people, a tribe of ripe martial artists, clearly sleeping in tents for a week, with overloaded bikes and our Berimbaus emerging behind our panniers. And how grateful we were to be welcomed into the homes of the likes of Contramestre Chin in Santa Barbara or Instrutor Rebelde in Santa Cruz. Mestre Acordeon tried his very best to keep us presentable, but that's not easy on the road.

Imagine you are enjoying a leisurely Sunday afternoon with your wife and two young kids and suddenly a ragtag bunch of smelly, unshaven bicycle hippies shows up, takes over your backyard, your kitchen, and, to add insult to injury, clogs your toilet.

All the California Capoeiristas wanted to show Grandé Mestre Acordeon their appreciation and love. They probably also wanted to make sure that the crackpot idea was actual reality. The hospitality of the Capoeira community is often astounding, but our hosts outdid themselves. Even Capoeira legends like Mestre Amen (Yes, the burly, curly Afro-Brazilian Capoeirista from *Only the Strong*) and family opened their homes and hearts to us.

LA UCA Contramestre Guatambu held his Batizado at sunset right along the board-walk in Santa Monica. We got off our bikes after a day of riding and started playing (watching).

Mestre Boneco of Capoeira Brasil also had his event in LA during our stay and Mestre Amen came out to be *padrinho* (godfather, giving the first belt) to a capoeirista. It was beautiful to watch all these highly accomplished martial artists sharing a roda together.

Then there was Mestre Boneco's night time roda in a dark, dank, and sweaty room at the CBLA academia. It was the perfect preview for the trip. For two hours the charismatic Boneco held the crowd in thrall with two chest pounding, earth slapping, berimbau in air thrusting chants of "DE MARÉ DENDÉ, DE MARÉ DENDÉ, DE MARÉ DENDÉ" and "MES ACORDEO-ON MES ACORDEO-ON MES-ACORDEO-ON!"

His students jumped up and down like they wanted to bring down the house. People screamed at the top of their lungs, kicks flew, I was in shock and awe. I could not imagine being in a better place.

Only one small blue light, high up on the ceiling gave just enough light so that you could see the shadow of a heal coming at your face, if you paid attention. People were so greedy to play that they kept pushing to the front, making the circle smaller and smaller. I don't think it was more than eight feet.

The Capoeira was fast and aggressive. Nobody went to the floor. In this game you are dead on the floor. No time for cute splits or back bends. You need to stand up, escape the kick thrown at your chin, and answer with your own. The energy pumps through your veins, you can feel the rhythm take you.

Mestre Boneco's roda was a primordial mob ritual. It was fucking amazing.

I, hell no, did not play. I went back a couple of years later though.

> *Iê, Viva meu Mestre*
> *Iê, quem me ensinou*
> *Iê, a capoeira*
>> Long live all the Mestres
>> Those, who taught me
>>
>> Long live Capoeira[3]

While we were in California, there was very little obvious communication going on amongst us. It's all very organic in the world of Capoeira, full of inherent ambiguity that I only came to understand better once I spent time in Brazil. You'd think B2B was hashing things out, planning what to do when it rained, what to do when someone got lost, etc. But in all of California we had only two meetings. To this day I remember with complete clarity what Mestre said to us in Leo Carrillo State Park just north of Los Angeles.

"Here in California we have a strict time plan because we have a lot of events. But once we cross the border into Mexico I don't want to have a plan. I don't want to know where I am going next week or which route I am taking. I want to ride south and see what happens. I want adventure."

Those words still give me goose-bumps. I loved our Grande Mestre then. I always will, even though, as the months wore on, he started acting more like a traveling, German of two minds, who was refusing to plan but then asked Diego

---

[3] It may be problematic, and possibly pointless, to speak in this strange ritualistic way. Yet, I must honor my lineage. These weighted speech patterns are the transmittors of oral histories that will die unless practiced.

every few miles how much further it was. Of course he knew how funny that was and appreciated that we indulged our mentor's foibles.

That day, when Mestre let us in on his secret master plan of not having a plan I decided to ride with him. With eyes wide open and heart soaring high I surrendered to fate's hands-off hand. Adventure, he said he wanted. And adventure is what we got.

Afterwards Tuchegas asked for a meeting without the Mestres and said, "Diego had an accident today."

Diego had looked for, and found, the ditch next to the road on a downhill.

She continued, "Luckily, this was when Amber joined us because Diego's front wheel was a doughnut. I think this is a good moment to talk about how we will help Amber for being our support car. Maybe whoever wants her to carry things in her car should pay her gas money, for example 500 USD."

It was a typical Tuchegas moment, standing up for the rights of another person, even though Tuchegas wasn't planning on donating since she wasn't planning on putting anything in the truck. Not sure if the pickup to fix Diego's doughnut would have been cheaper on Uber.

A few days later, in Los Angeles, I finally admitted defeat, got rid of my recumbent bike, and picked up a fantastic Surly Long Haul Trucker, *the* touring bike of choice as the long frame lends stability and the old school parts are fairly indestructible. Put some Schwalben Tires from Germany on it and roll forever.

I know, you are sad to see the recumbent gone from the story, you have grown attached to it, and I admit it was pretty entertaining - for everyone but me. So frankly, #zerofucksgiven

We continued to count our blessings and I continued to ignore that nagging voice in my head that told me to do something about Microsoft, because there was nothing I could do.

We enjoyed California, we enjoyed Capoeira, and we enjoyed riding our bicycles. All three arguably symbolic for what every human desires once surviving is settled - Freedom.

Welcome to Tijuana
Date: October 3rd 2013
Location: Tijuana, Border Crossing to Mexico

"You are going to ride where on your bicycle," he asked.

I said, "Mexico."

"Are you out of your mind?"

"Well, actually, we are gonna ride through Mexico, Guatemala, El Salvador, Honduras… all the way to Brazil"

"Have you not heard about the drug war?"

I thought I'd try humor, "Welcome to Tijuana, tequila, sex, and marihuana? Don't tell me you never crossed the border to have a little wink-wink fun?"

"How many people died so far?"

Since humor didn't work I tried data, "Because of the War on Drugs the USA incarcerates 708 out of 100,000 people. Which makes this country the number two in the world, ahead of paragons of democracy such as Russia and Ruanda."

He responded with, "At least 80,000. They are massacring each other down there."

The disconnect was simply a case of *sarchasm*, where the divide between us was so big, that no amount of sarcasm could bridge it.

Maybe love would work, "Have you heard about how Portugal completely solved its drug addiction problem? Love bro, pure unadulterated love, and total decriminalization," but I could see I wasn't getting through, "Well, in any case, we are riding to Brazil, and Mexico is in between here and there. So…"

Before we follow this story across the border to Mexico, let me make a note. There is a lot you will find in this book. Tons of Capoeira, adventures, history, politics, a couple of death threats, and just a bit of group drama. I try my best to insult most systems, institutions, and other collections of idiocy. There may be some sex, drugs & samba.

One thing you will not find is the word *colonialism*.

Words have power. The word colonialism sugarcoats what Europe has done to the rest of the world since the 15ᵗʰ century. Let us be clear what colonization means. Samoans arriving in actually empty Hawaii is colonization. White whalers and missionaries ogling nubile girls on surfboards two thousand years later is not. People walking an ice-age landbridge to pre-historic Australia is colonization. The Queen of England showing up 40,000 years later and calling it Terra Nullius is not.

There is a word for arriving in a foreign land and butchering everyone who lives there. The word is genocide. Shipping everything of value home to build palaces and churches proves that the motive for killing hundreds of millions of people was greed. It is more difficult to forget 500 years of murder if that is what you call it.

Of course this is a royal pain in the ass for a writer, considering that occupying forces, marauding empires or thieving plutocrats, to name a few options for replacing colonialism, are all mouthfuls. But who am I to complain about a few literary complications in the face of truth.

So, shit was about to get real. B2B was leaving the USA for Mexico - going from one country born of genocide to another, before hitting eight more with the same historic can-do frontier spirit. We were about to ride 12,000 miles through blood soaked earth. If some people heading south think about narcos, tacos, and Brazilian girls, I think about thirty million dead Aztecs.

Don't invite me to your Columbus Day dinner party; I tend to poop on it.

From now on Disneyland no more - only filthy drug lords, corrupt Federalis, and tweaked-out truckers. We were so mistrustful that we didn't leave our bikes out of sight, even inside the border building where we got the first of many immigration stamps.

Some of the B2B riders were disturbed by the immediate presence of large caliber fire arms, though violence is probably not directed at tourist cash cows in broad daylight. Looking at us dirty hippies on bicycles as tourist cash cows was somewhat of a stretch in any case. Also, many people in Central America use their bicycles as transport. To people who ride their bicycles twenty miles to a backbreaking job every day we looked like lunatics.

Nobody messes with lunatics.

Looking at the military grade weaponry on display one thinks that maybe there is something potently phallic about having to strap down that hip holster so that it doesn't slap against your thigh while you walk. Considering the recent demise of the various dictatorships in Latin America, strangely coinciding with the end of the cold war, the gun toting was historically logical. Hopefully, the snitches will soon all be employed gainfully instead of loafing around street corners with their dildos more or less on safety while the rest of us earn their pay and indoctrination courtesy of the CIA.

By the time we arrived in Brazil we took the boys with toys for granted. Anyone who travels a little bit off the tourist beaten path learns how to operate in semi-dangerous situations. But, mostly you are either in the wrong place at the wrong time, or not. All you can do is pay attention and try to remove yourself at the drop of a quiet pin.

Much more upsetting than the coming risk was to leave the people behind who weren't riding to Brazil. Amongst them were Contramestre Fabio and Instrutora Come Come, who rode their bikes from Brazil to San Francisco five years earlier and inspired Mestre Acordeon's idea for B2B. Their dog Hermes had patiently been riding in a cage on Fabio's rack since Berkeley and was in particular demand for hugs. Only today, after having finished my own tour, do I understand how difficult it must have been for them to turn around. I don't think I could do it.

Professor Mniska told me, "I am glad you are going Pirata. It's good that Mestre has you along for when the shit hits the fan."

I gave him a big hug and shed a couple of tears as Peixao looked on waiting to hug it out.

People called out, "We will see you soon," and, "I can't wait to ride with you in Brazil."

Those words gave us hope, but not much comfort. We were saying good bye to our tribe.

"*Vai com deus, o Senhor,*" (Go with God, Sir) tears ran down Mestre Mago's face as Mestre Acordeon walked his bike across a very final seeming border.

I was also saying good bye, unfortunately, in horribly unprofessional manner, to my career. Because of the normal speed of things at Microsoft and the annual company RARARA meeting I had not been able to reach my boss the past week. Additionally, the company was in upheaval because CEO Steve Balmer had finally quit. Of course he had to pick the same week as I. This inconvenient meddling was normal for Microsoft employees' relationship with Steve Balmer.

Incidentally, Balmer's departure raised Microsoft's stock price by five percent. The increased value of his own billions in stock holdings was enough to purchase his next toy, the Los Angeles Clippers. Without rancor one must admit that yelling at the Clips from the stands suits his personality much better than motivating DEVELOPERS.

Of course, the next CEO Satya Nadella immediately fired 20,000 people, who mostly did at least as good a job as Balmer. Nobody bought them a professional basketball team for their retirement toy. One day, somebody needs to riddle me this shit that stinks to heaven so bad that even the devil's toes curl up in disgust.

Under these circumstances, there was no way I could reach anyone there, and so I emailed my resignation two hours before crossing the border, which, like breaking up with your girlfriend over text, will get you blackballed rather quickly.

It didn't matter. None of it mattered. What mattered was that I was really doing it. After a month of limbo, after gambling my entire life on a whim so thin it floats on a breeze, I won the jackpot. I was free.

But I was not alone. Mestre walked with a bounce in his step, too. We both felt freed from a prison of our own making. Sometimes, it seems like we spend our whole lives in that prison, one that Michel Foucault would call a Panopticon: it promotes self-discipline through possible but not necessarily constant observation. Our modern economic system works that way as well. One could even say, quite successfully so, and without the need for medieval coercion, or the protestant work ethic. The Man just sits himself at the center with a big pile of dough and makes everyone want to get some. Is modern capitalism's biggest yet most dubious achievement our belief that we actually want to work?

I felt relief to leave this world behind. But traveling through poor(er) countries does not change this equation. You only resemble The Man more and so it is easier to imagine you are closer to the big pile of dough.

Though I tend to fall too easily into these esoteric and somewhat escapist economic analyses of my first world predicament, for Mestre it seemed less mumbo-jumbo and more of a quest. As if crossing into Mexico removed the fear that his *alunos* (students) will attach ten horses to his bike and drag him back to Berkeley, preventing him from making good on all the lost years with Mestre Bimba. I may have believed that I would never again have to answer 500 emails per day after crossing this border, but Mestre Acordeon, he was going home.

We rode the bridge across no-man's land to Mexico where Mestre Pelourinho amazingly welcomed us with a Mariachi band and a Roda on a street corner in Tijuana. The super flexible, big haired Mestre, his gorgeous, no-nonsense wife, and aluno Maré did an amazing job of guiding us through the streets of Tijuana after we played a few short games and prevented a few pick pockets from stealing us blind (nice work, Balão).

Mariano interviewed Mestre Pelourinho for the documentary later that evening, not only because he is an amazing capoeirista, but also because his background is instructive of Brazil's relationship with Capoeira and her slavery past.

"Mestre, please tell me how you started Capoeira."

"I saw a few people play in the Pelourinho and wanted to try it. So I went to ask my parents."

Mestre Pelourinho is as tall as I am, but silly flexible. He can play big and small, he can bend around you like that rubber super hero guy and tap you on the shoulder with his toe while kissing you on the cheek.

Mestre continued, "My parents hated the idea, especially my mother."

"But why Mestre, you are not so old that Capoeira was still considered to be bad."

"Even today many people have a prejudice against Capoeira. My mother was worried for my safety and image."

"Why about your image?"

"She thought that people would think I am a Malandro." (Street hustler)

"So how did you end up starting to play? Because obviously you did."

"I jumped out the window wearing my normal clothes over my whites and snuck to Capoeira class with Mestre Pelourinho."

"Far out! For how long?"

"For years."

I often wonder what it would be like to either live in a dictatorship of a country or someone's mind. I was lucky that I never had to fight for freedom. When friends from Lebanon tell me about trash stacking up in their streets, or I try to get Mainland Chinese to talk about their government I realize I can never know. I also realize how much we, as a specie, can improve.

As Capoeiristas it is our responsibility to know the history of our art, but I was lucky, as a human, not just as a Capoeirista, to gain a small insight into Mestre Pelourinho's life.

That night we slept in the first of many dark and dank basements to leave town early the next day along a ten-mile-long, mean with fumes and tight with trucks uphill ride.

As we headed south we left Mexico's dirty underbelly, which oxymoronically is right next to its upper, northern border with the USA. No wonder gringos think that Mexico is a total shit hole. All they do is look one mile across the border, not realizing that the good parts of Mexico are closer to that country's center and the bad parts, oops, right next to the USA, where NAFTA incentivized robber baron capitalism.

On the second evening we pitched our tents in a compacted sand parking lot that they called a campsite perched on a cliff high above the Pacific. The sun melted into the sea. We needed to play some Capoeira down by the beach and Maré asked me, "Tienes Berimbau?"

I didn't have a Berimbau because mine got broken in San Diego, so I went over to Tora who was in front of his tent searching through his 10k plastic bags.

I sat on my heels next to him and asked, "Hey Tora, can we borrow your Berimbau please. Maré wants to play Capoeira on the beach."

Tora shot me a look of disgust and nearly yelled, "No!"

I guess I asked him for his first born. Some Capoeiristas are very protective of their instrument and this is valid. Later, I found out that Tora's Berimbau was a replacement for his original one that Amber lost on the freeway when it flew off the top of her truck. She didn't bother picking it up.

Diego brought his Berimbau and we played some beautiful jogos to Maré's haunting voice under a blood red sun going to sleep in the Pacific.

> Foi na beira do mar
> Foi na beira do mar
> aprendi a jogar
> Capoeira Angola na beira do mar
> > It was by the sea
> > It was by the sea
> > I learned how to play
> > Capoeira Angola right next to the sea

Fuck My Life (and the Windows Phone)
Date: October 2013
Location: Ensenada, Baja California Mexico

We continued south along the coast, a dry stretch. In Baja you see what California would look like without Colorado's water or invasive species like palm trees, lawns, and silicone implants. Skeletons of recent, never finished real-estate developments litter the seaside.

Three days south of the border, in sleepy Ensenada we encountered Capoeira again. A French Professor of Capoeira had pitched his tents here. We also had internet for the first time since leaving the USA. When I opened my inbox I found emails from all my friends at Microsoft.

Yo Peter! Your boss is looking for you.

Where you at man. Your boss is about to launch a search and rescue operation.

Dude, answer! Your boss is about to blackball you!

At the most I should have found a pissed off email from said boss.

I checked my outbox, and found my resignation email there, quasi grinning, telling me that I had asked for it. Thank you Windows Phone, I didn't log it as a final bug.

A few hours later I finally reached my former boss on a skype call from a café with internet in a dingy mall. Funny, that. Couldn't reach him for a week straight, but on this shitty connection, pop, there he was.

In any case, it was to be one of the less fun conversations of my life. At least it's all on film, because the crew had found out about my predicament and wanted to film the occasion.

I said, "Hi boss."

Boss said, "Oh… Peter… Where are you?"

There was no way around it, "I am in Mexico."

Boss lost his marbles, "What? Why are you not at work? You were supposed to be back three days ago."

I stated the obvious, "You did not get my email."

Boss threw his marbles at me, "What fucking email?"

"The one where I tell you that I can't come back to work."

Pause - reasonable, I'd say, under the circumstances. How often do you lose your team's representative in the tensest war room in all of Microsoft that year? I could see him sweat bullets thinking of having to go sit in it. It takes way too much brass to look Harry, the mercurial Director of Development in his cold eye and tell him that you are bringing three code bugs, when you are really bringing five thousand linguistic fixes.

Boss croaked a weak, "What?"

"I am sorry."

"We are shipping in six weeks!"

Y'all better recommend my book to everybody you know, because I sure am going to need a new line of work.

Then came the no fun part. I completely understood. Sometimes following your dreams blows. I had to explain that this opportunity was beyond normal professional reasoning. After fifteen minutes of not being able to do that I, without knowing what came over me, said, "You should come!"

Stopped him right in his angry bird, catapult launching tracks, "Huh?"

"I know you bike and get out into nature all the time. How about the picture of you up on Mt. St. Helens? When you are done shipping, fly to where we are, and ride with us. You will love it."

Silence. Maybe I was getting through, or he realized I really went off the deep end.

"Hmm, you know, that sounds really great. But… I don't think I could."

I thought I caught a note of doubt in his previously righteous anger. And though I know he was still pretty mad, I'd like to think that asking him to picture himself in the situation helped him to understand how extraordinary it was.

Whatever it was, I was finally free.

Baja California
Date: October 2013
Location: Baja California

A few days later, we rode into San Quintin. More or less as a hoax, Mestra went to ask the Bomberos (fire brigade) in her completely non-functional Spanish if we could spend the night. They invited us to sleep on the ground next to their fire trucks. It was the first of many nights that we slept safely, courtesy of the intimidatingly named helpers in need.

I liked how matter of fact our group did this. There was no prissiness, there was no drama. We just put down our tarps, took cold showers, and played a roda with the bomberos. They had barbequed the largest clams in the world (at least to an Austrian land lubber) and some fish and shared their tasty bounty with us. About here is when we started wondering why these people of humble backgrounds were so hospitable to a bunch of crazy but also, to them, wealthy gringos. One of the new Mexican film crew members, who had joined after Mestre Beiramar and Penguin had left us at the border, drily pointed out that, "It's because you are white. This would never happen to a Mexican."

Here we also started the habit of repaying people's kindness with a small donation or similar services. We'd leave some little things, do some cleaning, anything we could do or think of.

Soon after San Quintin we turned inland at El Rosario and said good bye to the Pacific. We were about to hit the real desert. To prepare we took our bike's drive trains apart and made sure all the break and gear cables were tight. We expected no potable water or villages for the next three days and tried to figure out how to carry four gallons of water on our bikes. The people of El Rosario thought our brains had been prematurely - as in, before entering the desert - fried.

At the guesthouse I met another bicycle rider, Eagle. He was a gangly, wildly curled, and spectacled nerdy looking guy.

After introductions I asked him, "Where are you going?"

Eagle said, "To the Observatorio Astronómico de San Pedro Mártir."

"Interesting. Why?"

He did that thing where someone doesn't look at you when they are talking to you. Like the sky and that cactus are suddenly way more interesting than you, and said, "It's located in the middle of Baja. One of the best places to do astronomy in the northern hemisphere. I am going to ride my bike there and write an article for a science magazine."

Eagle seemed naïve about riding his bicycle into the desert. He had one half of a gallon of water and a crappy backpack strapped to his rack. Plastic bags dangled on the handlebar of his cheapo mountain bike. Normally, you'd take the bike away from a guy like that. I invited him to ask Mestre and the others if he could join us for a few days so we could keep him alive.

I was right to worry about him. While cleaning my drive train I saw him swapping a perfectly good tube. I asked him, "Why are you not patching it?"

"I don't have a patch kit. I don't know how to do it."

Instead he carried ten tubes that he planned on swapping whenever he had a flat. All this being a little strange, I tried to find out more about him.

"So, uhm, what do your folks think of you riding into the desert?"

"I don't talk to them."

"Oh, ok. Are they in the…"

He cut me off with, "I don't want to talk about them."

Everyone has their reason to ride bicycle around the world. Eagle sounded like his was being an axe murderer. On the first night, he proved that it may have been premature to invite him when he tripped us out by talking about taking our knives and offering blowjobs to some of the guys.

On day two, he was through his tubes and had to hitch a ride in Amber's truck.

On day three, she lost track of him. But before we could get too worried he overtook us in a car. Fairly good riddance to a liability that lacked the social graces to survive in a pack of wild dogs. No insult to canis lupus intended.

In El Rosario we also met 117-year-old Mama Espinosa, who famously impacted Mestre Acordeon. Mama Espinosa was remarkably alert, as opposed to Eagle and many others in the area whose state of mind seemed to be affected by the creep that comes with the heat - that creature that slips past the lids of your eyes and nestles right next to the membrane of your brain.

In the deep desert vacant or hard eyes stare as you ride by.

For days afterwards Mestre randomly yelled, "Hah, she called me Bambini! How about that? 117 years old, and still young and fit."

"I guess it means that we can do B2B at least five more times, Mestre."

"Piratata, you are right. Let's never stop."

Mestre talked about Mama Espinosa on occasion after that. As a Capoeirista you are constantly aware of age. After you turn thirty your body yells at you every day *It is all downhill from here.*

Most of us give in to father time sooner rather than later. Mestre Acordeon never gives in. He complains about having to sleep.

We'd try not to pass him on an uphill, and he'd yell, "Oh, MarianoMariano, I wish I had your legs, I would fly up this mountain."

"But Mestre, you are doing fine."

"Hah, I can't feel my legs. Soon, Piratata will make me eat bananas and salt again and I'll still have cramps all night long."

At age 70, his reflexes were still so finely tuned that I couldn't get past his defenses when we good naturedly threw punches to greet each other in the morning. I always ended up with his hand in my face or in my gut. Imagine how fast he would have been forty years ago. Nevertheless, noticing the decreasing physical and cognitive ability of his once supreme physical awareness must be one of the toughest challenges of his life.

There were times when I had to hold back tears because I saw him frantically looking around a roda, distracting people with some insane Berimbau solo from the fact that he had stopped singing mid-song. It was fear that I saw in his eyes then. Not understanding why he did not remember the words to a song that he's been singing for fifty years.

Maybe these things were on his mind, re-enforced yet somehow alleviated by Mama Espinosa, when he asked us to concentrate on introspection, to consider our position in life, as we entered the quiet of the desert. He wanted us to record those thoughts for the B2B documentary.

This is easier said than done when you ride your bicycle through 100-degree (38 Celsius) heat. When you think you need a gallon and a half of water per day and know that the next emaciated desert village that might have potable water is probably three days away. Here the only shade from the brutal high noon sun is under a tarp that you span from the saddle of your bike to a rock on the blistered ground. But if the tarp is above you, what are you sitting on? An important question since you want to sit on something because you can fry eggs on the ground.

The good thing is that all of this needless suffering helps you acquire new, though I admit, somewhat arcane knowledge. Like how much a liter of water weighs: 2.2 pounds׳, in case you were wondering.

׳ Or 1 Kilo. I know, it's a metric miracle.

Here you also learn that the human body is an exceptional machine, able to endure far more than our suburban existence lets us believe. Yet, as strong as the body is, it is the mind that keeps it going. Diarrhea being one of the tests, that I, like everyone else on B2B had to pass, so to speak.

On the third day of excruciating yet explosive diarrhea, your patience runs as thin as your digestive tract. You try to stay as hydrated as you can, you get pissed when Mestre asks the film crew to interview you about your condition, and you carry a lot of toilet paper.

After the first time scraping your ass with what is, hopefully, a somewhat round rock, you carry more toilet paper. At least that doesn't weigh anything. Mostly, you go about pushing your pedals forward one at a time, because that is all you can do.

Along California's Highway 1, or Disneyland, as we called it, because it was always fun and safe, there seemed to be no obvious assholes amongst the riders. A thousand miles later, the physical and mental challenges made them a lot easier to pinpoint.

When a group of martial artists discovers dark places within themselves, when their willpower is all they have left, then it is a wonder of self-discipline that they do not punch each other in the face every once in a while.

Yet, we all had to deal with each other because we were all determined to make it to Brazil and so the year ahead provided us with ample opportunities of surprising realizations about ourselves and our ability to function in a group.

I was pretty sure that diarrhea and punching each other out were not the thoughts Mestre had in mind when he asked us to film small conversation pieces about our introspective processes. So instead I talked about seemingly superficial things like learning to adapt our riding strategies to Baja or how happy I was to be with B2B instead of in Seattle, to which winter was coming. I did not yet know what Mestre wanted.

One of the people who could have helped me understand Mestre better was his long time student, Instrutor Parafuso, who I rode with one day. He was the last one left who wasn't sure if he was going all the way.

I asked him, "So what's your plan?"

"I don't know Pirata, it would be dope to ride to Brazil."

"What's holding you back? I know you just quit your job."

"I'm struggling man. I got things I want to do, I need to do, for myself. To tell you the truth, I don't know if following a group is right for me right now."

There was always this intensity about Parafuso. No matter if he played against some baby Capoeiristas in Ensenada or learning a song around a campfire, it always seemed like he needed to break out of a cage and if he couldn't he'd make like the Hulk and get all green in the face.

"Hmmm, I can see that you need to walk alone for some time. B2B, however adventurous it will be, won't be an individualistic exercise."

"Yeah, you know, I am still gonna roll out. Ima build myself a little traveling van, go surfing, roll around Cali."

"The man in a van with a plan," I said, smiling on the outside.

He was the last one to turn back north soon after. This bit by bit tearing apart of our small ad-hoc family added a sense of melancholy to our introspective processes. Yet, during the filming of those small scenes it seemed like Mestre and the film crew could never agree on how to shoot. The crew would rush ahead and find some perfect location to shoot, prepare the place by adding some obvious traveling implements like a patch kit or a water bottle, and Mestre would show up and yell, "Porra! All this stuff is so fake. Like it's been produced in a studio with lights and makeup.

"… But Mestre."

"Do I look like I am wearing any makeup?"

"No Mestre."

"I want dirt, sweat, and pain. And maybe some blood."

So Yolanda went to build a fire in a beautiful sunset spot, sans implements, for us all to gather around and share some words. Romantic explorer stuff - pink sky, desert vegetation, and all. Perfect, even for Mestre.

Then the wind killed the sound.

For Mestre himself those days were intensely introspective. Tuchegas thought it was nearly compulsive how he urged us to engage him with questions during lunch breaks. We would arrive at some shack in the middle of nowhere and raid whatever dry goods things that were available and then sit down in the shade of a veranda on the concrete floor, eat, nap, and chat the heat of noon away.

He spoke often of his relationship with Mestre Bimba, and most poignantly of not having spent enough time with him.

One of the more memorable occasions was an early evening in a sleepy fishing village on the Sea of Cortez. B2B was lazing in hammocks, swimming in balmy waters, and watching fishing boats return to their tiny harbor behind a haphazard quay of boulders. A couple of them came over to chat and offered us fish.

Diego set to spicing the fish with the home-made spices that a certain kiss-the-ground-beneath-her-feet girl had given me before I left Seattle.

While the fish marinated we went to where Mariano had set up to shoot Mestre reading the chapter *The Making of a Mestre* from his book *Capoeira, a Brazilian Art Form*. We sat on some fallen palm tree trunks and arranged ourselves around Mestre. It was story telling time. White sand, palm trees, and a tranquil sunset framed us.

During the final sentences of the story about finding an ephemeral Mestre Bimba, tears streamed down Mestre Acordeon's face and his voice broke. He could not continue to read about his quest to find his Mestre and walked away along the windblown beach with only his wife by his side. Amongst the dunes and the shabby-chic fishing boats he remembered that he chose to leave his Mestre to bring Capoeira to the USA.

These occasions were the beginning of a tying together. A slow growing of root and stock, of limbs that carry and a heart that binds. Mestre bound us, and often we carried him.

After the reading of *Making of a Mestre*, as he handed him a plate of freshly caught and grilled fish, Diego asked Mestre with a nonchalant grin, "How come you wanted to ride your bicycle to Brazil Mestre?" (It was the third time that Diego asked Mestre this question)

Mestre, always immune to his students' bantering, answered, "As you know, I wanted to go on this trip by myself. But then Suellen said she would not let me go alone."

And he gave us a knowing look.

"And then you all wanted to go, too."

We grinned at each other.

"Some of you even just showed up!"

Then he leaned back, stroked his beard with one hand, followed it up with the famous Mestre Acordeon #3, a self-happy two-handed pat down of his chest and declared as a matter of fact, "Of course, I would be much further ahead without you."

Pat, pat – on his chest.

"But I am very happy that you are ALL here."

He usually finished with that line, as if he needed to convince himself. And sometimes we believed him that he would be much further ahead without us. But always it felt like Mestra would take him by the ear if he didn't say that last bit.

Mestre Acordeon may be the boss of Capoeira Regional, but Mestra is the boss of kindness. Just don't look for kindness when her *meia lua de compassio* (low, heal leading, rotating kick) comes flying your way.

Despite these events Mestre and I took a long time to warm up to each other. To him I must have appeared like a real wild card, showing up uninvited and on a weird recumbent bike. I continued deep into Mexico to do everything possible to live up to my Capoeira name. Lucky for me, even though Mestre is a master at figuring out people, he doesn't act very quickly or according to selfish desires. Maybe he sees the good deep inside of us, the good we ourselves don't even believe exists. Maybe he knows it is his responsibility to help us unearth it.

Much later, when the A-team went off track a bit Mestra observed dryly "Mestre gives you a lot of rope to hang yourself with."

I'm sure my noose had gotten pretty sturdy after the weed incident on the California camp ground and my general need to blow off some corporate steam since then.

Mestre definitely had plenty of reasons to keep his distance from me, or rather, not to worry how our relationship would develop. I on the other hand, am rather suspicious of grand personalities. I needed to see if he was arrogant like other Capoeira Mestres or if he tried to keep himself in check. Of course, anyone who has spent time with Mestre Acordeon will happily vouch for him.

I learned a secret when I saw the old man do dishes in the middle of the night at Contramestre Chin's house: humility is a work of daily practice. He was never too lazy to get up and do a task himself even though five Capoeiristas argued with him that they wanted to help.

Mestre leading the B2B pack

Maybe I also survived because Mestre has a weakness for the weirdos and the misfits. Capoeira in general provides a home to those on the margins. How could we say that liberty is in our DNA and not grant everyone, no matter how talented or broken, the liberty to practice the art?

Bebum had an even greater aversion to the Capoeira arrogance factor, but he overcame that with his direct way of talking to Mestre. The two quickly became close. I would be remiss not to admit feeling a little envious since I sat next to Mestre without really knowing what to say to him.

What was I going do? Ask him about his wife and kids? She was riding with us every day. Also, my time in Capoeira had been way too short to even begin to think of a semi-intelligent Capoeira question. Being foolish is much worse than not knowing something. Not knowing is just an opportunity for growth.

You could say that while Bebum went straight for a solid sniff at the biggest dog's balls, I circled around the yard endlessly, sniffing some old poop, overpeeing some markings, and only slowly coming closer to get a smallish whiffling of a trace of an airborne breeze of some potent Mestre musk. As both, Bebum and Tora would find out later, it is sometimes best to leave the big dog's balls hang about unmolested.

Shuke It All Night Long
Date: I'd rather forget
Location: Some fucking place in Baja where I didn't have a good time at all.

That piece of salad. I should not have had. Though it was so inviting and tantalizingly fresh looking, at least relatively to a day of scorched earth, I should have stayed strong and said no to the green. Like ice cubes and non-potable water, salad is on the no-no-list for gringos roughing it in the land of Montezuma's Revenge. Unless you want to accelerate your acclimation rate.

We had arrived at this ramshackle hacienda by the side of the cracked road about six days south of Mama Rosa's guesthouse at the end of another stupidly tough yet geographically gorgeous day of riding. Our clothes bore dried salt marks from our sweat. You know you are on the verge of collapsing your circulatory system if your sweat, that you have been licking of your arm to get at some salt, starts to smell and taste like urine. You feel light-headed first and soon you swoon. At that point it doesn't matter how much water you drink because the lack of salt prevents your body from taking it in.

I ate three handfuls of salt at the hacienda. The fourth made me want to puke, my bro-scientific sign that I had replaced enough.

After the salt, we needed water, food, and a safe place to sleep. You couldn't call the hacienda inviting by any stretch of the imagination. Threadbare barbed wire didn't really form a divide from the endless desert, a donkey screamed his scratchy unwelcome, and the proprietress seemed less than interested in making a few bucks off the crazy gringos on bicycles. I think it was pure pity that made her cook up some sun-dried beef with rice and – that salad.

After eating and hanging around just long enough for her not to be able to send us out into the quickly freezing desert night in good conscience, she reluctantly let us camp in the wind-shade of her bungalow. Maybe she knew what that salad would do to me and she didn't want me on her land. Smart lady.

At eleven at night I woke up and realized from the pressure in my gut that my digestive tract was revolting like it was a tea party. I peeled myself out of my sleeping bag, unzipped the inside of my tent, then the outside tent flap, and crawled over and past my panniers that I had stacked up inside the flap to avoid having them stolen, eaten or rained on. A process as long-winded as this sentence. By the time I got outside, I really had to go, if you catch my drift.

I raced over to the outhouse on the other side of the compound to take a mighty and probably explosive dump, and, found it locked. Frantically, I searched for a key by the outhouse and it dawned on me that the Senora must have locked it. That desert crazy again.

While I tried to come up with a civilized solution to this situation my body suddenly made like a pretzel and as I nearly kissed my feet, the explosion happened from a bodily orifice that I did not think was part of the equation. Minutes later I was relieved from the mostly undigested parts of my dinner and tried to scratch some dirt and rocks to cover my vomit. I examined my completely unsatisfactory attempt in the gorgeous full moon light while realizing how lucky (haha) I was that I had to puke instead of shit because I had not brought any toilet paper from my tent.

I went back, crawled over my panniers, awkwardly turned to zip the flap, forgot to check for scorpions, got into my, by now totally cold sleeping bag, and zipped up the inside of my tent and my sleeping bag. A process as long-winded as this sentence. I tried to relax, but the only thing that came to my mind was that delightful piece of salad, burned into my consciousness. Funny, how you know exactly which piece of food to blame when the shit hits the fan. I also forgot that there was a pretty good (100%) chance of having to repeat the whole procedure again in, oh, about 22 minutes.

But one learns. Again, I woke up with a cramp in my gut that kindly helped me understand that this was no one-time thing. Very quickly (hah) I unzipped my sleeping bag and my inside tent, crawled awkwardly over and past my panniers, opened my outside flap, turned to grab some toilet paper (this is the learning part) and… froze.

The fucking outhouse was surely still locked. The pressure in my intestines kept building while I scanned the property for a likely spot. Not next to the outhouse, not next to Mestre's tent, not next to the donkey – last thing I needed was a donkey ululating in my ear while I puke or shit. As all those options were neatly placed in the corners of the hacienda, the only place left was the center, close to where a lot of us slept. I staggered carefully - you can't really call it walking when you are trying not to vacate from every possible orifice - over to a tree and held on to it as I bent over to get ready to puke. Oh shit, this time it was the other end. It was a freezing desert night and I wore everything I owned. So I ripped down my sweat pants, pulled down my capoeira pants and my long johns, held up my jacket, sweater and three shirts, and… well you can imagine.

It was like a watermelon exploding on the sidewalk right in front of you that some punk kid tossed from the tenth floor. But it felt kind of good, relieving even. Until a strange, unfortunately, now all too familiar cramping in my gut let me know that I had to - WTF - puke as well. I wasn't done shitting yet! As I bent over, I started retching like never before in my life. You can't retch quietly at this level. Mercifully at least the donkey did not join in my screaming. I leaned my ass against the trunk of the tree, held on to a branch for dear life, and, yes, you would not think it possible, shat and puked at the same time.

I shuked.

Apparently, necessity is the mother of all invention, though you should avoid trying to imagine the exact geometry of this s(h)ituation. Just know that that perfect, slightly slanted tree was a life saver.

After five minutes of this ordeal I didn't even have the strength left to stagger back to my tent. I literally crawled. Fuck the panniers and fuck the flap, fuck the scorpions and zipping it all up. I knew I was going to be out there again in, oh, about 22 minutes.

Rinse and repeat - except there is no running water - a few more times as the night progressed. It was atrocious. Most of us might have called it a day and taken the next bus home, if you imagined this to be your future for the next year. I preferred to think of it as getting a necessary evil behind me. Eventually my body would stop impersonating an Oktoberfest staple food and get used to the bugs doing Olympic laps in my cup and scaling my food like it was the Eiger North Face.

In the morning, I hid in my tent while the rest of the gang was breaking down camp. I finally managed to force myself to move, I needed some food in me. Even though I would probably not keep it down, at that point it was better to have something to puke than not. While I made black tea and ate some white rice and lentils Mestra Suelly came over and asked with a kind twinkle in her eye, "Was that you or the donkey that I heard screaming all night long?"

Love her for making me laugh when that is all you can do to stay sane. After telling the rest of the gang why I was going to ride in the crew car Bebum drily commented, "So that was you, shuking all night long?"

I strapped my bike and panniers to the roof of the crew car and got ready for an embarrassing day of puking and crapping my pants. I hated not riding bicycle with a passion. Yes, I had to ask the new camera person to stop abruptly a couple of times, but I resolved that no matter how I felt tomorrow, this would be my last and only day in a car for the rest of this journey. Seeing my mates ride this arid land only made my desire to ride to Brazil stronger. Nothing could be worse than not riding, not feeling the sun on my back or the wind in my face. I wanted my heart to pump in my chest and my legs to do what millions of years of evolution made me perfect for. It was up to that point the worst day of the journey, and it had nothing to do with the shuking.

Even by the already very high Baja California standards the landscape towards evening was spectacular. Around 3 p.m. we entered this Mars-like area with reddish 18-wheeler-sized boulders strewn haphazardly across a rolling desert. The fifty feet tall Cardón Cacti and tons of other shrubs reminded us that, for now, we were still on planet earth.

I felt well enough to get out of the car and jog around to find a likely spot for our tribe and we camped at the foot of a ninety feet boulder heap. I put my tent a little off to the side amongst some nooks and crannies to spare my mates a highly likely repeat of the previous night's performance of *Shuke it all Night Long*.

The sunset from the top was magical and apparently the sunrise as well, though yours truly did not get to enjoy the latter. I was still busy spray-painting the desert. During the course of the night I had made about eight trips around cacti, thorny brush, and various poisonous animals to an unobservable corner to continue cleansing my colon. At least I wasn't paying some quack hundreds of dollars for an apparently fairly natural procedure. On my last trip, just as the sun rose, I realized that I had created a rather abstract colorful painting in my little corner of poop. Thankful for some, on this group journey, unaccustomed privacy, I finished my unsavory business and hobbled back to my tent wondering how my (Bronto)soreass was going to feel in the saddle later that day. Bebum and Mariano greeted me with rather dumb grins on their faces. I knew right away that it hadn't been as private as I thought.

"So bro, how did you sleep?"

I could only raise a weak middle finger.

Mariano looked behind me in the direction of my escape route and cackled, "So that's where you have been going all night long!"

"Affff, whatever! You fuckers should be glad I got out of the way. That shit wasn't funny".

"Actually, it kinda was. We just saw your ass sticking out from up there," Bebum said and pointed up to the top of the heap of the boulders. I couldn't help grinning at that thought and felt sorry for them.

Bebum said, "You are pretty talented, Poocasso."

What Goes Up, Must Come Down
Date: October 2013
Location: Baja California Sur

We spent the night in that magnificent place. A landscape so profoundly unearthly that even the more practical members of our tribe could not avoid a small sense of romanticism. Maybe it had actually been appropriate to add some surrealist art to the mélange of desert beauty.

A journey into the wild, a space so wide open that you understand your own tiny, disappearing existence, your actual place in this universe, lets you discover a sense of freedom. Yet, while you know this, you also instinctively feel connected. You are one with this wild world. Your star rises with the sun. And it is entirely appropriate for you to connect to the stellar mother of our corner of the universe on this deeply natural and creative path that you tread.

Of course being called Poocasso will rather quickly do the trick of putting you in your small little place, too. That morning of the second day of fighting, actually, forget fighting, you only suffer through Montezuma's revenge, I was still weak and so didn't participate in the following conversation.

Bebum said, "Hey, so we don't know how soon we will hit another village. And we are all loaded down. Why don't we put another five-gallon jug into Amber's truck just to be safe?"

We all thought this was a rather logical idea, so Bebum walked over to where she was getting ready for her day of driving at the incredible speed of 20 miles an hour to ask her.

Amber said, "No."

Even Bebum's stoic nature was flabbergasted by the support car's unwillingness to, you know, support.

"Wait? What?"

"I said, no."

"Why?"

"Bébé is already too full. I don't want to put that weight on him as well."

"What do you mean? It's a Toyota Four Runner. It's built for this shit. It wouldn't even feel another five gallons of water."

"No, I won't do it."

At that point there was a lot of headshaking and walking away from the conversation going on. Instinctively we all knew that if we escalated this the group would have trouble to be cohesive again. After a few more minutes of further pointless arguing with Amber, Bebum gave up as well.

Due to my preoccupation with my art work entitled *Poocasso's Artistic Contributions to Desert Landscape* it took me a little longer than usual to get ready and ride in the morning. The only one slower to get a move on than I was Tora. Balão, always the patient soul, was waiting for him as I started down the winding road.

Judging by the sun, it was about 7.30 a.m. Way too late to be riding out into a desert. Though I mentally prepared for a day of grinding it out in the heat I soon fell into a comfortable cruising rhythm through the arid valleys and grand landscapes of this central part of Baja California. The distant mountains outlined the horizons like giant, blue sails turning the earth on the winds of the cosmos. This absolute stillness went deep into me. I miss feeling small as I sit and put these memories to paper.

The morning's hills were a challenge for my stricken, dehydrated body. I had to ration my water, because we were on our third day out of town and not sure if the next stop at roughly forty kilometers would have potable water. It was a point on a map but the people we talked to could not really tell us anything about it.

I was coasting down the winding road when I heard Bebum's characteristic *Hatchaaaaa*. There was a 400 feet tall heap of boulders to my right and sure enough I saw Bebum's Shimzzy parked in the shade of a McMansion sized boulder at the bottom and Bebum waving from the top. It took me about 15 minutes to climb up to where he was, but I must have taken a different route because when I was nearly at the top I was looking at a six-foot gap between the boulder Bebum sat on and me. I looked down and saw – nothing. The hole completely swallowed the harsh desert light. I had no idea how deep it was. For all I knew I'd be tickling Mao's ass if I fell in. I would have enjoyed jumping over Mao's ass but the problem was that Bebum's boulder was also six feet higher and the side facing me completely devoid of anything to hold on. I can climb, I can jump, but I ain't Spiderman. I looked around for an easy way to get up to him, but it seemed like I would have to climb for at least five minutes.

Bebum said, "Don't worry bro, I'll jump down to you."

"No you are not, that's way too far."

"Na, it's gunna be ok."

"Your knee ain't gunna be ok!"

"It'll be fine."

Knowing that it probably wouldn't be fine, I stood exactly in the place where he would need to land. I wasn't on a very large boulder.

Bebum is a stubborn fucker and said, "I'm gunna jump."

I hated that moment. I knew if I went to look for a way to climb up he would jump as soon as I moved. Or we'd stand there for an hour. I also knew that his knee was completely shot from his snowboarding injury and operation-free recovery. Bad luck does not feature in America's plan for your dream.

He gave me that stubborn Bebum look. That look that says, *Ima do what Ima do, and you can deal with it or get out of the way.*

I got out of the way. Bebum jumped, landed, fell over. And screamed.

He held his shin, pulled his knee to his chest, and lost all the tan in his face. At that moment I viscerally remembered my own basketball induced torn ankle ligaments twenty years before. Again I heard the *pop* ring through the gym like a gunshot when I stepped on that guy's ankle during scrimmage, ripping all three ligaments in my left ankle. I knew exactly how Bebum felt. A stabbing pain in the area, a crazy pulling on your suddenly disconnected muscles. He was going into shock. And we somehow had to get him off that bleeding stack of boulders.

Right then, Balão came riding by on the road below. He heard me whistle, stopped, and I called for him to ride ahead and get our non-water carrying support car to come back. Then I turned my mind to getting Bebum down the mountain. I had no idea how to carry him around, through, and over the haphazardly stacked boulders. He didn't seem to be in a frame of mind to analyze the situation either.

So we smoked the joint we had come up for in the first place. In Bebum's world you either rub some dirt on it or you smoke some green medicine.

For sure, I could not take him down the way I had come up because I had done quite a bit of real climbing. If Bebum followed the three-point climbing rule, he would not move at all, seeing that he only had three points available at that punny point.

In the end we had no choice. There were not going to be any helicopters throwing rescue lines, and no drones or gnomes would magically appear to save the day. We limped, carried, pulled, let down, and straight up dragged his lanky, heavy frame down the boulder stack.

By the time we reached the ground, forty-five minutes later, I was sweating as much as he. The air was shimmering on the road and the only shade we could find was low to the ground under a boulder with an overhang. I crawled under and dragged Bebum in after checking for desert critters.

The cold desert ground was a blessing for our overheated bodies and stressed minds. We ate some snacks and drank what little water we had. Thankfully,

Balão had left some extra for us. One hour later, Amber returned. We strapped Bebum's bike to the back and he got in. Considering how the day had started, it must have been a rather awkward first five minutes.

I started riding the lonely road, wondering if I had already lost my brother less than two months into the journey.

Brothers in a TukTuk

Brotherhood No More
Date: October 2013
Location: Baja California Sur

The days after Bebum's injury were strange for me. While the UCA crowd had slowly started to accept us we still had outsider status. Riding alone is sweet in its own lonesome way, but it's not advisable in the middle of nowhere. Tarantulas, narcos, wayward Saguaros, knife-wielding, cunnilingus-offering Eagles, you can conjure up any of many scenarios in which it would be preferable to travel in twos or better threes. So Mariano and I teamed up. Are two bros a brotherhood, or do you need at least three?

I realized then that he seemed to have been riding unattached up until that point. Strange, considering that he was part of UCA. In the long run this was a fortuitous development but at the time it was a delicate situation. He was just too obviously straight-edged for me in most instances, being second in command after Mestra. And likewise he probably had his reservations about this Pirate who just showed up to join a trip that he had been planning for years. But I soon realized that even though Mariano acts the straight guy when needed, he cuts loose harder and faster than most people I ever met, and I bartended in a Yakuza bar in Ropongi. Just saying. So, with me being the conduit, car-bound Bebum, Mariano, and I established a tight friendship.

Amber and Joaninha took to calling us "The Brotherhood", on account of us embodying the unapologetic male part of the species. Bebum is a redneck in a hippie coat, Mariano doesn't give a shit about your feelings, and I hate being labeled. We all love pushing buttons. So calling us "The Brotherhood", which started as a thinly veiled criticism for falling out of lily-livered, politically correct line. Bebum pubescently kept saying "testies-testies" during sound checks, quickly became much appreciated. We loved being brothers. Cooking lentils and arroz con leche (milk rice), smoking, riding, and chasing girls together (rather unsuccessfully, at least until we hit the big city lights). Those were the visible mechanics of our existence. You'd have to sit down by the fire to hear some bro-losophy.

One night, I asked Bebum, "You think when Joaninha told me last night that she thinks that I think that she is a fucking idiot I should not have not said anything so quickly?" (I should say, that I enjoyed her direct manner)

"Bro, I just spent a day with Amber. Spare me."

"So… you are already warmed up."

Bebum pulled a face, "Well, she did let that stray dog lick out the bowl that Yolo had just washed out to use for breakfast the next morning."

I continued, "And every time we are at a camp site she feeds the stray dogs."

Bebum said, "Yeah, but still bro…"

"What?"

Bebum and Mariano did a Mestre Acordeon #2. In which he spreads his arms a little, opens his palms and his eyes wide, and in this pantomimic way asks you, to please utilize the normally vacuum-filled space between your ears.

I said, "You mean instead of not disagreeing so happily, I should have tried to explain why I think that the local disease-carrying walking public garbage bins are not like the pedicured little lovies back home?"

Bebum's and Mariano's eyes opened wider, arms spread further, then came a smooth transition to a Mestre Acordeon #1. In which one hand comes back to the face to straighten the beard, sort of gently pulling wisdom out the bottom of it.

I said, "I tried that at El Salto. A dog ran after her for a mile when we left the campsite in the morning."

Bebum said, "Pirata, it's not like you used your inside voice when you talked to her about it."

I said, "I don't know man. I get the ego calming thing, but I feel like telling the truth goes a long way."

"But if you are coming from your own ego you will only end up attacking the other person's, and then they won't try to understand you. They will just attack you back from their ego. Which is what Joaninha did."

"Whatever Mr. Bro-losophy."

Mariano executed a perfect transition from Mestre Acordeon #1 to #3, in which both hands self-happy pat down on his chest and then spread, elbows at the hips, in full agreement.

And so we rode and I learned. Not sure if that lesson will ever stick though. Us Austrians can have a rather direct nature.

Whatever the good lessons had been, of course my boy Bebum had to go ahead and fuck it all up by jumping off a boulder. I knew I would miss "I just don't talk much" Bebum. Hanging out with him is like walking into a Clint Eastwood Western. Ugly dudes with few words and lots of firepower. But behind the stoic outside resides a patient street-wisdom, that will do great by maturing a little more, for a couple of decades or so, in order to reconcile a flip-flopping past into a coherent personality.

This is a good thing, if you don't look back every ten years and wonder what an idiot you've been, you aren't living and you sure as hell aren't learning.

Writing a book also gives you ample opportunity for this often very difficult exercise in self-improvement.

U-turn
Date: Late October 2013
Location: Bahia de Concepcion, Baja California Sur

His glasses were as thick as coke bottle bottoms. The old kind. The ones with real sugar. Un-regulated, highly caffeinated, and only available outside the USA.

His teeth were rotten, his nose swollen, and his skinny, lanky frame utterly undernourished. His appearance was a little extreme, even for Baja California desert crazy standards.

"*Que hace este pendejo gringo en bicicleta en medio de la pinche calle en la noche,*" (What is this pubic hair gringo doing riding bicycle in the middle of the night on the fucking road?) he yelled from his cab and proceeded to tell the gringo to toss his bike into the back of his pickup and get in.

In this case, the crazy gringo on the *pinche* road hailed from the cold steppes of central Ukraine and did as told. His name was Cantador (Opera Singer), our first official Sequestrado.

"*Quieres una cerveza?*" the physically oxymoronic driver continued to yell at Cantador. Apparently, he always yelled while he drove his truck. Cantador had only been riding with us for three days, and what an insane welcome to B2B this was for the Ukrainian scientist. Flies himself and his wife, two bikes, and tons of gear from Santa Barbara to the middle of Baja California, starts riding, and the first thing that happens is a crazy man yelling at him.

So Cantador reached deep into his bag of Spanish vocabulary and answered, "*Si hombre,*" and grabbed the two beers offered.

The driver's next question was, "*Quieres fumar,*" offering the joint he just dragged on.

Now Cantador wondered if the middle of the pinche road might not be the safer place after all. They were on route to our campsite, which was another Baja nature wonder along the *Bahia de Concepcion* on the Sea of Cortez.

In the meantime, most of the gang was swimming in the bio-luminescent waters of the bay to hide from the sunset swarming mosquitos. Since I don't believe in having my head gnawed off by hordes of bloodsuckers, I stayed on land wrapped in layers and so I saw the rusty, forty-year-old pickup truck turn into the sandy expanse of the campsite's half moon bay and roar straight at our camp. I got ready for trouble. Mariano was in the water and Bebum in the support car.

But then, Cantador emerged somewhat dazed with two beers and a reefer from the cab of the truck.

When the driver emerged from his truck I was immediately reminded of Billy Bob Thornton's character in the movie U-Turn. Laughing loudly, disgustingly dirty, and somewhat untrustworthy. Did he have pigs in his backyard?

A minute later, Bebum, Amber, and Cantador's wife showed up. They pulled out a case of beer and four huge fish. But before we could start grilling the fish we needed firewood. U-Turn offered his and way too many (all) of us piled into the back of his truck. Maybe we were all looking for adventure. Would you rather be Sean Penn or Jennifer Lopez?

U-Turn ran his mouth a million miles an hour as we rocked past the beach and the gringo trailers at the end of it. I knew this kind of jibber-jabber from

Japan. The Shabu (meth) does the talking, embracing the world for days on end. The paranoia sets in later.

He stopped at a barbed wire gate, Mariano opened and closed it behind us, and we continued driving on U-Turn's private beach to his trashy trailer. The stars streamed their light in perfect silence. Geese and chicken hung out in the small bay.

We helped him unload his truck as he turned on his rumbling generator and tacky Christmas lights to light up his trailer trash. Then he offered two joints (I hoped there was no smack in them), drove us to his firewood, yelled at us about the pinche corrupt Mexican government, dropped us and mountains of wood off to our campsite, and disappeared into the night after inviting us out to his place for whenever.

We needed to be friends with U-Turn.

That night, Cantador and wife grilled their fish for us. Little did we know how good they were at seafood, apparently the Ukrainian scientist likes spear-fishing and, of course, once you get into that you should know how to prepare your catch. Mariano's specialty, Arroz con Leche over campfire rounded out the feast. We passed out from food coma.

The next day, half of B2B went to catch up with early riding Mestra and Mestre after we played a few games of Capoeira on the beach. Mariano, Bebum, Yolo, the Sequestrados, and I rode out to U-Turn's beach.

We arrived at his RV and shockingly his coke bottle bottom glasses were gone. What? He didn't look like he'd feed us to his pigs anymore (not out of malice, you understand, but a rather finely developed sense of economy).

He let us have one of the Palapas, an open-sided shelter with a thatched roof, and went back to leveling an acre next to his trailer, by hand! U-turn himself would have said, *"En medio del pinche dia caloroso"*. No matter that it was in the fucking middle of a hot day, soon he would have the flattest spread on the block. We set up at the Palapa and Mariano and Cantador headed over to invite him to lunch. They returned without U-Turn but with a full set of spear fishing gear.

Mariano explained, "His name is Marco. He used to be the Chief of Staff for the President. They framed him for murder, threw him in jail, and the key away. He just got out last year after 10 years. Bought this place to get away."

You laugh, but you should know that the desert heat will fry your brain and the wind will carry it away.

Mariano continued, "Then he invited us into his Tarantino trailer, sunlight streaming through fucked up blinds 'n shit. Told me to find his spear fishing gear and smoked fucking crack out of a light bulb right in front of me and Cantador. Cantador was about to bust a vein in his eyeball."

An hour later, we were grilling two Halibut and other morsels of the sea that Herr Badass Cantador speared in the tranquil bay at the end of our world.

U-Turn was still leveling. And he wasn't going to be sleeping or eating any time soon. Two of his friends showed up and they got to work, too. Until sunup. At which point the spread was flat like Dubya's world.[5]

Despite his tweaking days and yelling ways, he was another example in a long list of Mexican hospitality that we were forced to compare with the local escapist gringo friendliness, which usually went down like the chat we had with one on the next day.

---

[5] I wrote this chapter in the happy days when George Bush was the worst US president in recent US history. I think it is historically important to leave it that way.

"Yeah, we live down here most of the year, gotta get away from things, you know?" said the man with a knowing look. I didn't want to agree with him. I dislike these chummy *you and I are in the same boat* assumptions.

He continued, "So you guys are riding to Brazil, huh. No shit? Hey, that's great. What an adventure. Is there anything you need? Can I help with anything?"

I said, "Hmmm, no we are fine... Well, maybe some eggs?"

"Oh... how many are you thinking?" he asked, looking at the horde of hungry looking cyclists behind me.

"Up to you, sir."

"We juuust came back from the store, well, we have some, but..."

He paused.

"… you guys look like survivors, you'll get on. Yeah, sorry, no can do."

No comment.

In the end it turned out U-Turn was apparently not another crazy Mexican dude mad at the government. I googled him, the interwebs never lie. He did get thrown into jail for murder and seemed to have been involved in a murky real estate transaction.

A few months later, someone hit me up online, after having read my blog post, claiming to be related to U-Turn. I hope I didn't fuck up his retirement out of the lime-light.

Far be it from us to say who is guilty of what because of course in prison everyone is innocent. Should we have been glad that we had his spear in our campsite over night? Hindsight is like wearing glasses the size of coke bottle bottoms. The old kind.

Amore Mexicano, or why Hemingway was a Drunk
Date: Early November 2013
Location: Bahia de Concepcion, Baja California Sur

Amore Mexicano came into my life like a long lost lover – a rush that you didn't see coming. The day after we left U-Turn's beach, Mariano, Bebum, Yolo, and I ran into Amber at Nathan's Playa Bonaventura. She had stayed back to get her ride on while the riders rode on.

Nathan's cool little Palapa style beach hangout in that small bay on the Sea of Cortez south of Bahia de Concepcion should be in a brochure called *Gorgeous Beaches far off the Beaten Path*. Of course then it wouldn't be off the beaten path anymore. The slightly run-down joint reminded me of the *Titty Twister* from the movie *From Dusk till Dawn*. Minus Machete trying to get you in the door, and minus the titties, or the vampires. Wouldn't be surprised if Salma Hayek swings by every once in a while, though.

When I walked in, the floor creaked, the saloon door banged a little behind me, and a lone crusty Mexican desert dweller sat by the bar, nursing this earth-dirty drink out of a tall tumbler. Too strange to not ask about, because the drink should have been red if it was a Michilada,

I used my outstanding (ridiculous) portengnol[·] on him, *"Buneos tardes Senor, como vai?"*

"Muy bien, gracias," he rasped.

"Tenho una pregunta senor." (I have a question)

[·] A mix of Portuguese, Spanish, and English, being as unintelligible as it sounds.

"*Vale,*" (Sure)

"What drink are you having here?"

He smiled, said "Ahhhh," and, "Now, that is a good question for a gringo to ask."

I liked the old man.

Then he said, "*Café Mexicano!*"

I failed to understand, he pointed at the menu above the bar. *Michilada, Margarita… Café Mexicano,* they were all there. My gringo mind remained too dense. Finally, he made me taste it.

It was a revelation, a symbiosis, a synergistic 2 + 2 = 5. Café Mexicano tasted like Tequila. Paradigm shifted. Thank you very much.

And, with all considerable respect due, I realized why Ernest Hemingway and Stephen King were alcoholics. A couple of Café Mexicanos sent my brain on a zinging, pinball machine creativity overdrive. Over time, I also accumulated a little Tequila belly, as Mariano called my paunch. Quite the achievement on a bicycle journey. I sacrifice such so that real stories may be born in the eyes wide open haze of *Amore Mexicano.*

That was the name Mariano and I bestowed upon Café Mexicano. We planned to make a million dollars with it on our return. Except now, that I have spent a year on the road, I am even less into the idea of business for profit. So go ahead and make something out of it, it's yours. Just don't over-sugar the thing, like Petron does. And remember where to send a yearly supply.

From that point on you'd find me with my Mexican Lover and a joint on most rest days. All, you understand, in the name of art. Try it sometimes, maybe it turns you into a riding, writing, treasure seeking fool as well.

A few months later, in Salvador (the one in Central America), I had gotten over my need to blow off corporate steam and I started contributing more to Mestre's goals. But the weed and the bottles of local booze stayed. After all, Bebum and Pirata had an image to maintain.

On day ten of Bebum's incarceration in Amber's truck, Mariano and I gunned it down a nutty downhill. You will never know joy until you fly down a winding road after you rode uphill for three days. We were waiting at the bottom when the support car passed by, with Mestra in it instead of Bebum. In those early days she didn't like going downhill at high speeds.

Mariano asked, "But where is your bike?"

She only laughed and pointed up the mountain. A second later Bebum came flying down on Mestra's bike like a lunatic. Grinning like a mad man too.

Only the most famous B2B Facebook video of all time ensued. Tora filmed Bebum, with his Brazil sarong draped like a cape around his shoulders, riding Mestra's bike, one-legged. Right hand steering and right leg pushing the pedal. That much was normal. But the bad left leg rested up on top of the handlebar, and with his left hand he pushed the left, now leg-less, pedal with his walking cane. I can't even describe it properly. It was a mirage of physical inventiveness. There might have been some Cheech and Chong involved. In one word: Bebum Bebum'd it.

What started as a quick little trade gave Bebum the idea to see how far he could ride one-legged. You want to be in a Clint Eastwood flick with ugly dudes? You better have a big jaw to take punches with and determination for days. He never looked back and rode the 400 miles to La Paz on one freaking leg.

One day, we were riding up a baby hill, he started hollering. I sprinted up to him to make sure he was ok and he yelled, "The mosquitoes are catching up to me."

I laughed when I saw the evil suckers swarming around him.

"I am too damn slow to get away, and I don't have a hand to slap them with."

I love my brother but some things you gotta do on your own so I hit it hard and left him and his blood sucker friends behind.

He laughed, "Fuck you Pirata."

It was to be one of our last innocent, joyful moments.

On a journey of any kind, but specifically on an adventure halfway around the world the hardships and risks will take their just count. That Bebum would miss most of the trip was one of my greatest disappointments.

From the beginning, somewhat arrogantly, he and I had assumed that the two of us were physically and emotionally best equipped to make it. Sadly, the same asynchronous personality that made Bebum perfect for the arduous journey also was his undoing.

Once we took the ferry from La Paz across the Sea of Cortez to Mazatlán he went in the car to Guadalajara with Yolo. She had decided to call it a day and go to work on her dream project of filming a documentary about the experiences of a quadriplegic homosexual prostitute. This might be an indicator why her and Mestre where not really matched up well for the B2B project.

Bebum went ahead to get his knee looked at and found out that he would need an operation. He would recover under the care of Instructor Guerrero care for three months. The same amount of time it took for us to ride through Mexico all the way to Guatemala.

Peace in La Paz
Date: Mid November 2013
Location: La Paz, bottom of Baja California

Most days in the Baja Desert were brutal. In reality, it's not a place for humans. I guess that's obvious since nobody lives there. Especially, the Mestres were looking forward to leave the heat behind. "It's because as the body ages its ability to adjust to heat diminishes," Mariano, old metabolism nerd, explained.

Mestre constantly suffered from nightly leg cramps, no matter how many bananas and how much salt I forced on him. Two days before we reached La Paz, it was over 100 degrees as we rode through an undulating landscape. Mestre struggled all day. We were used to seeing his ramrod straight back, a perfect physical expression of his indomitable will ahead of us.

"Just keep on moving," was his mantra for these occasions.

But that day it seemed rather like he wanted to shove a rod up whoever said the wrong thing.

I rode up and asked him, "Mestre how you doing today?"

"Hrmpf!"

"Here is a banana."

"Thanks Piratata, you have the first bite."

Mestre gives nicknames to everyone (he likes), on top of our Capoeira Apelido. There was Dieguito, Tuchegetas, Balãonzinho, ToraTora, MarianoMariano and Piratata.

"It's alright Mestre, I just had one. You know me, I live of Amore Mexicano and bananas."

I was lying, but Mestre needed all the potassium he could get and he would not eat otherwise. I knew he could see to the bottom of my sneaky soul.

"You know Piratata, today it's really hard for me."

"It is pretty hot Mestre. Maybe we should take a break."

Except there was no shade. Not even a boulder or large street sign. Both had provided shade before. Obviously, there were no trees around, it's, you know, a desert.

"Let's lean the bikes together and make a shade with my tarp."

I couldn't believe he was still carrying it. While we were building, the rest of the crew arrived. Once finished, we all crowded under. It was a game of twister trying to fit all of us under there. Whatever body part stuck out got baked.

Suddenly, Mestre said, "I feel like I am having a stroke."

Not the words you want to hear from your 70-year-old fearless leader.

"Let's just wait until the sun goes down a little more, Bira. I see some clouds in the sky."

The clouds never came.

A couple of hours later, we rode on but Mestre kept struggling. Mariano and I stuck close. Finally, he pulled over and asked us to check his bike. To me it looked more like a *Mestre Break* (a break to gain some rest time without admitting exhaustion), but it turned out that his disk break was stuck. Mariano giggled, Mestre had a good laugh at himself, and "I think I am having a stroke," became a running joke like "It's all downhill to Brazil from here."

If any of us looked a little too winded, there was Mestra cackling, "You got a stroke, huh?"

Better than being asked if that was you or the donkey screaming. Just saying.

Six weeks after leaving Tijuana, we coasted towards La Paz. The sun set behind us, the road, sometimes obscured, sometimes visible, gently wound downhill into the dusky light ahead of us. One last perfect moment in the desert that had been our home for six weeks. *La Paz*, The Peace, a romantic name for a quiet port, bid us a kind welcome.

Mariano and I smoked a victory joint at the top of the ridge above town. Our view of the Sea of Cortez was as wide as our hearts open. For the first time since leaving Berkeley we let ourselves feel a small sense of accomplishment. Maybe we could really do this. Maybe Brazil didn't seem like it was on another planet anymore. A thousand miles of desert turned us from Sunday riders into road warriors.

Part II

Mestre Zeus throws Bolts
Date: November 2013
Location: Mazatlán, Sinaloa, Mexico

We hit Mexico's mainland via ferry from Baja California. The Capoeiristas around Mama Teresita welcomed us to her cozy hotel in Mazatlán. They helped us overcome a ceviche induced diarrhea attack and organized a police escort for the first two days after leaving town. This was crap your pants, El Chapo homeland, Sinaloa. We weren't sure if the police escort was a good idea or not.

On the first evening in the coastal flats, a hopefully well-meaning Capoeirista led us astray and we spent a bumpy 45 minutes in the bed of a pickup going to a shitty beach. If you want to piss Mestre of, make him ride bicycle in the heat for eight hours while worrying about the Cartels, and then put him and his stiff back in a pickup just so that he can enjoy your dirty, mosquito rich beach.

Once there he called a meeting. I sat down next to him, which proved an unfortunate choice.

After some rumbling by Mestre, Tora said, "I waannt to saaayyy thaaaat soooome peooooople…"

I interrupted him, annoyed by his continued indirect bitching instead of just coming straight out, "Tora, why don't you talk to the person direc…"

Tora cut me off, "Shut up Pirata!"

I shut up.

"In myyy coompaniieee, weee aaaaaalways maaade cuustommeeeers haaaapyyy byyy…"

I don't get mad if you step up to me. Especially not if…

Mestre unleashed Zeus. He banged his toilet cover sized hands on the rickety table with the force of a sledgehammer.

BAMMMM!

And yelled at the top of his lung, "Tora, I don't want this shit."

Mestre's face was the color of a stop sign, a purple one, veins popped on his neck. The hair on his head, and even his beard, stood off like he had his hand in a power outlet. Lightning bolts may have sprung from his eyeballs.

I sat there trying to hold my breath; I thought I smelled ozone. The force of Mestre's temper had shaken me in my boots (ok, flip-flops) even though it wasn't directed at me.

One more time he stormed, "I don't want this shit."

I don't know how Tora survived. Must be some kind of training Japanese kids get in the face of absolute furious domination. I would have dropped dead like an Australian Aborigine whose shaman pointed the bone at him. Tora, instead, had that look on his face when he doesn't understand, but he might also not have any fucks to give.

So Mestre turned to Tuchegas, "Tuchegetas, please translate for Tora."

She rolled her eyes and started, "OK, Tora, did you understand any of it?"

Pre-school teacher Tuchegas' duties included, amongst many other items, translating matters of state to small children and language challenged folks.

Mestra sat on my other side. Her only comment was, "Just take it to the roda."

I wondered if she was implying that we should Code Red each other, like we can Handle the Truth, like we are in the Marines, whose group cohesiveness ethic is probably pretty similar to that of Capoeira.

I started to look forward to the next roda.

The next day we were going to head up to the Mexican Cordilleras, our first real mountain stage. Google map profile told us that we would have to climb six thousand feet in less than thirty miles. We didn't really know what was about to hit us.

At lunch the probably good police escort turned back and we continued towards an ominous wall of green on the horizon in front us.

And then, on that sweaty, suddenly intensely emerald afternoon we turned a corner and the road ahead simply pointed straight into the sky. No gentle rolling hills prepared us for what was about to happen to our quads. No Sireee. It went from flat to *I am going to murder your legs until you beg for mercy* in one little innocent turn.

The worst thing about that climb was the straightness of each segment. Every time we came around a hair pin turn we looked at a mile-long ascent of 300 feet. It was completely demoralizing. We had no idea how many of these we had to overcome. It was like hiking the Grand Canyon. Each plateau you reach might be the last one before getting back to the rim, but it probably isn't.

Three hours later we finally hit the outskirts of Tepic. The local Capoeiristas welcomed us, gave us hope for warm showers and tasty, yet, at that point still gut-watering, ceviche. And then said, "It's a little more uphill to get to our house."

Mexico was finally showing her true colors to the gringos who meant to insult her with their silly little bicycles.

Mestra giggled somewhat deliriously.

Mexico
Date: November 2013
Location: Querétaro, Mexico

A couple of days, and a few much cleaner colons, later we left Tepic to make our way across Mexico's central high plateau towards Mexico City and had many opportunities to discover this extremely varied country.

If there was a competition for the most misunderstood country Mexico would own it. Unless you could vote for your own country, then everybody would be a winner.

Open any US newspaper on any day and you'll find a glaring headline about ten million illegal immigrants being driven to the US to steal jobs and benefits by Mexican drug gangs cannibalizing the country.

My personal truth about Mexico is simple: It's amazing. This shouldn't come as a surprise, considering that it has been the home of continent-spanning empires for millennia while the Brits and the Spaniards were still hovelling along in their short, nasty, and brutish existences. Mexico astounds us with ancient technologies that are so advanced as to be inexplicable.[7] It has a growing middle class, everybody wants to get more educated, and commerce is popping. The Distrito Federal of Mexico City is a *superchingon* (super cool) global metropolis and Mazunte in Oaxaca a black hole. Plan to stick around longer than you planned.

---

[7] Go ahead, make my day. Hand build a largish rock heap in prism shape, 79 feet tall, the cardinal directions thereof align so perfectly that on summer and winter solstice the sun transforms the stairs on its side into a snake that appears to slither up or down the side of the pyramid.

There are so many facets to this country that you could spend years here and never be bored. The further south you go the greener, more developed, and cleaner it becomes, often with a rich civil life thriving around beautiful town centers. Of course if all you see are the NAFTA polluted ten miles south of the US border, you might think Mexico is a total shit hole, but this is forgetting that the further from the USA you get, the nicer the country becomes. Strange, isn't it?

Unless you've been lucky to hang out in one of the little central Mexican towns, joking around with locals, eating ice-cream, and fixing flats, you probably won't even believe me. Considering what you hear on the news you'd expect empty, eerily quiet towns. But out of the seventy odd towns and villages we stayed in during our traverse of the country only one was scary. We came across it on the way to Leon in the state of Guanajuato.

Mariano had pulled five flats that day and we were getting frustrated at not being able to ride for more than ten miles at a time. When your rubber runs out you appreciate its heretofore solid stoicism in the face of constant friction. Mariano was on *Continentals* at the time while the *Schwalben* I rolled with had not had a single flat in well over 2000 miles. Give a German unlimited time and budget and she will apparently build you a thingamajig that will last forever.

The group was split up. Due to the flats, Mariano and I came late to an un-obvious left turn where everyone was waiting for Diego to bring the Mestres back from a Mestre Shortcut.

We stood because the ground was too hot to sit on. When Mestre finally grumbled past, everyone got on their bikes and followed sniggering.

Mariano pulled another flat.

We told the rest we would catch up. After laughing at the silliness of riding for one thousand miles without a flat and then having five in a day, we continued on what we hoped to be a (real) short cut instead of following the group. Unfortunately, the road we chose had much crazier truck traffic and no shoulder at all. And so, after getting run off it a couple of times, we decided to turn back to the main highway. Of course, now we had to ride into the wind.

After Mariano's flats, the Mestre and our own shortcut it was 4 p.m. We were not going to catch up, so we turned into the next town.

And there it was. Tombstone at high-noon. Tumbleweeds rolled in the dusty streets, reminded me of Daily City Bart station. Dudes in jeans and boots loitered on corners, staring at us from underneath their Stetsons. Mexicans in Stetsons are like Magyars belting out, "The hiiiiillls are alive with the souuuuuund of muuuuusic!"

They were leaning against walls in those lazy, confident poses that louts think threatening. Our inquiries at the local, small dried goods grocery store about a guesthouse were met with incomprehension. As if no one in their right mind would want to spend the night here.

We needed to increase the price for messing with us. Out of sight someone might cause problems, but in public there would be more of a barrier. The front door of the small church on the square was locked but to the left of it we found a small doorway through a thick, white-plastered wall into a courtyard. We moved our bikes in, deciding to ask the good lord for forgiveness later.

An employee of the church found us and did not make us leave until Father Ronaldo returned later and offered us his dorm for the night. We were happy about the way our day ended, having only to fend off ravenous suckers on church property (mosquitoes, what were you thinking?) instead of louts in Stetsons.

Days like these are always exciting. Instead of sitting in the office thinking about whether to have coffee or soda we were forced to engage in a more primordial existence. Did our hunter juices flow freer because we could not be on autopilot? Or maybe we were just happier because we were free to let them flow.

At 5 a.m. the next morning we bailed. We had some catching up to do.

And it seems, many people think Mexico does as well. Yet, the country's central high plateau has been home to some of the first empire states on the planet. Complex, resource-rich societies supported mega projects like Teotihuacan which formed the foundation for four millennia of Mexican high culture.

In the 8ᵗʰ century, when the Spaniards were learning things like math and other civilizational advances from Muslims, which certainly laid foundations for the Renaissance, the Mayans were busy creating perfect celestial calendars.

This sentence alone should illustrate why humans should all just get along instead of pretending superiority to one another.

In the 16ᵗʰ century, only 800 years later, Hernan Cortez came upon several highly developed city states in the Yucatan where people used gold for ornaments. To the conquistadores the fabled Fountain of Youth, or at least Eldorado, must have seemed just around the corner and so their plan went from conquest to enslavement faster than a modern-day news cycle.

Spain's occupying forces built their thieving vassal state on top of an empire that thrived during the time of Marcus Aurelius' death in Vindobona (Romans started the settlement that was to become Vienna). The only European culture that came even remotely close to that level of development at that time was ancient Greece. Greece didn't build 300 feet tall temples or calendars predicting Venus' location 5000 years into the future. Democrazy is pretty cool though, despite having been described as the least of all evils.

We get mad at the Taliban and ISIS for blowing up ancient temples, but we easily believe the *Justifiers*. Those who tell us that the conquistadores brought civilization to the Americas, instead of burning up temples and melting down Aztek gold artifacts – because it was easier to ship gold bars home, which would then be made into gold artifacts for the churches of Europe.

Those brave Castilanos surely were much more advanced, higher evolved even than the Taliban.

Apart from thinking that Cortez was a god, proving indubitably again that religion is just never good for you, except should you be stranded in a cartel stronghold with louts in Stetsons, the Aztecs lacked certain inventions and disease vectors.

The commencing thievery of humans, gold, and novel resources such as rubber, sugar, and potatoes was of a titanic scale and *justified* with the ludicrous idea that the so-called savages were actually profiting from all this misery. Mostly by gaining entrance to heaven, posthumously, you understand. Spain and Portugal presided over the largest genocide in history with that most ferocious of fervors - the golden, godly kind.

In 1519, thirty million Azteca lived in Mexico, despite some rather cruel sacrificial practices. Fifty years later one million was left.

The best brains in the just about to be enlightened old world left us with marvels such as this one from Voltaire: *Latin America is inhabited by lazy and stupid*

ᵃ The castes in society that help us understand why we are supposed to kill and be killed in the name of our god, our king, or our nation. Longest serving members: religious minions.

Indians who live side by side with pigs with navels on their backs and bald and cowardly lions.

Navels on their back? What does that even mean, Sir Justifier?

Bacon, Hume, and Montesquieu declined to recognize the "degraded men" of the new world as human beings. And with the moral backing of the future thought leaders of the renaissance, the dis-ease ridden, witch-burning, and illiterate white man arrived on the shores of the Aztec empire. He killed their men and, in their homes, he took their women to his smallpoxed bed. He made their/his children slaves for his death trap mines.

I am sad to have to write that nothing has changed in the last five hundred years. We still swallow every piece of propaganda bullshit whole as if it was a prize strawberry. We do not question Colin Powell when he stands in front of the UN with a vial. People in the developed West do not question why people in the Middle East are upset even though every piece of ammunition Israel has dropped on her neighbors in the last 60 years had "MADE IN THE USA/FRA/SVE" stamped on it. Russians do not question why they suddenly get to enjoy all that Crimean sun. Israelis do not question their government's assertion that nothing but building a Nazi state around Palestine will work, while Muslims do not question their leaders' lies about the Holocaust. This abrogation of the truth on all sides, this willing following of today's *justifiers*, is why you can sometimes find me impatient with religious and stupid folk.

For the sake of the universe I hope that a great filter waits for us somewhere out there. If not, maybe Skynet could help us out and put us in a zoo before we civilize ourselves, and the rest of this joint, to death[.]

Just about five hundred years after Columbus failed to discover India, I witnessed the results in every town I bicycled through: A nation climbing out of the pits of poverty, yet multiple gilded cathedrals praise a distant god in each little farm village. The other half of the bounty went to build palaces and finance religious wars for an equally distant Queen Mooch.

The assertion that the Renaissance and the Industrial Revolution, enabling today's Western standard of living, were financed with the wealth stolen from the *Open Veins of Latin America* does appear factual when you visit the former gold veins of Guanajuato.

The town is set in a tight pot shaped valley. To reach it, you drive through subway-sized tunnels. Those used to be the mines. They have public buses running through them, which is what we took to reach the city. There were intersections with stop lights and signs. It's a huge road network under a mountain. Someone hacked all of this out of the mountain by hand.

That's how much gold the holier than thou Spanish looted from there.

Once you exit into the cobblestoned streets of the *Centro* you can look up, past richly decorated facades, gorgeous frescos, and angels pissing off rooftops, at a huge statue of a priest on a hilltop, surveying that which lies beneath. Fittingly, Father Hidalgo started the Mexican Revolution here, which might have been the first labor action in history. Was Karl Marx, like tomatoes and beans, a gift from the new world?

Guanajuato is a jewel of a town, and that is the other legacy of the occupiers. Beautiful palaces, the latest fashions, and four dollar cappuccinos. Walk through it, and you think you are in Madrid.

We only had one Capoeira session there and played tourists the rest of the time. It was the first town on our journey with some serious history and so we

---

[.] Thank you Dr Ryan.

walked around all day long, checking out the dumb[10] mummy museum and shot a video of Balão singing one of his gorgeous, heartbreak songs up by the revolutionary monk.

Mariano and I spent the last night in the centro, getting lost, rolling with Pretzel from LDM who true to being a peerless Mexican host helped us to achieve complete inebriation while dragging us from one Beer Case Dance (Cumbia) joint to the next. I must admit happily that the second half of the night is rather a blur. Happily, because I was tired of humanity's dark side.

The next day was a good day for all of us to ride later than Mestres, even though usually at least a couple of us rode out with them. Due to Pretzel's (not afraid to blame him at all) ministrations I may have still been a little drunk, but I rode anyway. No matter how little sleep, and how much Tequila, Marijuana, and dancing I enjoyed the night before, I always rode.

Two hours later Mariano received a phone call "Mestre got hit by a car."

On the one day that the Mestres take advantage of not having a bunch of over-worriers stuck to their back-wheel, Mestre gets run over by a car. Are you fucking kidding me?

For all we knew he was bleeding out on the side of a lonely Mexican freeway. We punched pedal on a whole new level and started to burn down the road. Adrenaline cleared our foggy heads in a flash. We arrived in the medium sized city and found them close to the main square. Mestre was fine.

He said, "I got hit from behind, BANG flew through the air, did an *Aú* (cartwheel), broke it like I got a *Cabeçada* (headbutt), PRRRAPPPAP got into a *rolé* (roll) and ended up on my hands and knees. Took a second to check myself. Padded myself down and realized nothing was broken."

Total, utter seventy-year-old Capoeira Mestre amazeballs.

Mestra was white like a sheet.

I asked her, "How you holding up?"

"I heard this horribly loud crash from behind me, stopped, but I didn't want to turn around. I looked a little bit behind, and I saw one of his panniers on the ground."

Her hands flitted to her brow, rubbing it, as if to make the sight disappear from her mind, "I was sure I would see him there…"

She didn't give voice to her worst fears.

"…When I finally turned around, I saw Mestre on his hands and knees. The bike mangled on the side of the road and his bags all over the place…"

We hugged. Mariano tried in vain to fix Mestre's bike. Fortunately, we were supposed to stay with some Capoeiristas that day. Mestre had called them and they were coming to pick him up. Later that evening he quipped, "I can move much better. I think the accident fixed my back pain."

To finish off a day from hell I found out that Bebum needed 4000 USD for his operation in Guadalajara. 46,000 USD less than what it would cost north of the border, 4000 USD more than he had. I ended up wiring him 9000 Pesos. He was my brother. I don't leave brothers behind. The conversation I had with him about which account to wire the money to, was the last time I heard from him for a long time. That was rough.

The next day, it turned out that Mestre's bike frame was broken. Mestres were forced to take the bus from Queretaro. The rest of us rode on with our newest

---

[10] Because a museum about the revolution or the mines is more appropriate, you'd think.

Sequestrados, Professor Mata Mosquito, UCA Berkeley and the Wright Brothers[1], LDM Mexico City. The ride out of Queretaro was brutal. The steep uphill three-lane, shoulder-free highway we were one was not the right place for humans on bicycles to be. We rode next to monster diesel trucks fighting their way uphill. Relief spread amongst us once we made it to the top of the five-mile climb and finally had a shoulder to ride on.

Of course, life is never supposed to be easy, and soon a truck of squealing pigs blew past, kindly re-interpreting the meaning of a golden shower for me. I was glad I got to share the banho d'ouro with Mata Mosquito, though.

Yeah, that happened. If I was going to where the pigs were going I'd piss myself, too.

On a bicycle you learn many valuable lessons, thankfully not all of a scatological nature. For example, that in defiance of 500 years of slavery and pillage a strong indigenous element remains in Mexico. Even after all that time appearances of people were different from town to town. People were tall and skinny in one, and short and round in the next. I saw different skin shades, different facial bone structure as well as different clothes. This genetic and cultural strength is extraordinary in an increasingly mongrelized world. I for one am happy to be greeted by Mayan and Aztec faces, even though their names knot my tongue.

Mexico's history impacts its present self-image but the country seems to be moving in a good direction. I am sure to some this sounds like a naïve statement, but during four months of riding we slept at the Red Cross, at fire and police stations, municipal halls, gyms, (former) prisons, restaurants, hotels, mescal distilleries, and on roofs of *paleterias* (ice cream shop). Countless Capoeiristas shared their stories, ideas, and thoughts on a better future. The country seems impatient to improve.

Yet, development, democracy, and civil society take time. Many countries in the world did not take these steps easily or gently. Having a two-thousand-mile border with the world's only super power is going to get you fucked with as well.

So please, dear Mexico, please be patient with yourself. Neither Rome nor the Ming Dynasty were built in a day. Cut yourself some slack. Life seems to be, like riding your bicycle, a marathon.

And Mexico, keep your hospitality, you are amazing.

But stop warning me about the dangers in Guatemala. It makes you sound like a Gringo.

Capoeira en México
Date: December 2013
Location: Mexico City, Distrito Federal, D. F.

And then there was Mexican Capoeira and B2B. Mestre Acordeon coming to a small town near you. We were a Capoeira bicycle train with a super charged twin turbo diesel engine. Much later I realized again how big a deal Mestre Acordeon really was, when the trip was over and I had to find my own food, my own bed, and my own Capoeira. It was like being Steve Kerr playing with the

---

[1] Because they flew down the road on their professional mountain bikes. Also, their Aztec names are unpronounceable to unskilled tongues.

Suns after having rolled with Michael Jordan for five years. An average white guy with a decent shot who can't get open for the life of him.

Throughout the entire trip Mestre's star power gently trickled down like mana from the heavens in the form of ceviche, pupusas, and churrascos (Brazilian BBQ). And always we found the most important thing for weary road warriors: open arms and hearts. And Capoeira.

And did we ever play Capoeira in Mexico. It started on a street corner in Tijuana and continued when Professor Irak randomly found us eating Tacos in Baja California Sur. We did workshops on the Malecón of Mazatlán, in the square of Tepic, with Mestre Xuxo's group Signal de Santa Cruz in Guadalajara, and with LDM in Leon, Guanajuato, Queretaro, and Mexico City, where we stayed for nearly a month. Puebla, Oaxaca, and Chiapas down to Guatemala followed. You name it, we rode it and we played Capoeira there.

In Mexico City I spent many hours with Professor Aramé, who introduced me to his family, and showed me where he used to get into fights before he started Capoeira.

He told me, "Mestre Cigano saved me. I would be dead without him."

I heard Mexicans talk about Mexico, about Capoeira, and about Mexican Capoeira. Mestre Acordeon set out to discover the roots of Capoeira in the Americas. And that's what we did.

Mexican Capoeira is intimately linked to Mexican culture. You can take a taco guy out of his taco truck, but you can't take the taco out of the taco guy. Even if he becomes a salad guy, he will toss your salad as fast as if he were still making tacos.

Right.

And nowhere was there more Capoeira than in the mushrooming suburbs of the D.F., although, similar to Mexico's northern states mostly without Brazilian instructors. The leaders of large groups often had less than five years experience and were under the supervision of Mestre YouTube.

It was mixed, messy, and happy. Yes, some of these groups seemed zumba-ized. They may not know how to play pandero (tambourine). Or that the *toques* (Berimbau rhythm) in your roda are the toques to your life.

But, as Capoeira grows, in the nooks and crannies of this dense humanity, should we prefer some Capoeira over other? Considering that none of us know an absolute truth of origin, a base, do we have the ability, the right, to know the destination?

And how can Mexican Capoeira find its base, when Mexico itself has been working, justly, for centuries to find and accept its own?

Each revolution in formerly subjugated lands left a legacy of deeply ingrained cultural memes. Do you wear fur or feathers for equinox? Are you a Minute Man or one of the Child Heroes of Mexico? Where is your past located and how does it impact your present?

Wherever you live, these narratives leave a lasting impact that is beyond my experience and understanding to interpret. It is difficult to imagine any part of humanity that does not contain such cultural signposts. I remain with questions: How does Capoeira as an expression of anti-subjugation mesh with Mexico's founding mythology? Does Mexico's self-image allow room for Capoeira, which is part of another nation's creation myth?

One of the statements we often heard about Mexican Capoeira is that players don't "speak" to each other which is a central aspect of Capoeira. Each attack and defense is supposed to form a question and a response, a conversation. Mexican

Capoeiristas didn't speak their mind. They either played parallel to each or threw punches.

Yet to speak one's mind, one must first know it. One must know one's foundation. And so this stasis between a game of mutes or a fight remains. *Mas não é um bom jogo* (but it's not a nice game).

It is as if Mexico were caught in finding its soul between its tortured history with Europe, its brief infatuation with the USA, and finally, itself.

Stuff
Date: December 19th, 2013
Location: Mexico City, the D.F.

By now you know that I decided to go on this crazy trip two weeks before the thing started. Yes, it may have been better to plan this a little longer.

The first inkling of what I was getting myself into, was an excel sheet that "why do today what you can do tomorrow" - Bebum sent my way on the day of his fateful phone call. It was a monster of an equipment list that the B2B crew had put together. I stopped counting at 200, and started thinking about what I could do tomorrow.

Insect repellent, biodegradable soap, water purification method A B & C. Stove, pot, cooking utensils - which fuel is best for Honduras? 500 and one things for a medical kit, clothes, sleeping bag (not too hot/cold), tools, patch kit, bike replacement parts. Bear spray, dog whistles, bike bell, reflectors. Pepto-Bismol & condoms.

I don't know how (thank you, helpful friends), but when I lined up on the first day of my new life I managed to have everything strapped to my ridiculous recumbent. I was prepared. Nothing could harm me.

Of course then Bebum and I camped on the beach on the first night and the rest, especially our gear, was, as they say, history. Though my sweet Dutch friend wired me a little money we did not have access to any real resources until my replacement cards arrived in Los Angeles. We could not buy clothes, gear, or tons of food.

So we made do. And we learned that we didn't need most of the stuff. For a month, one of those water proof Trader Joe's re-usable plastic shopping bags was my second pannier. It was a pain in the ass, spent five minutes strapping it on and off each time I needed something. It worked.

Before minimalism was the new black, I packed all the belongings that I wanted to keep for my return into two bags. I kept some knickknacks, clothes, books, and a blender. Call me Homo Blendus. This points to an essentially functional relationship with stuff. I need to wear stuff, I like to read stuff, and I blend stuff.

How much stuff one needs to be happy varies widely. Some need more to be comfortable, some less. It was the same on B2B. I was rather sensitive about how much stuff I had because it was me, not a horse, a dog, nor a woman or an enslaved person carrying my stuff (You laugh, or you are insulted, but that is who, historically speaking, carried stuff for men).

And yet, over the course of a year-long bicycle journey, stuff accumulated, again. It was as if stuff, like mosquitoes, magically appeared out of thin air when I least wanted it. Periodically, I went through my stuff and, you guessed right, gave stuff away.

If you are tired of reading the word stuff, you can stuff it.

That fourth t-shirt that a Capoeirista gave you? Donate it, remember him in your heart instead. Biodegradable soap bottle? Donate it, bar soap is lighter. Wash your hair with it, too. Third pair of sports undies? Donate them to hazardous waste. Headlamp? You have a bike lamp that magically gives light, too. You only need a headlamp because you are doing so much unpacking and repacking in the middle of the night. Toss the cutting board (are you kidding me?), get a skinny plastic sheet. Unless you go to where it's cold, toss the tent, get a hammock. Keep the knife, stove, pot, and your Indian maybe-girlfriend's spices. Keep your summer sleeping bag, it doubles as a pad. If it's cold at night, wear all three shirts. Keep your bike tools, a sowing kit, and electric device chargers/adapters.

Still getting a flat per day? Your bike is too heavy. Donate more stuff.

The lighter I got the easier I felt. Bike riding is not only a gloriously meditative and healthy activity. It's also a direct feedback loop on why possessions are bullshit. I asked myself: Other than clothes, food, and a place to sleep what do I really need? And is my normal life any different? How does my second TV increase my happiness? Do I need ten towels? How many pairs of jeans do I actually wear?

So be more Dutch. Move into a smaller house. Channel your inner Japanese. Do what you love, instead of wasting time on work so that you can buy stuff that you never use – because you don't have any time for it, because you are working so much to pay for all the stuff you buy. Work thirty hours instead of fifty and hang out with your kids more.

For those of you who already do this: great stuff. For those of you, who want to tell me, "fuck it, I like stuff," that's cool, too. Everyone is different. Just know that when you are eighty you will not look back and say, "I wish I had bought a Mercedes instead of jumping into that alpine lake with my kids." Not completely without coincidence, one must note that if we all keep driving Benzes much longer, there won't be any alpine lakes left for anyone to jump into.

Tora had all the touring stuff under the sun. He organized for two hours each day, often waking us up with his plastic rustling noises at 4 a.m. You'd be one moody motherfucker, too, if you only got six hours of sleep after riding eight hours every day.

I did not have much stuff to organize and went for many swims, looked at the sun and the stars an unreasonable amount of time, did unnecessary bouldering, played flute for a lot of local kids, as well as the moon, wrote a bunch of things and watched that grass grow or that small town plaza flow.

In the end we all are the makers of our own happiness. I am not the keeper of your spare time and Tora is not the judge of your effectiveness.

That being said. Get rid of some stuff. One day you might have to carry it.

Stranger in a Strange Land
Date: December 24ᵗʰ 2013
Location: South of Puebla, Mexico

It is typical of Mestre Acordeon to spend three weeks in Mexico City only to leave two days before Christmas, to my pleasure[12] not caring much about anyone's sensibilities about the season of giving the gift of consumerism.

I loved the D.F., that agglomeration that churns, melts, dissects, and re-forms day and night. In its burrows humanity makes magic. Around daily Capoeira activities I took in as much of museums, local culture, and people as I could. I walked around Frida Kalo's hood, got lost with Mariano on the way to Xochimilco (what is left of the wide ranging canal system of pre-Cortez Tenochtitlan), and checked out the university library's gigantic fresco modeled after Aztec carvings in the fantastic National Museum (also a definite must-see for visitors). I froze my balls off in a mothballed manor house with a capoeira feminist and smoked pot on the roof of a body builder nutritionist. Now I am confused what's more feminine. I drank a toast in a hotel of my family's lore and wondered if the Zocalo's Cathedral could sink any more. One evening, it snowed.

We said good bye to Mestre Cigano and Longe do Mar, as is customary for B2B, at the crack of mid-afternoon. On the day we left, B2B picked up four permanent sequestrados. Instrutor Banano was the new camera guy, Ken offered Mestre to drive the now crewless crew car, Indi (Bebé Chorrão) and Tartaruga (Juanjo) wanted to ride.

From here on out B2B would shoot the B2B documentary because the film crew would not continue with us any longer. Mestre was going to have visions, Mariano tried to find them, Banano shot them, Balão did sound, Diego edited film, Tuchegas logged film, Tartaruga fixed the B2B website, and I wrote scenes, articles, and Social Media things. It's clearly magic that enables Mestre Acordeon to randomly collect exactly the type of skills that he needs for his journey across the world.

When B2B left town in cars, because we did not want to die in traffic, Mestre asked me to go in the crew car with Ken and Indi. Rasta-haired Ken sure seemed to sweat a lot that day, even by his moist hippy standards. Bug eyed, he constantly pushed his piss-color tinted aviator glasses back up his nose. Within meters of leaving Mestre Cigano's house I knew why. He stalled the car five times on the first block.

"So you told Mestre you know how to drive, huh," I asked him.

Ken gave me the look of a Shih Tzu puppy that somehow, without meaning to, had attached itself to the tail of a raging Bengal Tiger.

I continued, "Stick or automatic?"

His high pitched voice imitated that of all Mexicans in Hollywood actions flicks, "I donn knoooow mano. Isss maany jears."

It was becoming entertaining, "How many?"

But I was only teasing him. How could I, an often falling down and frequently stoned pirate, be mad at him for trying anything possible to join Mestre?

---

[12] When I was thirteen my mom asked me, "So, you and your brother don't believe in this Santa Stuff anymore, right?"
Proudly thirteen I said, "Pffft, of course not."
"Good, because your dad and I are going trekking in Nepal for three weeks over the holidays."

That didn't mean I couldn't give him a hard time.

"Do you even have a driver's license?"

Indi, from the backseat, cackled at the top of his lung, "*Licensa por chingada tu madre.*" (License to, well, never mind)

I shouldn't have, but I took pity on Ken and over driving. Partly, because the joining of the Mexican sequestrados, except for Banano, was sort of my fault.

It happened like follows: after one of Mestra Suelly's workshop in Roma, central D.F., Juanjo asked me, "Oi Pirata, where are you from?"

"*Yo soy de Austria hermano.*" (I am from Austria)

"*Que chido, mais tu vives en Estados Unidos?*" (Cool, but you live in the USA?)

"*Sim, no Seattle.*" (Yeah, in Seattle)

This sort of language mishmash was normal in our group. I was learning Spanish and Portuguese, the Chilangoes were learning English, and the lucky rest already spoke all three languages.

"Oh, you don't live in San Francisco?"

"No."

"*Mais tu esta com grupo de Mestre Acordeon?*" (But you are in Mestres group?)

I pointed at the Candeias logo on my tight, white Capeoira pants and said, "No."

"*Como?*" (What?)

"I am from Candeias in Seattle, it's a group from Goias in Brazil, Mestre Suino."

"*Mais...?*" (huh?)

"I kinda just showed up in Berkeley. I had written Mestre a letter asking to join, but in his response he didn't specify yes or no. So I just went. And now I am here."

"*Pinche tan loco.*" (fucking crazy)

"Gracias amigo."

He hesitated, "*Entonces, yo quero viajar tambien.*" (I want to go too)

"Oh, verdad? Well, what are you waiting for?"

"I can't, I work as a Project Manager for Software in a large company."

"I used to work at Microsoft."

"What the... and you gave that up? *Pinche maluco gringo*" (fucking crazy gringo)

"Hah, I've heard that a few times. But really, if you want this, talk to your Mestre, then to Mestre Acordeon, pack your shit and go."

I had a similar conversation with Ken during our stay in D.F. but never thought that the crazy hippy looking guy would have the balls or resources to go.

The rest of the trip Ken and Juanjo often attacked me with hugs and said, "I am only here because of Pirata. I love you man."

I don't know if Ken in particular still felt that way at the end of our journey.

Yet here we all were; leaving Mexico City and my new-found friends behind. We passed portentous Popocatepetl and iridescent Iztaquatl, the two active 15,000 feet volcanoes named after two Aztec gods in dramatic yet impossible love, on the bowl shaped periphery of Mexico City.

They were still as unpronounceable to me as they had been 25 years earlier, when my dad drove us past them. Once again, like on the Pacific Coast Highway, Mestre Acordeon traced my family's vacation routes. Of course back then, being Austrians, we needed to get up as high (Physically - as far as I know, my hippie parents never touched pot in their lives) as we could, so we took the road that runs to 12,000 feet between the two volcanoes instead of the regular road to Puebla.

And of course once we reached the highest point, we didn't return the way we came. Oh, no Siree. Backtracking would be timid, possibly even cheating. After all Puebla was on the other side. To attain the proper central European adventuring spirit one must engage in at least one twenty-mile hike and/or deal with something unknown that happens unexpectedly per vacation. So naturally, we followed the unmarked dirt road down the other side. To where? Well, nobody knows. Probably the unknown. Expectedly.

I told you, none of this is my fault.

There I was, thirteen years old, sitting in the back of a sometimes (never) reliable 1980's Oldsmobile rental car, driving on an always (always) four-wheel drive dirt track down into the heart of the jungle on the wrong side of a mountain that no white person in five hundred years has been able to pronounce right. Unfortunately, with three other Austrians, whose only hope in this very verdant hell was my mom's six months of more or less not very intense attempt to learn Spanish.

I can just hear the conversation between my folks.

Mom, "I want to go to Mexico on a vacation."

Dad, "And you just sort of thought of this *Schnapsidee* on waking up today?"

"No, think of the Aztec and Maya ruins and the beaches. It'll be great for the boys. And it would drive your mom nuts."

"Hehehe, if you learn Spanish."

In technicolor I still see the sweat running down the Indio's face, who was asking for smokes outside my rolled up car window and the exotic looking kids pointing and giggling at my equally exotic, to them, blond hair.

The so-called road down the back of Popocatepetl was atrocious. Considering what we put it through, it was amazing that the rental survived. I will never forget the look on the Hertz guy's face when we returned the beat up thing in Puebla.

To get a chance to pass the Aztecs' eternal guardians again, twenty-five years later, put me in a melancholy mood remembering places known and embraces missed. My parents set me on this road of almost compulsive exploration. The road that lets you know you so much, and so little at the same time. The life that makes you wonder if you keep on running away from, or towards something.

This life also teaches you that you must always help a fellow traveler. For better or worse, Ken and Indi were now my fellow travelers, and so I drove stick past the tombstones of my family's past.

The next day, on the 23ʳᵈ of December, on a mildly cool winter morning, sun blazing into our eyes, we rode bike. After having been stuck in Mexico City for nearly one month it felt like we floated on a magic carpet. Finally, riding again with my gipsy family, enjoying the sensation of the wind flowing around me, smelling the sun on my skin, feeling my muscles and my heart pump was incomparable. You just cannot describe eating miles of open road on a day like that.

As I rode, I heard a well-known beat coming up from behind, *tststs tststs* and knew that Diego was about to roll past me.

"Bro, man, I am so freaking happy!" he hollered as he flew past, blasting Cumbia on the speakers mounted to his bicycle. To Tuchegas' consternation he played the same playlist every day, albeit only for the two hours that his juice lasted. I liked it, though most days I tried to get away from him because music and nature don't mix for me. But when I needed some beats to keep me bumping he was good to ride next to.

I hollered back, "I know man. I just love riding bike!"

Over his shoulder he yelled, "We are made for this shit!"

That day was the moment of truth for Ken. I talked him through engaging and releasing the clutch as I rode next to him. Slowly he got the hang of it, on the open road only stalling the car every third time. Otherwise, Ken was super helpful. He often waited by the side of the road with water, a word of encouragement, and a joke. A welcome change from Amber's erratic support philosophy. A few weeks later, he asked for and received a small stipend for his free road trip to Brazil from Mestre. As soon as he did, he became a lot less helpful. Soon Mariano was helping him out a lot instead of me, because I am not patient enough for that sort of attitude.

It was also the moment for Indi to earn his new apelido Bebé Chorrão (Cry Baby) from Mestre Acordeon. He was on the silliest bike we had ever seen. It had two top bars and a handle bar that was strangely sideways curved, kind of like a water buffalo's horns. He was the guy showing up to Mt. Everest base camp wearing bedazzled flip-flops.

We rode him hard and we showed him kindness by helping him fix whatever broke every five miles. His panniers slipped off, I gave him a bungee cord. His saddle kept turning, I tightened it for him. His tires, I kid you not, slipped off the rims, I pushed them back on, and helped him pick better wheels. But he didn't show any inclination to learn how to fix his own bike.

Mexico City is at 6000 feet altitude. The ride to Oaxaca went up over 9000 feet. Brutal days. Made me feel at home to ride through alpine areas where the sun was hard and oxygen in short supply. *Juarez*, another temporary UCA sequestrado, from, you guessed right, Juarez, was doing fine. He was prepared and had been training. Unfortunately, he only stayed for ten days.

Even Balão felt the burn.

"Yo man, do you feel weak?" he asked while we rode some nasty inclines, punctuated with dry karst-rich vistas and five hundred feet roadside cliffs.

I said, "Hmm, I don't know Balão. I think I am ok. How you doin?"

"I am not feeling as strong as normal. I don't know what's up. I know these mountains are tough, but it's not usually this hard for me."

"Did you drink?"

"Yep."

"Salt?"

"Yep."

"Might just be the altitude brother."

Crossing these lonely mountains during hot days and cold nights marked the week around my birthday, which we spent at nearly 9000 feet in a stony and bleached out village a few days south of Puebla. The locals directed us to a lake to spend the night and for my trouble I got tossed into it. Somehow, magically, The Wright Brothers procured a bottle of Tequila for their favorite Pirate to warm up with after the freezing lake experience.

On your birthday it is customary to have a birthday roda with your group. You play as many games as your age. Appropriately, we played mine in a former jail, watched by a bunch of drunk local cops a day later. At 9000 feet. 40 games.

If that was the half point of my life, and let the record state that I disagree with that notion, it was a brilliant way to spend it.

Oaxaca

Date: January, 3ʳᵈ 2014
Location: Oaxaca

"Let's go get some Tlayudas," I said to Mariano.

"Let's go get some Tlayudas", a high pitched cartoonish voice repeated my words. I turned to see Banano smiling at me. He had arrived on the bus from Mexico City the night before. I didn't know if he was fucking with me because his smile was kind of shy but with a twinkle in his eye.

Tlayudas are an Oaxacan delicacy; a pizza sized crispy corn tortilla, with toppings to order. For example, fried *Chapul*. Yes, those would be crickets. Wash it down with Mescal, a special Tequila from local agave. I found the idea of visiting this cultural hub while eating fried insects and drinking tequila with floating worms oddly appealing.

We had arrived in the gorgeous, tourist infested town after intense riding from Puebla and stayed at Instrutor Golias' hotel in the center of Oaxaca.

Soon Banano was annoying the shit out of us by constantly repeating everything we said. I thought it was some kind of tick until I realized he was trying to learn English. Once I understood that, it was just another thing to be tolerated like Diego repeating inane questions multiple times to see how often people would answer.

"Hey, when we get there, do you think they'll have *Churrasco*?" (BBQ)

"Probably."

"So we should ask if they have Churrasco, right?"

"Yeah."

"You think Mestre will want Churrasco?"

"Fuck you, Diego."

"What?"

Bananito is a consummate Capoeirista who had to fend for himself on the mean streets of Mexico City since he had been a teenager. He also is an incredibly tactile person who constantly fondles you somehow. (That might come across wrong, so I'll leave it in.) Before B2B he made a living with fashion photography and teaching Capoeira classes. He had a knack and absolute ruthlessness for taking pictures, bossing little kids around to get the perfect shot. And, he repeated everything we said.

"I want to get some Mescal."

"I want to get some Mescal."

"I want to punch you in the face."

"I want to punch you in the face."

Then he'd grab my constantly hurting wrist and start massaging it. Maybe so that I couldn't punch him in the face.

We planned to stay in the State of Oaxaca for ten days. Mestres had business to take care of, and so the rest of us were, as strange as this may sound, on vacation. We decided to do some bike-less traveling. Chacahua, a hippie beach on the outside of a lagoon on the Pacific, was our first goal. Ken insisted on taking us there first, while Indi insisted on also visiting Zipolite, another beach town further south.

The Chilango Sequestrados and I left a day after the UCA crowd. My Spanish became a lot more super chingon on the day-long road trip to the coast. But maybe that is just my memory, which today seems like a hazy kind of fear and loathing type language lesson. We arrived at the lagoon after dark where Ken procured a speed boat to take us across to the beach.

Bioluminescence illuminated the wake of our boat from within. In tears of gratitude I floated on a river of light under a full moon. To live this way defies description.

Every once in a while we manage to open ourselves to this rollercoaster called life, the one full of unexpected turns of open heart and secret passages to our soul, that sometimes throws us violently down a gravity well. There we awaken to power. How could I ask anything of my future if the now was so perfect?

Soon, a dense mangrove forest closed in on us. The watery path became tighter until it was narrow like a country road. Apparently, that was no reason for the driver to slow down. Maybe he just wanted to freak out the gringos. The first mate (his kid) came to stand with me in the bow and lit the way, or I should say, searched for openings in the labyrinth with a not really powerful flashlight.

The beam searched left and right while we bore down on a solid wall of green. Only at the last moment he remembered which way to go next, pointed the light at it, and then the driver ripped his powerful engine in that direction. We sped past a wet grave too many times that night.

Upon arrival, we found the UCA crowd at the southern end of Chacahua's palapas. The five-mile-long beach was deserted because it was after New Year and the hippies had gone home to D.F. to be middle class folk again.

We ate homemade mussel tamales and coconut sweets purchased from an ancient local Indigina babushka who walked the beach every day. We found moonshine mescal and delicious local fish dishes in a back yard that should have been in Africa. Albania, whose father was a communist, softly whispered, egalitarian poems into my ear next to a beach fire, one dark night.

This Pirate was not able to resist her charms.

At sunrise, a conservationist set hundreds of baby turtles free; a completely cute yet terrifying spectacle. The baby turtles struggled and fought into the waves with their tiny flippers, got turned over on their backs and carried back up the shore by small waves that must have been like tsunamis to them. They never stopped.

Alas, four lazy days later we left paradise heading south in search of more festive atmospheres. When we passed Mazunte on the way to Zipolite, I had cell phone service for the first time in a week and a bunch of messages popped.

Pipoca from D.F. told me about a Capoeirista who wanted Mestre to come to Mazunte, but since we could only disappoint we kept on going to Zipolite which was the place Indi really wanted to visit. We arrived late and grabbed a random beach side hostel. Mariano and the Chilangos slept close to the building, while I went to the beach.

Sometimes I wonder if it's the remnant of some kind of genetic memory that makes us feel so at home when we are close to the sea. The sound of the waves, the salty air in our lungs, and the stars twinkling above are the most wonderful lullaby. I missed Bebum.

A gorgeous bay bid me good morning as the sun rose over the left end of the broad, yellow beach. The water was balmy and far from me, and my stash of very little peso cash, cards, and flute still dug into the sand under me. Yep, learned that lesson in San Francisco.

But when I looked around I noticed something. There were only men walking the beach. Alone or as couples. With or without shorts. Wait what? White dudes on their morning stroll in their birthday suites? In central Mexico? Maybe I was still too groggy, so I wiped the sand out of my eyes and saw, yes, those guys were distinctly checking me out.

Of course someone sleeping on the beach is always weird to people, beats me why, but these were more insinuating stares. By any means there is nothing wrong with men staring at me, I take it as a compliment. Unless I got sand in my eyes and can't see who is behind me.

A gorgeous bay bid me good morning as the sun rose over the left end of the broad, yellow beach. The water was balmy and far from me, and my stash of very little peso cash, cards, and flute still dug into the sand under me. Yep, learned that lesson in San Francisco.

But when I looked around I noticed something strange. There were only men walking the beach. Alone or as couples. With or without shorts. Wait what? White dudes on their morning stroll in their birthday suites? In central Mexico? Maybe I was still too groggy, so I wiped the sand out of my eyes and saw, yes, those guys were distinctly checking me out.

Of course someone sleeping on the beach is always weird to people, beats me why, but these were more insinuating stares. By any means there is nothing wrong with men staring at me, I take it as a compliment. Unless I got sand in my eyes and can't see who is behind me.

Indi insists to this day he did not know because he had come here as a kid with his parents. Of course, since some Mexicans tend to be a little less tolerant of people's sexuality we needed to make fun of him.

"Indi," I hollered as I got up, "Now I know why you wanted to come here."

We headed over to the small tourist street, found a 3.5 liter (3/4 of a gallon) plastic coke bottle of clear Moonshine Mescal to make Amore Mexicano with and an internet café. We were on vacation, damnit. Tax season was also up, so Mariano and I spent a day doing infrastructural things. May the supreme being of your choice bless the interwebs, letting us do our taxes online while getting six sheets to the wind in a small boy's town on the Mexican Pacific Coast.

After the possibly unkind, and certainly politically incorrect, ribbing Indi had to endure all day we went back to the beach for sunset, at that point sufficiently inebriated so that even the Chilangos could enjoy the, now much more diverse, crowd. Afterwards we were planning to head up to San Pedro del Pacifico, a mountain village known for its powerful shamans and magic mushrooms.

Mariano yelled, "If everyone's naked, let's get naked, too."

I politely declined, no need to provoke, as Mariano pulled down his shorts and ran into the Pacific. He apparently was in a generous mood and pleased the crowd by coming out and doing a full on *Parafuso*, with not only his legs performing a rainbow kick high in the air. It just so happened that three pretty girls came walking in our direction just when Mariano did his big show. Still, and as usual, it fell to me to be the extrovert and talk to them, which I gladly did. Doesn't get any easier than talking to a girl, or three, if your friend just flashed the entire Pacific coast in a rather, how shall I put this… athletic way.

A tall, statuesque French girl, a cute curvy Latina, and a black shorty. Before we even started walking down the beach the tall blond was checking out Mariano, somehow the black girl ended up chatting to me, and the curvy one was giggling with the Chilangos. Don't ask me how these things happen. We were travelers, gorgeous humans, all of us, in one of the last anonymous spots on the planet. Blessed to live a moment of abundance and kindness, and hopefully aware of it.

They took us up to a rocky outlook sixty feet above the northern end of the beach and I put the world to rest with my flute. Our new friends asked us to come to Mazunte with them. We did. In Mazunte they wanted to keep partying in a bar, and that was ok, too. But when the shorty (she *really* was short, this is not misogynist) was having troubles concentrating on the good times ahead, I started talking to this interesting, tall gringo with long hair.

He said, "Hey, gut to meet you, ja. No, I am not from zis town. I live in San Cristobal de las Casas."

He was obviously Austrian, so I said, "*Servas, du I bin da Peter, I bin aus Wien.*" (Hi, I'm Peter from Vienna)

He said, "Na leiwand, oida." (Hey cool bro)

Excited to meet him I asked, "What are you doing here? This is pretty far from the old world."

"My brother lives here."

"Oh, both of you are here?"

"Yeah, come down to the Architect tomorrow, the backpacker on the beach and you'll meet him."

Right then Mariano yelled, "Pirata, let's roll."

Since I couldn't take any more Amore Mexicano, and my own travel date had gotten cold feet, I was not too unhappy to follow him and the gorgeous French girl, but there was romance in the air and I didn't want to be third-wheelish.

Mazunte beach was much smaller than Zipolite and right in front of some hotels. I didn't feel up for crashing there. Maybe waking up to a bunch of dudes staring immodestly at my ass the day before had something to do with it. So I looked for and found an alternative, a doorway that led into a janitor's corridor with some brooms and mobs. I turned a corner and saw three doors, two locked, one open. Jackpot! A dorm style room with beds. I went back out to tell the love birds that I would be sleeping in there.

She gave me a look and said, "Let's all sleep in there."

She may have had a French accent.

I checked Mariano, he shrugged, I took the lead. As she walked behind me she grabbed my ass. Remembering where I woke up that morning I happily decided that the world knows justice after all.

Mosquitoes don't though. The room was swarming. In the dark we may have slapped each other more than even a random Mexican encounter justifies. When it was time for condoms, I pulled mine out in a jiffy. Mariano started patting down his imaginary shorts in desperation.

"You got another one?"

"Sorry bro, it's my last." (It really was; you don't think I would do that to my brother)

Since I was an invited guest to the party I offered him mine.

She said, "Hell no."

A woman's mind can be a wonderful mystery to a man, mostly because my specie tends to emotional thickness, and in the state I was in I wasn't quite able, or willing, to question her logic. But, after a few minutes Mariano really didn't like the situation on his end anymore and decided to find some condoms.

Minutes later he arrived at the car to find Ken amorously engaged with the Latin girl. Mariano tapped the window, Ken did not stop his gyrations, but instead looked over his shoulder and mouthed WTF to Mariano, who in turn mouthed and mimicked, "Camisetta!"

Ken still didn't stop and mouthed, "Mano?!?!?!"

Mariano continued to beg, and since Ken had to help out when he could, because otherwise we'd stop feeding him, he opened the door and stretched his hand out to give a condom to Mariano, when suddenly, right at that moment, out of the dark night sprinted Banano, grabbing it before Mariano could, and took off cackling.

"That's my Camisetta, pendejo," yelled Mariano.

"That's my Camisetta, pendejo!"

I'd give my left testies-testies to have seen the look on Mariano's face.

Such is the life of a traveling hunter-gatherer tribe. The next day, we nursed a mighty, yet completely acceptable Mescal hang-over at the Architect. We got some food into our bellies and enjoyed re-living the night. Apparently, all of us were meant to have a good time, even Mariano, after I had excused myself to sleep of my exhaustion. Mutual human love, discovered and experienced on a level playing field of dreams is a gorgeous thing.

We were kicking it there, when I saw a tall, long-haired guy walk in. Remembering the Austrian from the night before, I walked up to him.

"Servas Alter, alles klar heute," (Hey man, how you doin?)

He said, "Huh? Have we met?"

I examined my memory and realized that I wasn't too sure what he looked like. But there can't be that many 6'2" white dudes with hair to the middle of their backs running around Mazunte.

"Yeah, man, last night. You must have been even more fucked up than I was."

He laughed and realization came to his eyes, "Ah, you were talking to my brother."

Soon the brother showed up. They looked ridiculously alike. Both had that long hair, not a gram of fat on their bodies, and the easy loping gate of running warriors. They each sported two scars on their pectoral muscles. I was intrigued since I knew one earned those during Native American Sun Dance Ceremonies.

He asked me, "So what brings you guys to Mazunte?"

I had not shared our journey with anyone for a week. It was nice to be incognito for a change and without our bikes that was actually possible. But these guys were from the homeland. We had been jibberjabbering in German. I wanted to share.

"We are riding our bicycles from San Francisco to Brazil."

His eyes ripped open, his face made a huge OH, and he yelled at me, "Are you riding with Mestre Acordeon?"

Now it was my turn to be surprised, "How do you know?"

"Is Mestre in town?"

"No, he is in Oaxaca. Well, I think he is in D.F. right now. How do you know about B2B?"

"Man, I have been trying to get Mestre to come here."

"Oh, shit, really?"

"Yeah, I asked Pipoca to hook me up with you guys."

Small world, isn't it.

We spent a day playing and teaching capoeira to our curvy/statuesque/forgetful friends on the beach. A few of the backpackers from the The Architect got into it with us as well.

The backpacker itself was ingeniously designed. It was built into, around, and on top of a fifty feet tall rocky outcropping, like a baby Sugar Loaf, in the middle of Mazunte bay's fine sand. Winding paths and staircases lead to various levels, rooms, and outdoor showers. Hooks under the open sky awaited the weary traveler's hammock. It was a cool 3D labyrinth and when you found your way to the top you knew you had arrived at the secret treasure: A flat area set above the turquoise tranquil of the bay. Strong iron chains suspended wooden platform beds from rustic frames along the rim of the horseshoe shaped top of the Architect. Each platform was semi-obscured by a white mosquito net underneath which you could relax on black futons, while floating a couple of feet above the ground.

She remembered then, the good times that we were supposed to have the night before. The warm sun, short naps, and the hidden spaces in between melted into one slow and sweet, lazy as molasses day dream. Sadly, she left an hour later. Made me feel a little wham-bam-thank-you-man'd, like I was the last pin missing in her Oaxacan collection before she had to catch the day's bus home. Apparently, and as my mother loves to point out to me, the world is not a one-way street.

Later, during the waning afternoon, the Austrians took us to hike to the right end of the bay where a rocky point reached straight for the setting sun. With my flute, and Austrian bro's Berimbau we saluted her as she bid us another golden evening. Happily, I'd play my flute in churches and to the setting sun until the day I die.

Once no more than a shadow of dusky light remained, and Luna gently spilled her cool vibes down on us, we walked back from the tip of the rocks to find three elder locals chanting. The Austrians stopped to listen. Soon, the woman offered them to lead a chant.

After some time she asked, "¿quiénes son tus amigos" (who are your friends?)

"They are riding their bicycles from the USA to Brazil. They are Capoeiristas."

She appreciated that for a moment and said, "You should play."

He got up, took his Berimbau and strummed the slow, hypnotic rhythm of Capoeira Angola. Luna and the chanting woman watched over us as we played Capoeira games of friendship and brotherhood under an eternal, starlight canopy.

The next day we left to San Pedro del Pacifico. In my mind, the drive back from the coast forms a memory like a rapid, artistically flashy raster of hair pin turns, sips from bottles, drags from pipes, Ken hacking at a car tire with a machete to get at the *aramé*[13], a piercing sun above white clouds, and the emerald mountains. We arrived late on a freezing, oxygen-poor night, 10,000 feet above sea level.

No wonder this was a center for Mexican shamanism, you are already high because of the skinny air. Throw in some shrooms and you are sure to visit the blue planet. The next day we were going to procure the necessary ingredients for our appointment.

From the beginning of B2B, Mariano and I had thought that experiencing even the more esoteric expressions of a nation's spirit world was required for proper cultural immersion. Yes, the Virgin of Guadalupe was part of this journey, but so was the Bruxo, and his name may have been Castaneda. Billions believe in catholic, muslim, hindu, and buddhist hocus-pocus, while thinking that the Shamans are just getting sky high, kind of like L. Ron Hubbard. From the outside it seems that the main difference is a couple of millennia of time. Is it not better to examine each miracle, each passion, personally so that we can call all of them liars in good conscience, or change our heathen ways?

In the morning, we hiked out and after some time a parched mountain local pointed us in the direction of a forested path and we started hiking. Was a proper pilgrimage to dimensions unknown to follow? Well, not at the first house nestled in a small, well-cultivated valley. Instead we were pointed to another one just over on the other ridge. Walking on a forest road in that direction thirty minutes later, we met the oldest person I have ever seen, other than Mama Espinoza. I swear if he came up to my navel I'd be calling him tall. He wore way too many layers of dark, alpine felt-type clothing and a wide brimmed hat. Bent at the waist he shuffled along, holding a duffel bag and on to a cane for dear life.

Soon, Indi was writing a response to a letter from a distant relative that the man had carefully unwrapped from cellophane after pulling it out from deep under his many layers. He could neither read nor write and such was Indi's gift to bond that the old mountain man simply asked him to read the letter and respond in his stead. He cried when he heard his family's words come from Indi's lips. We all did.

As if on a World of Warcraft quest we then received the information we desired, which was where to find the best shrooms on the mountain.

A bit of walking later, we arrived at a mossy log cabin perfectly placed on a shoulder under a couple of trees overlooking a juicy green, wide open alpine valley. The whole setting reminded me of Alto Adige, where my grandfather hails from and where I spent many summers with my family. We were greeted, you guessed it, by a couple who were extensively shriveled yet strong as bears. They offered us moonshine Mescal and the strangest kind we ever smoked: dark black, stringy buds with skinny orange velvety flowers and a skanky smell to it. Though fairly typically ornery mountain types, these two clearly had experience with random gringos showing up on their stoop.

Alas, it wasn't shroom season, and so, after exchanging some more gifts, we opted for a sweat lodge, and went back to Oaxaca the next day to continue our ride via Chiapas out the bottom right corner of Mexico into Guatemala.

We may have missed out on the blue planet, but The Land of Many Trees awaited us.

---

[13] Wire for Berimbau.

Cana
Date: February 2nd, 2014
Location: Guatemala

"Mano, onde va sobre su bici?" (Dude, where are you going on your bike?)

"Pra Guate," I hollered, flying past the Chiapas road workers who were offering me a smoke from a plastic bottle bong. I turned around to have a chat.

Hombre asked, "You goiinn to Guaaatemalllaaa? *Tu eres loco?"* (Are you crazy?)

Shrugging and smiling I smoked their schwag.

"Hermano, that place, it iss krrazzy!"

I asked, *"Mas loco que Mexico?"* (Crazier than Mexico?)

"Siiii," they started cavernously deep but ended high pitched.

At the border to Guatemala, Bebum waited by the side of the road for us. Just sort of showed up like a mirage after he had spent three months in Guadalajara. He was riding a strange circus looking Schwinn bike and said, "I traded my Shimzzy for this classic."

"Shimzzy got stolen," I asked him.

"Yeah man, out of Jacaré's yard. Mestre Xuxo's Santa Cruz Capoeira guys gave me this one, didn't have good wheels though. The only replacement I found for free was too small, so now I don't have front breaks."

Bless his vagabond soul.

If people in the USA think that Tijuana is a fucked up border town, then you know what we rode through on the Guatemala side of things. A really small, fucked up border town.

Even the Mexican Capoeiristas got in on it, telling me to warn Mestre about Guatemala's dangers, *"Fala para Mestre, Pirata! Precisa cuidado!"*

And I always responded, "Yes, I'll tell Mestre to be careful, but you know how it is. Mestre will go and I'll follow."

As we crossed, hard eyes stared holes in our backs, lusting for our gringo wallets. Hustlers and hookers roamed the streets, at lunch. I sensed an easy violence in people's steps. Iron bars made cages out of windows and doors. Physical disabilities that the West only sees in text books abounded.

Still, we should not assume that cities in the USA don't maim the spirit the way a Guatemalan border town does. I suspect were we to bother visiting certain neighborhoods in the western world we would find them to be similar. As if to prove my point, on my return to the USA, I found tent-cities growing under her freeways.

Humanity's dirty underbellies draw me. They remind me that outside of the popular volunteer havens not all is rosy with our queer little species. You can't make things better if you don't look to see what's broken.

It certainly is an improvement to send the Peace Corps instead of the CIA, even though the Kennedy's contribution to world peace is apparently the very conduit for silly spy games. It was still an inspiration to meet dedicated young women being the change they want to see. Women like Ms. Pleasants, who started a small library and works with Voices on the Borders in remote mountain villages. Or Lua, who educates local populations to use existing law to fight for their rights.

Guatemala with attitude

Upon entering Guatemala, we immediately saw something new. Every truck had a guy riding shotgun - with a shotgun. You better learn quickly to notice these vital security facts when riding bike or traveling in general. The roads were tighter, the trucks dirtier, the trees taller, and the guns more in our face. The tree thing makes sense, since Guatemala means *Land of many Tree*, but what was this violence born of? A beast so random and savage that a truck carrying pinto beans needs an armed guard. To protect it from who? People so poor that five pennies a pound beans are worth robbing for?

We rode through fields of cana. Sugar as far as the eye could see. Every last possible speck of monochrome green stretching to the horizon was dedicated to the white powder. Like tulips, potatoes, and marijuana it should be included in *The Botany of Desire's* list of hyper successful species.

Hyper successful species are not good for the rest of the planet. They tend to crowd things out. Humans being a case in point.

Nothing moves here. No insects *buzz*, no *chirp*, no *ribbitt*. Only this eerily swishing ocean of eight feet tall cane stalks. I don't know if this is as disturbing to me as the wheat factories of the American Midwest, but a mono culture of sugar cane, or bananas, while exotic to my gringo eyes, is still a dead zone.

There is one difference between Midwestern and Central American mono cultures. Men instead of satellite guided machines work the fields. Men wielding machetes. The sugar for our table is brought to us by the sweat of someone's brow.

Bebum told me later that he tried to make money harvesting pineapples in Costa Rica. When he heard the pay was five dollars a day he went to work on a sustainable farm in exchange for room, board, and magic mushrooms.

In Guatemala the pay is thirty cents per ton. You can harvest ten tons and make three USD per day. Have you ever tried to lift ten tons? This produces ninety liters of alcohol, worth 200 USD. The itinerant workers get paid in kind (moonshine) and are always in debt to the company store. They are slaves to my sweet tooth.

They had no shoes.

I wanted to take pictures. But something held me back. My shame? This modern *Grapes of Wrath* scene upset me too much. I thought of all the sugary sweets I have eaten. Bad for my teeth, for my body, and bad for my conscience.

I expected the good, the bad, and the ugly on this journey. If Oaxaca was the good, riding in tropical rainstorms over insane mountains the bad, then this inequality was the ugly.

For a week we traced the west coast past sugar cane, banana, and rubber. Then we turned inland to ride up a brutal mountain. Lake Atitlan awaited us.

Before we took on the challenge we rested in the small town of Patulul for a day. In the evening, when the crowds came out to enjoy some snacks and social life, we trained in the main square to show those kind people something completely exotic to them.

The next morning, we gathered at Mestre's hotel around eight. Tora stuck a plastic bag of trash right under Mestre's nose.

"I no know why people no clean up. I want leave good impression when we stay in town hall."

The Chilangos had forgotten to clean up after themselves. Something we all (except the good kids) did occasionally. I know I cleaned up after others, and the same favor was done for me a few times. Mestre looked like he was about to bust a vein in his eye, but he didn't seem to be in the mood to do a repeat Mestre Zeus performance.

He called a meeting. I found a spot on the periphery because I didn't want to sit in the line of fire again. Though we didn't usually film during B2B meetings Mariano pulled out his camera. He was not to be disappointed.

Mestre talked about being kinder to each other, addressing me specifically as someone who should learn to be less confrontational – point well, if obviously with difficulty, taken. He also spoke of being respectful, asking the Mexican Sequestrados to man up in this regard.

Mestre continued, "However… You don't know me... I know we have been riding together for four months now. You think you know me, but you don't."

Mestre sounded seriously threatening. He didn't yell. You knew it was on. He did not mention Tora. This is a strategy that Capoeira Mestres employ. They don't call out the offending person directly in a group setting, but rather use the incident to teach a general lesson.

"Don't fuck with me. You don't know who I am. You don't know what I will do."

We were shocked. Mestre never dropped F-bombs. Mariano giggled behind the camera, but got it all on tape. I kinda doubt it'll make it into the movie, that's why you had to buy this book.

Mestre repeated, "Do not fuck with me."

I thought Mestre let us off too easy. People don't learn unless they know what they did wrong. But I guess that's why everybody and their dog cries about Piratata being too direct.

And so we started one of the toughest days of the year in a shitty mood of epic proportions. This may have had something to do with me burning up the hill as if the devil, using Lance Armstrong's doping regime, was on my heels.

Five months into the trip my childhood cyclist's muscles had solidly re-established. I wanted to measure myself against the heat and the potholed, stupidly steep road. You have to be a little nuts, and want to find out exactly where the outside edge of your envelop is, in order to actively enjoy this. Yet there is certainty in every push of your burning legs, in every labored breath. You may not know how much farther up it will keep going, but you know you have the power to ride it out.

About two thirds of the way I took a break and watched colorful and overloaded chicken buses (re-incarnated US school buses) trundle past at walking speed.

That's when I saw the old man. He was emaciated, bent at the waste. Gingerly, he stepped out from a hidden path and walked towards me. His name was Poverty.

Poverty carried twice his own weight in wood on his back. His wide-brimmed straw hat hid his face from the sun and my prying eyes. Paying neither me nor my bike any heed he passed me slowly. I vowed to complain even less about tough days of riding or other first world problems.

Ten minutes later I saw two younger men also carrying wood, in company of a woman. The woman wore traditional Indigina garb, ankle length skirt, and colorful patterns stitched on the front. You know the one. Every gringo tourist with a semi-legit lens goes gaga over it.

The Oh, so artisanal past was still alive here, as opposed to our own countries where we replaced it with plastic spoons. Except, there is a problem with our fantasy. Not just that it's patronizing, because how would you feel if random Japanese tourists constantly stuck their lenses in your face because they want pictures of you and your SUV, since people driving SUVs is just so incredibly exotic to them. But the real issue is that these are not the traditional Indigina outfits you thought they were. In fact, Spanish conquerors forced the tribes to wear different outfits so that they could divide and conquer easier.

The effort to reach Lake Atitlan two hours later burned away any energy to deconstruct group dynamics or subsistence economics. Atitlan sits like a glorious centerpiece on a necklace of volcanoes, sparkling at high noon, mysterious at sunset, gleaming with hope at sunrise. Even if you didn't scale forbidding mountains to get to it, your mind would still be blown by the spectacle.

The next morning, we rose from our campsite on the lake shore to birds singing their song of the new day. They happily investigated the group of smelly bipeds who showed up under their trees the night before, and seemed to wonder why we tied our nests (tents) to our horses. And why do the horses have wheels instead of hoofs? And who is this poor biped (Bebum) who doesn't have a nest[14]?

Nature energizes our mind and body like a fusion bomb of positivity and joy. *Celestine Prophecy* only verbalized what we instinctively always knew. A powerful setting lifts our spirits to the sky. Then we feel as though Gaia fairly whispers peace into our core. Maybe, if you live in a place of mountains, or close by the sea, you know this feeling of energy slowly imbuing you from the earth up to the very top of your head. A wellspring of love speaks directly to your ancestral roots then.

And still, it is difficult to explain this to my old self, whose feet barely touched the earth. The self that spent years laying in bed, sitting at breakfast, in my car, at my work, in my car again, and at dinner to finally lay down in bed again. Only experience let me realize this.

I can't tell you how it feels to sleep under twinkling stars, or to wake up in a pristine paradise and eat just harvested food, you have to try it yourself. Writing these words, I realize that I am trying to understand why I was so happy without a bed, a toilet, a shower or conditioner for my explosive yeti look.

Maybe you are nodding when I tell you to live this way at least once in your life so that you may re-feel some of the human in you. The creature that is born a part of this earth and yet tries so desperately to be apart from it. But like someone who hasn't been in the military can't understand the deep level of camaraderie born in combat, we don't understand what it means to live like our hunter-gatherer ancestors. Until we do.

I kept returning to humanity's roots to attempt to explain my obnoxious happiness. Despite being chewed up by mosquitoes, despite the group dynamics, despite the dangers and boredom of the road I was happier than ever in my life.

These roots of us evolved over billions of years. It took further roughly six million years to come down from the trees and move into caves. Only in the last 100,000 odd years have we moved beyond living more or less like animals, and it seems like solid roofs over our heads really only became cool about 10k years ago, with the advent of farming. Maybe that is why we all, no matter which creed we belong to, collectively "head out there", "recharge", "escape". And maybe that is why we are quite bad at managing our societies. We are, after all, civilizational babies.

I can't help but think that our modern unhappiness is a result of leaving behind our roots, our tribal existence. An existence we evolved for and into. If we want to be less connected and more materialistic, yet stay happy, we might need to change some of those super cooperator genes.

---

[14] Not having space on his new classic bike he gave away his tent.

We have built a world of placebo motivation on top of a very few basic needs. To be happy do we need more than food, a roof, and time to do with as we please? Instead we work to have three roofs, don't have time to enjoy them, and compensate ourselves by eating too much bad food, because it so happens that the bad food was the one we evolved to crave in order to survive, except you only got mammoth burger every once in a while.

I hear of a new generation that values enjoying the moment rather than owning it. I hope that you take advantage of this opportunity to step into you. Walk freely and walk with buckets filled with happiness swinging in your hands. Slosh them around, spray the people around you with gaiety, leave little rainbows of love trailing behind you. Give more hugs.

Here in Central America that wild, romanticism inducing, natural beauty is still very much alive. Except for the coasts, the land is too mountainous and rugged to do much with. Volcanoes stick out of all kinds of bodies of water. Fiery sentinels encircled the horizons of our world.

And like the tall volcanoes and the deep lakes, the gorgeous beaches and the steep roads, the hard eyes and the smiling faces, the opposites remain. Light and dark. Wealth and poverty. Heirs of occupying power and Indigina. I imagined the people of Central America to be similar in temperament to the ever friendly Mexicans (just, you know, don't steal their hot sauce). But people here are harder, more closed off. Years of torture turn the sunniest disposition into a protective shell.

Sometimes people hollered, "Gringo go home." When you are riding that's OK, but when you are walking you are more vulnerable. As I strolled through hundreds of small Central American towns I formed the habit of frequently changing sides to look behind me. Made me feel like 007. On occasion I realized a potential danger. It depended on the situation whether I'd stop to explain that I am not a gringo or get the hell out of dodge. These were instinctual decisions that carried consequence. Mestre Acordeon drilled us that we needed to be aware at all times. We even ugly-fied our rides by taking off decals and spraying dirt looking concrete paint on the frames. But paying attention is something you learn, like everything else in life, by actually doing it.

I know that painfully well, because during my years of global vagabondage I was often lucky to be exposed to, let's call them, awareness raising situations. There was that gang enforcer in Tokyo, there was that time I lost an opportunity to be an FB stock millionaire, and there was that Grizzly in Yellowstone. The list of my fuck-ups and close calls is rather never ending. I mean who, in the name of sweet baby jesus, gets bitten in the ass by a poisonous centipede while sitting on a rotten bench overlooking a thousand lingam carved into a river in Cambodia?

A small town in El Salvador was another such place of learning. A guy followed me up a semi quiet side street and yelled something about gringos. I realized that he was alone, though at least as big as I. In Central America that's Yao Ming status. Since it was the middle of the day with people around, I did not feel too threatened and started a conversation.

I said, "*Buenas dias Senor. Desculpe, mais yo no soy gringo. Soy de Austria. Un pequenito pais en Europa que gusta tortas, café e pax por todo mundo.*"

I think I stunned him either with my terrible Spanglish or my explanation of being from a small European country that exports coffee, culture, and cakes, because he kind of just stared at me.

I tried again, "*Usted sabes Austria, pequenio pais como Guatemala? No somos gringos, mais creo que, los gringos de EE UU son pendejos con certeza!*"

Even telling him that I agreed that gringos are assholes, especially since I am not one of them, as I am from a small country like Guatemala didn't work.

He asked, "*Como?*" (Huh?)

Of course it's not that easy for a Guatemalan and a guy who mangles Spanish on a good day to discuss centuries of occupation or the United Fruit Corporation.

So I tried something else, "*Yo no estoy tourista amigo. Yo estoy haciendo un viaje en bicicleta desde California para Brasil! No tenho casa, no tenho dinero, no tenho amor.*"

When he heard that I am on a bicycle tour and that I don't have a home, money, or love, he finally grinned and said, "Ah, you are a crazy gringo. You want a beer?" (cont'd in Spanish)

Happily, I agreed, "Gracias amigo. But I have a question, why do you call people from North America gringos?"

He cracked open a can and said, "It's because they wore green uniforms when they first started showing up in Central America in the 1950s. We would say, *Green go Home*, and it became gringo."

I love a good history lesson while swapping a cold knife in my back for a cold beer in my hand. Maybe this was a good opportunity to ask my new friend about Guatemala's recent past.

In my usual indirect way, I said, "So tell me, why is Guate still such a fucked up place? After all the gringos and the conquistadores have left a minute ago."

He kind of rolled his eyes, "What would you do if Massachusetts had been raped, pillaged, and plundered for centuries by England only to be used as a punching bag during the Cold War? You come from a peaceful land while all I know is violence. Be happy that we call you gringo instead of slitting your throat, just in case."

Of course, just because I escaped difficult situations by sheer luck and pluck didn't mean he didn't have a point. Gringos have been responsible for his suffering for too long.

And yet, while I mulled over these miserable human things, nature cradled me in her arms of glorious, uncaring perfection. My brothers and I flew down the wide open roads towards the Pacific Ocean. The wind carried promising notes of distant shores and arid reminders of nearby burnt earth.

Centro America
Pablo Neruda

Land as slim as a whip,
hot as torture,
your step in Honduras, your blood
in Santo Domingo, at night,
your eyes in Nicaragua
touch me, call me, grip me,
and throughout American lands
I knock on doors to speak,
I tap on tongues that are tied,
I raise curtains, I plunge
my hands into blood:
O, sorrows
of my land, O death-rattle
of the great established silence,
O, long-suffering peoples,
O, slender waist of tears.

I wish I had taken the picture of those men harvesting sugar in Guatemala. Sweat pouring off their heads, ripped clothes & flip-flops, hacking away at the cana, their broken backs bent. As coincidence will have it, Banano did. So that we can cry over it together.

For only a human can make another human feel like an animal.

Mestra and Mestre
Date: March 2ⁿᵈ, 2014
Location: Nicaragua

That first time I talked to Mestre back in Seattle was shocking to me. You are not supposed to meet men like that in the real world. Santa Claus, the most interesting man alive, and Zeus all rolled into one. Obviously, these three figments of our imagination have one thing in common: the beard - that hairy madness that, like Samson's, can't ever be cut.

Even by the highly eclectic standards of elder Capoeira Mestres, Mestre Acordeon is in a Renaissance man league of his own. Dangerous Capoeirista even at 70. The entire world of Capoeira is glued to his lips when he speaks. Multiple Capoeira National Brazilian Champion. 500 songs to his name and plays bossa nova like a boss. Somebody once breathlessly told me that he did the first backflip in a Capoeira game, though Mestre giggles at that. Definitely, first Capoeirista on the USA's West Coast.

Who has all these accomplishments to their name, and then decides to sit their ass on a bike for a year on their 70ᵗʰ birthday? It's like winning five hundred million in the lottery and putting it all on black

People are what drive Mestre Acordeon and Mestra Suelly. You can see it every time an old friend shows up. Mestre's eyes light up, a big smile splits the Santa beard, and a drawn out "EEEEIIIIIIIIIIIIHHHHHHHH" emerges from deep within that cavernous chest. Mestra gives you a kiss, though you never know which side she wants. There is room for everyone in their hearts. If you have the urge to be taught and mentored, you are in the right hands.

Just be prepared to be called on exactly what you don't want to be called on. Which is incidentally also exactly what you need to be called on.

"So, Piratata, how is Pirata working out for you," Mestre asked me.

We were in Leon, Nicaragua at a café on a corner of the large, and unusually, for Central American standards, unattractive main square. It lacked the cozy little spaces amongst flower and grass beds. Trees were willing to give shade but their roots were covered in concrete.

On the terrace of the café, water mist kept customers from melting, lazy fans spun high up under the stuccoed ceilings, and the bartender was able to make Mestre's Papaya Batido (smoothie) just right.

Each of us filmed four conversations for the documentary, picking a topic of our choice about personal growth throughout the journey. Of course, if Mestre was the interviewer he chose the topic.

In Leon, I knew exactly what Mestre meant. So I tried to buy time, "Hmmm Mestre, it is a complicated topic for me."

Mestre did a Mestre # 2. Opened his eyes wide, leaned back a little, spread his palms. Generally, urging me to use the obviously empty space between my ears. Then he moved a couple of things around on the table in front of him, creating order for our minds, and looked at me.

I said, "You won't believe it but I am actually quite none-confrontational these days," Mariano giggled behind the camera, "For my standards anyways. I used to have a girlfriend who'd get mad at me for always calling people out."

"Well, I do see an improvement with you since we have been on the trip."

"It's still a complicated topic for me."

Mestre said, "Tell me."

"I like being honest. And I like fairness. I also think that we can't improve without feedback. I like knowing when I am an ass. I think Tuchegas is a little bit like me. She can be direct when she wants to."

Now Balão giggled from under the table where he was holding the microphone.

I kept going, "Remember in Baja just before that tropical depression ran across our path. You started preparing me to read *Making of a Mestre* to the group there."

Mestre nodded.

"One night I walked into the little eatery and sat down with Tuchegas and Diego. TV was blaring. I am not used to TV advertising at all, stuff drives me up the wall. There was only one other guy there, so I got up and turned it down. Tuchegas snapped. I think to her it was a typical example of a white guy imposing his values."

"So what happened?"

"Nothing Mestre. She just turned it back up again. I don't mind if people get at me forcefully. Like Tora telling me to shut up in Mazatlán before you ripped his head off."

We laughed as Mestre opened his eyes wide; doing an impersonation of Tora looking like a shark just ate his lunch.

"The next morning Tuchegas apologized. I told her there was no need for that. But I think these sort of group interactions are making me try to be kinder to people."

"That's good Piratata."

"I just don't know if I want to be less straight. I think there is value in calling people out. Like Tuchegas did with me. We are in a small group, 24/7 with direct feedback. Most of us are learning to be better because of it. But in the real world this doesn't happen. People live in their ego-bliss bunkers and do not interact with others who would potentially call their ass out."

"It's not an easy life Pirata."

"Ain't that the truth Mestre. But I am trying to be more polite about telling people that they are idiots."

Mariano cackled, "It's not working Piratata."

As you can tell from these pages, Mariano was right. Mestre was, too.

> Navalha quer me cortar,
> não corta não, não corta não,
> não corta
> Navalha é a língua do falador,
> navalha não me corta não senhor
> Navalha não corta não
> > The razor wants to cut me
> > Can't cut, can't cut
> > The razor is the tongue speaking
> > The razor can't cut me, no Sir

At the age I started riding with Mestre Acordeon people don't usually look for a mentor. Before I was either too stupid to value a mentor, or never came across a suitable person. In the year we spent together we built a mentor/mentee relationship. Concrete is patient, and so is Mestre Acordeon.

I appreciated his drive and his lust for knowledge, his stories about getting robbed in Barcelona and mugged in Brazil. I loved his silly humor, making us laugh by making up words, and I understood his faults, like his impatience. Most of all I appreciated that he had a knack for getting through to me.

He helped me write better, although this book is the exact opposite of what he often asked me to do in articles – remain focused and to the point, which is why looking at these pages may give him a conniption, he may tell me, that it's too much, too complicated and convoluted, because each sentence contains too many separate pieces of information, bouncing around, if you will, like a ball in a pinball machine, and too many commas, and words, and he'd tell me that I need to cater more to my audience, about which of course he is right, and it is actually how I started out, but now I need to admit that it's got a couple superfluous flourishes here and there, which I like, because I want to break this fascination with four word sentences and their dreaded cousin the four letter word, that Bushite domain, which tramples over any nuanced argument and, frankly, kills brain cells, so instead I try to resurrect the sentence in a sentence, the Aú sem Mão that aggrandizes a game of Capoeira, the daisy poking it's pretty little head around the corner of a grey, much too straight, yet efficient, literary wall, the red balloon that paints the sky.

What?

Anyone who knows Mestre knows that he is a highly strung character. He minds his duties and is a straight shooter. He doesn't drink more than one drink, he doesn't smoke, he eats in moderation. Yet, he does not impose his own believes on others.

He is fantastically intense. He keeps on moving, because you might as well cover some ground. You do not achieve his kind of global success living in a foreign country by sitting on your ass.

These days many Capoeira Mestres live overseas. They bring a range of skills to enable their success: they are amazing Capoeiristas and showmen, they teach percussion, and they dance like the fleet-footed, hip-rolling gods that they are. Still, some of them succeed while others don't. In my opinion, all the above qualities being equal, there is one determinant for a Capoeira Mestre's long-term success: their partner.

I know you laugh. You say that women do nothing but struggle in this macho-driven Latino martial art, with its hedonistic tendencies, with its balls to the wall lifestyle. But two obstacles are often the downfall for Brazilian Capoeira Mestres in the West. They can't demand mafia style loyalty from their students and they can't constantly screw a bunch of Capoeira groupies. A mother will not send her kids to a martial arts school in which either of those things are going on. Instead she will send them where respect is not just spoken about but lived.

Most of the Mestres outside of Brazil eventually marry a local girl, and not just for their Greencard. If she is an equal partner who brings a calming, inter-cultural sensitivity to the table they will likely succeed together.

Mestra Suelly

I doubt Mestra Suelly ever needed to make Mestre Acordeon more successful, but she does calm his temper down.

When Mestre yelled at Tora, "You are fired Tora, FIRED," in El Salvador because Tora ignored instructions not to film while being filmed for the umpteenth time, Mestra rode her bicycle past all of us to have a word with Mestre who himself was storming off in the lead.

"Mestre," she yelled. He didn't stop, she yelled, "Biiiirrraaaaa," but he kept going.

So she had to punch it harder to catch up, while Mariano and I slowed ourselves and the group down so that they could have a fight, I mean, a word in private. Mestra talked Mestre down, and he continued teaching the unteachable who was probably not even aware that his life had just been saved by an angel who can knock you out with a dance move.

I probably (definitely) also had the pleasure of Mestra's invisible support when I smoked pot and partied too much or when I always had a little shot of Cachaça[15] ready for her after a stressful speech that Mestre made her give.

"Hey Pirata, can I have a sip," she asked me in São Luís at the Tambour de Creol, where three drums beat a staccato rhythm, women out of your dreams swirled in flowery dresses, and the night was bright over the river.

"Sure Mestra. Oh, but wait, you know its straight… uhm… Cachaça"

"Really Pirata? What a surprise," she laughed at me being obvious, took a sip, and scrunched up her face.

It was my turn to grin.

"51, *Como um golpe em la cara, Mestra*," (It's 51, like a punch in the face, Mestra).

The Mestres love you, you feel it in your marrow, and you miss them when you are not around them. Professora Come Come came to an event in Seattle two months after I returned from Brazil, and just talking about missing our Mestres brought tears to both our eyes. They embrace you with love and care, which may seem strange to the uninitiated because the next thing you know you lie on your ass with a foot print on your forehead. What can I say, it's a tough love thing.

When Mestre is at his best he gently ribs you until you understand there is some room for self-improvement. When he is at his worst he will mess with you in order to get his point across.

That tough love made me examine what happened one night in El Salvador. The Chilangos (minus Tartaruga) and I had gone out, and when you go out on the town with Indi you find all the things your mother warned you about. Ken and I returned earlier but the hotel door was locked.

Next day Mestre asked me, "Pirata, was that you banging on the door last night?"

"I don't think so Mestre, the other two came home after us. I don't think we were that loud."

Just to make sure I asked Indi later, "*A que hora tu regresa al hotel?*" (When did you get back?)

Indi said, "I dunno man."

"Did you get in ok?"

"Yeah, door was open."

It was time to go apologize to Mestre. I looked him in the eye, shook his hand, and told him, "Sorry Mestre, won't happen again."

And it didn't.

Still, he giggled like a little boy when Balão nailed my pannier with his slingshot later that day on Mestre's orders. I think he must have outright laughed when I stormed off in a huff because I thought Balão could have easily hit the pannier with my cellphones.

Mestre teased me for months about it. To see him imitate me, pulling my shoulders back, huffing and puffing to my bike, and riding off helped me learn to let things slide, and become more patient. What am I gonna do, yell at Mestre Acordeon?

---

[15] Brazilian rum made from sugar cane. Use liberally for Caipirinhas.

I stopped partying to the extent that it affected the group and started contributing.

And so, Capoeira and Mestre Acordeon's patience finally managed a tiny little bit, on a sunny day, with all stars aligned, to do semi-successfully what forty years, one love of my life, and several multinationals could not: civilize Pirata.

Capoeira, because if you are not very good at it, you will get your ass kicked if you play as confrontationally as your personality is. And Mestre, because in his wisdom he found the right words at the right time.

Throughout the months of living, riding, and working together we slowly built a rapport, which came to fruition on the slow boat down the Amazon towards Belem when he said to me, "Let's have a couple of beers and write Piratata."

For days we discussed the narrative of the documentary. Though it was such a pleasure to work with and learn from Mestre Acordeon it is other things that will always stay with me. Like the Mestre Acordeons #1, #2, and #3. Every UCA student does them perfectly.

And that whenever I asked how he was doing he just answered, "I just keep on moving, Piratata," even though his second most uttered sentence was, "Man, I did not sleep for shit last night, damn cramps again, Piratata."

He must have hated that each time he complained about cramps I'd respond with, "Did you eat your salt?"

He'd look at me disgustedly, and I'd follow up with, "Mestra, has Mestre been drinking water and eating bananas?"

It took me months to have the guts to make these suggestions to him, but eventually I felt comfortable enough to tease him about the animal growing on his face or about not having any patience.

Most of all I will never again be in a roda without hearing him yell somewhere in the distance, "Levanta perna Pirata!" (Lift your leg)

When he will finally part from this earth he will leave behind a hole of a size we can't yet imagine. It is a privilege to learn from a man like Mestre and a woman like Mestra. I hope to never take it for granted.

Do not forget his words of instruction, "Jinga like you walk. You don't slink along, you don't side-wind to where you want to go. When you walk, walk with conviction," and, "Kick to break your foot on the other guy's face. That's what my Mestre told us," and, "Brrrrrraaapppp."

A year later, after the trip, we were back in California, sitting in that cozy little nook in his house. Again, we were discussing how to tie it all together for the documentary, the months of riding, the lessons, the terabytes of material. I asked him if he was any closer to knowing the answer to the biggest question of them all.

"Mestre, after all that time on the bike what do you think now? What is Capoeira?"

He only chuckled gleefully, and said, "Piratata, I wish I knew."

I laughed with him, even though I wanted to be annoyed at not being able to nail this important part of our work down. I love him when he is so mischievous and laughing at his own foolishness.

But then we sat quietly. We watched the setting California sun throw patterns on the floor and thought about the time we had spent together. He honored me with his vulnerability that day.

"I wish I had stayed with my Mestre."

Rica
Date: March 25ᵗʰ, 2014
Location: San Jose, Costa Rica

In Central America we finally met some other long distance riders. The most unusual was Kim, the Korean. Many of you think that Mestres were crazy, but Kim proves that there is always someone out there who is, faster, stronger, and, in this case, crazier. A good thought to keep in mind should you consider yourself to be sliced bread.

We met Kim on the stunning coastal road (think Big Sur in California) of El Salvador's northwest. He came pushing his bike up a hill that we would ride down as soon as Mestres woke up from their shared hammock lunch time nap at the road side eatery. It's kind of adorbs how attached the two are to each other. If I'd be riding with my girl for a year, I might be happy to chill in my own hammock for a minute. Not those two, they are like teenagers in freaking first love.

Sweat streamed off Kim, he wore an oversized shirt and shorts that sort of perched on his frame like the dresser fucked up Carl Lagerfeld's runway show and put a size 0 on a size -2 model. The Korean looked as hippie-ish as his people can without dropping dead from progressive fashion mortification. I say this because he wore a red bandana around his neck. His bike was a piece of shit mountain bike, the kind the locals had. We had no clue what the plywood box trailer on a couple of cheap wheels attached to his bike was for.

Then two boys walked up the hill behind him. I mean, little green men beamed down from an UFO.

WTF were these two little Asian kids doing in the middle of nowhere in Central America?

I needed to ask some questions, and after we all met and chatted a little bit I did, "Where have you been?"

Kim, "All over the world. I am riding to North America now. That will be the end."

I looked over at his kids playing with Tuchegas. They were maybe six.

"Your sons have been with you the whole time?"

"Yes, the whole way."

"You have been everywhere? Africa? Asia?

"I started in Asia"

"How was it there?"

"It's our favorite, and Europe!"

You don't ride around the world in less than three years.

"How many years?"

"It's been nearly four."

I can't really describe the look on our faces when he told us these, to him, seemingly completely natural, *insanities*. Because we were on a bicycle tour ourselves, we knew what that life meant. To do it with a couple of two year olds? He was kind of inspiringly mad, and made Sisyphus look like a female organ, the name of which is no longer fashionable to use in this context. Since the male organ is busy describing mean people, that doesn't work either. I guess I'll just let it hang. So to speak.

Speaking of Sisyphus, I needed to ask, "How do you get up these hills? Is that what the motor is for?"

"Motor is too weak, only works in the flats. Now that the boys are bigger they have to walk. I can't pull them uphill anymore."

"Now," I asked weakly, and, "bigger?"

I guess I had a certain stupefied note in my voice. His kids were hardly three feet tall. There was really only one more question to ask, "Why?"

What he said in response made complete sense to me. I don't know if that makes me crazier, or him. Or you.

"I want my sons to spend their formative years in a global environment, without nationalistic or jingoistic fervor."

I had one more question after all. I thought I needed to frame it diplomatically, though.

"What about their mother?"

He responded, "Some decisions I have to take by myself."

Woah!

Have I mentioned that there is always someone stronger, smarter, and crazier out there?

Kim also shared some wisdoms about environmentally friendly yet gringo infested Costa Rica. Apparently, the country's name doesn't so much signify its none-existent natural wealth but rather how much stuff costs.

He was right. As soon as we crossed the border from Nicaragua, a bottle of water cost couple of bucks instead of fifty cents. We decided to ride through as quickly as possible.

Locals can't afford the prices in Costa Rica.

After entering Costa Rica from Nicaragua, or Nica, as the locals call it, we hung her right and headed down to a peninsular on the western coast. Instrutor Parafuso from UCA had a friend with a high-end vacation property there who offered it to us. When I say us, I mean Mestre Acordeon, the rest of us where lucky to ride the magic carpet coat tails. Like I said, Steve Kerr on the Bulls. Still working on getting open.

If you look at the peninsular on a map you think it looks like it has roads and it's Costa Rica, so it's got stuff. After all Homo Gringo Locustus is an infestation here. Remember, water is two bucks a pop. There *have* to be silly tourists around to be able to pay those prizes.

Think again. We got to south of Samara, and we hit dirt, and it wasn't pay dirt. For three days we rode dirt roads up silly steep angles, down slippery slopes, and around howler monkeys throwing poop. Ok, they didn't throw poop, but they howled.

Here my old propensity to fall over at the most inopportune moments, like when I am trying to balance on the edge of a dirt road in order to avoid the ridges in the middle, raised its stupid ugly head again.

For the first time even Tuchegas, who I think was pound for pound the strongest rider, had to push her bike. Instead Tora rode up in a bolt of strange energy. It all reminded me of Mestre telling us in Leo Carrillo that he did not want to plan. That he wanted to see where the road took him. That he wanted adventure. Well, there was no road. And we got adventure.

Late on the second day, of riding these mad mud tracks we spent some time waiting to collect everyone together at the top of a hill. The sun was prettily, yet inexorably, setting behind us. We needed a spot for the night but we had not seen any villages all day, and to the left and right of us was only jungle, no way to camp. Though some motorcycles passed us, we were not sure how far we needed to go. Finally, Tora showed up. He stopped, stood still, and started crying. Not little tears of quiet face-saving Japanese sorrow. He was sobbing. Mestre came over to where Mariano and I were trying to console Tora. But even Mestre's ministration did not help, so he started riding again. Mariano and I waited. Five minutes later Tora was OK to ride his bike again. Without much of a word of explanation. I guess if I had to carry all that weight, I'd cry my eyes out, too.

A few days later he told us, "When I am like that, I mean crying. Please don't touch me. Don't talk to me. Just leave me alone."

At the top of the next hill a motorcyclist stopped and asked us what we were doing riding our bicycles in the pinche middle of nowhere. We told him and he invited us to his jungle casa in the next town. Once again, the kindness of strangers saved us a certainly difficult night. We ended up sleeping on the fine property that he himself had hacked out of the, for crying out loud, jungle.

Feeling somewhat restored, the next day saw us getting up and down ridiculously steep dirt roads, again. We foolishly gunned our bikes through rocky, knee deep river beds, we laughed at ourselves getting stuck, and we cried no more.

At the end of this grand day, filled with small difficulties and big triumphs, we rode a dirt road that turned into a dirt track, then into a sandy path, and finally a beach with nothing but the blood-red sun setting into the gentle waves of the Pacific. I stood there, in silent amazement in this tranquil place at world's end and, in my heart, thanked Mestre Acordeon.

We threw ourselves into the cool waters and admired the setting sun, sure we would sleep alone under the heavens that night.

Then Mestre said, "Alright, let's go."

We just stared in amazement, turned around to look at where the sun had just set and back at Mestre who got on his bike.

Diego said, "But Mestre, where are we going? It's getting dark."

"Well, you know that we need to find this road that is supposed to lead away from the beach somewhere south of here."

Mariano chimed in, "Do we know how far?"

Diego, the route planner said, "I think it's about 10k, maybe more."

Mestre tried to ride but the sand was too soft. So he started pushing. Mestra followed. And so did we. Try pushing your bike through the sand sometimes. Then put sixty pounds on it. It's just about as much as fun as it sounds. After about forty-five minutes, the tide had been out long enough for the sand to firm up enough to ride on, if we kept our momentum.

Without the moon it was pitch black. I rode blindly in the perfectly scary, yet beautiful dark. The Milky Way formed a bright necklace across the heavens to gently guide me south. The only sounds I heard were the soft purring of my chain, the treads of my tires creaking on the sand, the ocean to the right, and the waves of the universe lapping at the shores of my soul.

Riding blind under a starlit equatorial sky was an extraordinary spiritual experience. We arrived at some small beach side huts exhilarated, high on nature's blessings. We laughed and hugged, gladdened by our luck and our friendships.

In a low, raspy voice Mestre said, "That was nice," and moved on.

The next morning, we continued towards Villa Mariposa, our luxurious resting place. I don't think the kind soul who wanted to lend us his place realized *how* dirty we would be upon arrival. The grime from three days of jungle dirt roads was extraordinary, even by B2B standards. Mestre asked us to wash off outside before taking a shower inside.

Three days later, well-rested and better fed by Balão's and Diego's BBQ magic, we continued our ride. Another one of those insane uphills into the Central American Cordilleras awaited us. Tuchegas and I were excited. But first we had to catch the ferry towards Puntas Arenas.

Keep your eyes on the road and your hand up on the wheel
Date: March 30ᵗʰ, 2014
Location: San Jose, Costa Rica

The next day, I was riding a fast downhill, when I came on a 90 degree left turn above a cliff with the ocean to the right. I had just flown past Banano who was riding with his camera in hand to film Mestre on the winding road. I barely managed to brake my bucking steel-horse into the corner of the opposite lane and out the other side.

Immediately, I was worried about our photographer, but I figured he would be fine. I rode on for some time until I came upon Mestra. Together we continued for about three miles. We were going at Mestra's pace so Mestre, Mariano, and Banano should have overtaken us soon. They did not. Mestra and I decided to wait by a bus stop. Five minutes later a motorcyclists pulled up, "Hola, tu amigo. Un accidente." (your friend was in an accident)

Our hearts did a smallish flip-flop. Memories of when Mestre got hit by a car came rushing back.

I asked him, "Quien? El viejo?" (who, the old man?)

"No, era el gordito." (No, the fatty)

Of course later on we teased Bananito endlessly about this, but in the moment we jumped on our bikes and started racing back. Soon an ambulance came flying by. You can imagine how positive that made us feel.

The video on Banano's go pro (always mounted on his handlebar) tells the story. He came around the corner one-handed and way too fast, lost a little control, ended up on the rough shoulder next to the road and flipped forward over his bike ending up doing a few front flips and a little roll before, thankfully, not flying off the cliff.

Mariano and Mestre provided first aid. All the skin and meat on top of both of his big toes was gone. Shredded on the rocks and concrete, because Banano rode in flip-flops. Abrasions that would make a fallen motorcycle racer proud scarred his elbows and shoulders. There were small pebbles embedded in his meat. Instinctively he had rolled over his shoulder to protect the camera he held in his hand during the accident. Still, the lens was broken and for his effort he had a huge bruise on his left ribcage.

The next day Banano rode in Amber's truck while the rest of us started uphill from Puntas Arenas to San Jose. It was brutal. We thought we were used to riding into the high plateaus to find Capoeira in the capitals of Mexico, Guatemala, and El Salvador. But there was a new wrinkle to this uphill. Traffic. You would think that a more developed country like Costa Rica has better conditions for bicycle riders. But the higher level of development didn't mean more safety and better roads. It meant more diesel trucks and more cars stressing out. The steepness remained the same though.

After six hours of straight uphill, we finally reached the edge of the plateau that San José sits on (to this day I have no idea how Mestres rode these monsters). We still had twenty kilometers to go.

So the wind started howling in our face.

Tuchegas and I usually rode uphill the hardest, until the Walatowas with their fresh runner legs showed up. I enjoyed mountain days. Nevertheless, that day nearly broke me. Kudos to all the B2B warriors. When we met the Cordão de Ouro (CDO) Capoeiristas under Instrutor Dorado at a burger joint in San José we were ready to lie down. They told us we had to continue riding through the traffic snake pit also known as San Jose, the over-capacitated and unfortunately hilly capital of Estado do Gringos en America Central (Costa Rica's real name according to Nicaraguans).

Riding high in San José, Costa Rica

We resigned ourselves to having to ride some more, somewhat energized by the burgers that everyone except me (gluten-intolerant) had eaten, but as soon as we rode adrenaline kicked in. It was awesome flying through town. It's a special pleasure born out of a combination of danger and being in the public eye of thousands of people staring at you dumbfounded as you fly by with your saddle bags, your berimbaus, and your smell. In the end, we safely reached CDO's Fanny's amazingly luxurious place, where Mariano, the Chilangos, and I were to stay in utter happiness for a week. We had hot showers.

Then Instrutor Dorado said, "Mestre, maybe do you want to go to the academia and do a roda?"

Instead of waiting for an answer we got our whites. We knew Mestre would do anything to make up for the kindness of putting up with his ragtag bunch.

Mestre started with music and did his usual routine

Mestre, "Everybody together now, sing with me AAAAAA." (Teaching the Capoeristas to sing in harmony with his Berimbau). Banano and Mariano filmed while Balão did sound - holding the mike and passing out, which is what he usually did. He said listening to the sound on the headset, which is how he controlled the quality, was like a lullaby.

Mestre wasn't happy with the singing. Don't take it hard Instrutor Dorado. Mestre is never happy with the singing. That's why you walk into UCA in Berkeley and think you are visiting the Vienna Boys Choir.

So he did what he often does in those situations. He divided and conquered the Capoeiristas' awful vocal cords.

"Ok only the girls sing now. You are the violas. None of the guys sing."

As usual Mestre was speaking in a mixture of English, Spanish and Portuguese. Of course some of the boys didn't realize that they were supposed to be quiet instead of trying their Falsetto with the ladies around Mestra and Tuchegas. And sure enough those well-meaning dudes sang a kind of fake high pitch, attempting to make the windows and Cabaças in the academia explode.

Mestre grinned sheepishly, but then the grin grew wider and I knew what was about to come. Mestre had been talking in Portuguese to me, in English to Mexicans, and Spanish to Brazilians since the beginning of the trip, it's like he means to confuse the hell out of you just so that he can yell at you *Do what I want, not what I say.*

Obviously being aware of his brain's muddled linguistic geographies he started to tell a joke, "There once was a Capoeirista who came up to all his friends in Bahia hanging out on the beach and told them 'Cachaçeros, drinks are on me!' Which of course they all loved, but they asked him why he was suddenly rich."

Mestre, the old showman, did a Mestre #3 and continued, "The little malandro laughed and said 'Well, I just made two million dollars over the weekend!' And of course the rest called him a liar and asked him how he did it."

I loved the coming punch line even though I had heard it before.

"Oh, it's nothing; I learned how to translate Mestrish. Nobody else understands it, so I can charge whatever I want."

And since I often had the pleasure of sitting next to him for five minutes pretending that I understood his Portuguese I enjoyed it even more. Of course my own Portengnol (Portuguese, English, Spanish) is much worse, in particular since it has that certain Arnoldian quality to it. I generally pretend to not notice my accent; otherwise, I would never speak.

While Mestre did his thing I sat in the back of the academia, eating a small bag of raisins to get my starvation sugar levels back up.

Suddenly, Tora sat down next to me and hissed, "Pirata stop eating!"

Even by Tora's standards this was surprising. I was baffled and only looked at him inquiringly. I may have put another raisin in my mouth.

Tora got more agitated, "Stop eating, you can't eat in someone else's academia."

Thinking about the day I just had, I definitely put another raisin into my mouth.

Tora said, "Don't make me kick you!"

I was hangry, but stayed cool. Then he slapped the raisins out of my hands, spreading half the bag on the floor, presumably what he wanted to avoid in the first place. I collected the raisins, put the now inedible ones aside, and continued eating.

He stood up - cables on his neck popping out - wrung his hands in front of his face and hissed in uncontrolled fury, "Doooon't maaake meee kick you!"

Twice was at least one time too many, so I stood up as well, and motioned Tora to please have a go. It would have been way more disrespectful to fight in Mestre's workshop than eating raisins, but what was I going to do, sit and wait to be kicked in the face? I was hoping Tora would throw a punch.

He didn't. Instead he walked away and I sat back down.

Thirty minutes later Mestre started the promised roda. I assumed Tora would come to play. He didn't.

You can be sure that over the following weeks I asked him at every opportunity to put his money where his mouth was. The one time I was able to buy his game in Panama, Tuchegas bought me out within seconds.[16]

After a few weeks of Tora realizing that his mouth is bigger than his balls I let go of my own stupid hurt ego-feelings and forgot about kicking his ass in the roda. Made me feel better right away. It was typical for us to get into little tiffs because we got antsy when we were stuck in cities for too long, though Tora started this one a tad early.

We stayed in San José for a week. On the third day, we started to feel human again, we had an interview with, what I thought was the University TV station at the University.

We shot a roda and Mestre was interviewed by the reporter who had perfect skin; the camera liked her more than Mestre Acordeon. She was also the first black girl I had seen in Costa Rica. The country might be bio-diverse, but human, not so much. Clearly, I needed to talk to her.

"Hi, I am Pirata."

She giggled, "My, y'all are weird, but I'll put up with you since you shaved."

Her voice made me want to curl up like a sexy, large-maned kitten in a lot of velvet.

"So you work for the University Radio?"

"Uhm, no, I work for Station 7."

"Which is what?"

"National Channel, I do the morning show."

I gulped, "That's not all you do though, right?"

"I sing jazz. How did you know?"

"Your voice."

"Come to my show."

---

[16] Let's say two people are playing a game of Capoeira and you want to play against one of them. You would carefully enter the roda while the game is going on and stretch out your hand, open palm towards the person you want to play. You just bought into the game.

Capoeira Function (roda) in Costa Rica

She was so busy though, and so was B2B, with more interviews and Capoeira functions to attend. A few days later I did have a chance to hear her sing in a concert. I was floored, though who doesn't have a weakness for seduction by sultry voice?

Then she had a chance to take me up above the mountains of San José one night. We looked at the stars above and the city lights beneath, and she sang me a song. I fell in voice love. So I told her how I crashed four times in front of the entire world when the trip started. Why was this the first thing I told her about me? Why do girls like us more when we cherish our foolishness?

Finally, the stars aligned and we spent a much too short a night together. It was a perfect start to… unfortunately nothing, because the road was already calling.

The next day her interview with Mestre Acordeon aired. It was fantastic. They really made Mestre, B2B, and Capoeira look like a million dollars. B2B watched together, loving the love that the National TV Station of Costa Rica showed us.

At the end she showed a graphic of positive Capoeira aspects that Mestre always mentions: Flexibility, Strength, Confidence, Community, and Culture. To our surprise she added one of her own: Sexual Stamina.

Maybe day time TV isn't so bad after all.

Mestre bailed town the next day. I hated being a Sailor of the Sands then and felt low, but B2B rode higher and higher continuing from San José towards the Atlantic. We crossed the continental divide and went from bone dry to wet green. Sixty feet tall jungle walls closed in on us. We flew down the mother of all down hills. The traffic was crazy but I still overtook a bunch of trucks and cars, even a cop, more because it is so difficult to break a heavy bike rather than being brave and/or crazy. I had a flat in the middle of the downhill and forgot to re-engage my front breaks after the fix. You can imagine it's a bit of a surprise when all you hear from the direction of your front wheel is an empty *klick* as you desperately clamp down on your brakes because you just accelerated around a truck and another one appears around the corner ahead of you. Sorry mom.

Three days later I stood at the Atlantic.

Life. Unbelievable. Rica.

Adventures of a Modern Hunter-Gatherer Tribe
Date: April 15ᵗʰ, 2014
Location: South of Bocas del Toro, Panama

A few days later, in the evening we rode up to a little hamlet on a dirt track. We were looking for a place to camp; out of sight so we could sleep securely and not worry too much about our bikes. It helped that we had our gear tied down and oiled up so as not to make too much noise. You never knew when it was better to politely alert a potential host or to have the option to quietly escape. As usual we ended up finding a good spot, which was definitely needed in order to re-accustom ourselves to wild camping after having enjoyed San José's and CDO's civilizational qualities for a week.

Many evenings started this way unless we were in a town with a paletaria; give us ice cream on a stick after a day of riding and we forget about sleeping in a sweet hamlet. We'll just go eat three plates of food in a cheap eatery and pass out in a guest house. Better for Mestre's back anyway.

Whichever way we secured a safe sleeping situation, once we did, I usually went vegetable hunting & cooking, while Mariano did some filming.

At the beginning of B2B, some of us had certain expectations: Maybe we thought we would become capoeira super heroes –in reality we trained less than ever. Maybe we would compose Berimbau Symphonies – nope, too busy fixing flats. One expectation was certainly fulfilled; it was an incredible opportunity to learn from a Capoeira legend like Mestre Acordeon for a year.

Some of these expectations were over-rated, some of them were true, yet others we did not see coming at all. This one, that we would be living in a modern day hunter-gatherer tribe surprised me.

Every day, we rode till dusk and then spent the evening fixing bikes, cooking, shooting film, eating and finally sleeping until just before sunrise. Often we slept at a fire station (in a concrete court yard), a municipal building (in a concrete court yard), a gym (in a concrete court yard), or a former jail (in a concrete court yard).

In the mornings, we rose early, packing and cooking breakfast simultaneously. Usually, groups of twos or more cooked together. Everybody kept an eye on Mestre's progress. Sometimes we trained before riding.

When Mestre was ready, we moved our steel-horses out, tied down our saddle bags, and checked the hoofs. Then we quietly rode through fog and wood fire smoke, past slowly awakening fields and animals.

Picture this caravan rolling through verdant landscapes. A little rustling here, birds calling good morning there, the ticking of our well-oiled chains adding the only human noises. Soon, the first roadside food stalls opened up to sell tropical fruit and all types of local breakfast street food as if it all was meant purely for our comfort and confidence.

This was our routine for a year. For better or worse we were as close to a modern hunter gatherer tribe, unless you follow Jared Diamond to Papua New Guinea, as possible. Albeit, one with service-less cell phones and sporadic internet connections.

Training at sunrise

What did that mean? Did we groom each other's pelts and munch on each other's fleas? Only a couple of us. Did we have a dominant male and everyone else tried to take his place? Yes, and no.

Yet, one has to recognize that this journey was so out of the norm of our previous existences that it necessarily impacted us, leading to changes in our behavioral patterns.

Time stopped to matter and confrontations with the real world's schedules startled us. We wondered why it didn't all just flow in a common rhythm, hopefully according to the seasons and the strength of our glutes. We became patient. In Capoeira we watched more and kicked less. Our emotional connections took on a subconscious strength. We resembled cultures with less emphasis on individualistic points of view.

This was the biggest surprise and lesson for me, because I had thought it would be very difficult to be stuck with ten people for a year. But instead, I don't think I have ever been as utterly blissed out before (Except for that one time when a for real Kinder Surprise Egg was smuggled across the Canadian Border). Falling into pack mode, moving as one, and relying on each other was beautiful, easy, and even peaceful.

Yet, as much as we learned how to function like a modern hunter-gatherer tribe, we didn't know each other's life story. It seems we wanted to shed those old skins. The past was only labeling and we ignored the future for we never wanted the present to end.

The now was our holy grail.

Instead of our stories we knew each other's habits; like who needed a cup of morning coffee, who did better in the heat or in the cold, and how fast and far we could ride. We knew who needed sugar and who needed salt, who paid attention, and who was attention challenged and had to be looked out for in a new town. Liking or not liking each other didn't matter. All we cared about was knowing each other's probable actions, because those actions determined our success and safety.

Our quasi hunter-gatherer tribe also didn't have the problem of majority rule. Mestre Acordeon looked for our input and then made a decision. Most of us had no issue with not having any real say about where we went, how long we stayed, or other obvious travel conflict points. This was a significant difference to our daily existence, which is filled with constant individualistic decision making processes. Of course, if you had ten people riding together democratically, they would soon fight over the color of the sky and split up. I would go look at some ruins, Mariano would meet an uncle, Tuchegas and Diego would start a none-profit, Balão would start a dog shelter, Bebum would live of coconuts and suckers, and Tora would be un-and repacking somewhere in California. Mestre would already be much further ahead.

In this environment we learned that the true formative factor of our existence is how we face a tough situation with nothing on the line but our honor, when all the trappings of civilization, all the titles and the gadgets have fallen away. That is what makes us. That is how you speak to the world of you.

Just, you know, most of the time, when you speak to the world of you, don't take yourself too seriously.

We only cared about riding, food, sleep, and capoeira. And we completely blissed out. This was in stark contrast to our previous lives. Like most people in the west we had created a world around ourselves that suited our need as much as we could. Don't like where you live? Move. Don't like that person's political opinions? Never going to see her again. Don't like your partner? Get a new one. Even our offspring and our parents, our very blood, have become expendable in our quest for personal fulfillment.

We build ourselves individualized privacy bunkers and the only time we are forced to deal with issues or people that we may not like is at work, which is ameliorated by context and political correctness.

But then why was it so easy to fall back into more ancient modus operandi? Is it because these tribal instincts were still close to our emotional surface, even after a few thousand years of civilization?

Would we be happier to live in a tribe instead of in our ego bliss bunkers? A tribe of our choosing, of a good size, and with as little gossip as possible, yet one, that forces us to face our own foibles and fears.

Do you miss your tribe without knowing it?

Hamster Wheels
Date: April 20th, 2014
Location: Panama

> One day, your life will flash before your eyes.
> Make sure it's worth watching.
>
> *Gerald Way*

That mountain. The colors played on my retina like an earthen rainbow. I was wondering if Mariano took it in as well, FAF when I saw him ahead of me waiting to share some water.

"Did you see that mountain Pirata? Wasn't it nuts? It reminded me of that sunrise in El Tunco. Remember, when Mestre made us get up at 4.30 for Banano to film the sunrise on the beach and then fucking Tora nearly got fired because he kept filming while we were filming?"

"Yeah man, though when I think of El Tunco all I can think of is Israel."

"Pirata, man, why you always gotta come outa left field?"

"She made my knees weak, and I don't think it was the gluten."

Mariano rolled his eyes and said, "That mountain though. Gracias Universo."

In this much slower existence we had time to pay attention to small pleasures, to be in the moment. However the more gorgeous citizens of the state of Israel affected my lower extremities, one thing was clear; we couldn't help but examine our circumstances more closely once we changed our environment, once we slowed down our mind. The new input demanded that we re-interpret our preconceived notions. It woke up our conscious thought processes. Pretty good reason to travel, if you ask me.

When I still had a job[17] I sometimes caught myself driving to work on autopilot. Neuroscience says that in this way we reduce active thought bandwidth so that our subconscious mind gets to use more of the brain. Sometimes we have the best ideas in that space in between, when we are singing in the shower or jinga-ing at Capoeira class.

Yet gurus growing their toe nails in Himalayan caves, as well as Oprah tell us to be more aware, to be fully conscious at all times, to really pay attention to brushing your teeth, or mopping the floor because in constant attention lies true happiness. The moment is the mantra.

Only somewhat in jest I ask "What's what?"

Are we supposed to space out or be present? Should we concentrate on our chi or go with the flow? Maybe I am best off with split personalities since there is clearly a conflict of interest between my brain and the self-help crowd.

Or does it make sense that we need to do both? Should we really pay attention to spacing out? Or is the actual Dalai Lama trick to leave space for both activities, but separately.

Maybe another reason for our happiness on B2B was that it was easy to live in the moment as well as to space out. Call it cyclo-meditation. Each moment held something enthralling. But each day also generously offered so many hours of calm pedaling that at some point our brains simply shut off. Part of the reason why I did not like riding with headsets on is that it prevented me from spacing out, as well as from being fully in the moment.

And so, all that new input and time to space out led to a storm of analysis and subsequent dopamine highs in little old Piratata, itinerant schlepper of knowledge, infant quasi-bro-losopher, interpreter of many things useful and not, and finally, lover of life in all its grand and garish fatness.

The results of which, I am entirely happy to admit, I am sure glad that you are spending time and money on to read.

Our brains have evolved an amazing pattern recognition ability. This enables us to look for blueberries efficiently while noticing the out of place tiger who wants us for his breakfast. And so a lot of the stuff that we think we see is really filled in by our memory, rather than actually seeing it with our eyes, sending the information to our brain, and interpreting it there. This ability is also what enables the spacing out.

The automation of repetitive tasks makes room for cool new stuff, and tigers. But we should not cruise on autopilot all the time and avoid new input, because than we are limited to what we are already know.

---

[17] Do I ever love writing this!

I support and work against this function by re-inventing my life every few years. Through moving to a new country, I change careers and find new friends and things to do. It's not because I am special, it's merely what makes my brain happy. So that's what I do, because fighting my biology would be calling Don Quichote uncommitted. A smart woman once called me a chameleon, I am pretty sure it was in anger, but she was right to label me that way, as long she meant the cultural way.

You don't have to go to such an extreme to change it up, but many of us seem to be tired of the daily grind. Yet, why do we keep following a dirt track even though, just over yonder a bedazzled highway, with our very own name on it, blazes towards a shiny hamlet surrounded by happy trees and bees? All we'd need to do is look up and step out of the rut.

On B2B, we were blessed with a bedazzled highway full of rosy sunsets and jungly greens. And we spaced out in the stillness of the open road.

Yet, it wasn't a foregone conclusion for me to arrive in this quiet place. I had been a cog in the machine and needed to ride thousands of miles to clear my cobwebbed mind. In the first months, of the journey I kept thinking I needed to attend a meeting soon, or I always felt like I wasn't taking care of some duty like writing a weekly report, or putting together a slide deck for the boss. If a guy who is riding down the Pacific Coast Highway in fulfillment of all childhood glory dreams is having phantom meetings, like an amputated limb that hurts, you have to assume that he was a tad strapped into the corporate hamster wheel.

Similar to the changes I experienced on the B2B journey, the Microsoft environment had also impacted me. There I was data driven, emotionally hardened, and more confrontational because you don't get anything done at a company like Microsoft if you don't stand up for what you believe in.

But then I found Capoeira and through the years of playing I started to change, again. I became more mentally flexible and easier accepting of other people. My mind changed with the way I moved my body.

These examples show, at least in my case, that our daily routine dictates how we act, and thereby who we are. Our mental and physical activities shape our personality. To me this means we must be more conscious about our choices because what we do in life affects not just our existence but also our actual personality.

You can't be a hardballer without hard balls. You can't be a number cruncher without turning into little zeros and ones. This might be why everyone who enters a system in order to change it from the inside finally becomes corrupted by it.

The conclusion is that we should not be in jobs just because they pay the bills. Rather, we need to align our work and our lives with who we want to be and treat our work as a sacred cause, instead of an ends to a means. Even if it's the most mundane thing in the world. Otherwise, we become unmotivated and depressed.

The one activity that affects us the most, because we do it the most, is work. Glorious, happy case of the Mondays. So why do we say that our families and friends are our first priority, yet spend five times as much time at a job as with them? When I was still gainfully employed I told myself, *If you have to put in eight hours a day, and most of us do, you might as well get as much (money) out of it as you can.*

But that is what the damn wheel is for. The hamster wheel sells us the ever greater challenges, but really, nothing changes, the wheel just turns faster, but we can also run faster, and therefore our experienced level of accomplishment is the same as on the first day of work.

When you see a hamster running in its wheel do you think it's going places? Now imagine a picture of my head montaged on the hamster, like one of those cute kitten gifs. Except now it's not so cute anymore. Suddenly that rodent is from 1984.

There won't be no pannier
on your last ride out of here

I have not met many people who categorically say that they hate the idea of traveling for a year. Open any online dating profile, and next to "spontaneous and up for adventure" there is always "love travelling". It has become the mantra of the perpetually young and middle aged to want to explore the world, two weeks at a time. But what keeps us from fulfilling this yearning to take off for a few months, a year even?

Don't ask *Doesn't your ass hurt from riding?* or *How do you afford it?*

These are the wrong questions. Walking away from your secure life, from your hamster wheel, is much more difficult than riding or saving a few thousand dollars to travel with. We think friendships and family matter most, but it is the box of our mind that keeps us locked in place.

Don't accept this chastity belt of your life, don't hold on to these images to the detriment of seeing a brighter light and hearing a richer song. Choose the bedazzled road over yonder.

Look for your true self. You might find it in front of a Volcano in Nicaragua.

During our temporary escape from the real world, simple moments took up much space and graced our minds with peace and tranquility. When all you have to discuss is the fish you caught for dinner and the color of the sun on the ocean waves. When you don't have a plan other than getting on your bike and riding south. When you don't think further than your next mile and your next meal. Why is it then, that you feel an unmatched peace come over you? A happiness that you might find in the embrace of your family or in the days of calm stretching before you. A beauty, that you will want to remember at the end of your life.

And so, I proudly advocate for bicycle touring. For taking that gap year. For letting the soul dangle a little bit. I didn't consciously understand it back then, but that's why, only one month into the trip in San Diego, I told my brother Pixador, "Go ride your bicycle bro. Don't even go anywhere. Just go."

Stairway to Heaven
Date: April 02ⁿᵈ, 2014
Location: Panama

All you need to know about crossing this monster of a ridge, slung carelessly across Panama's Central American spine like a sleeping dragon's tale, is that Mestre and Mestra got in the car at the bottom of it. It was a verdant nightmare. The predator alien guy would have said *fuck it* and turned around to lay down and drink Cuba Libres with a pretty person (this was "girl" before my editor suggested to not define the fella's sexual preference) under a palm tree.

The contrast to the previous week of lazily rolling from Costa Rica into Panama along the Caribbean and spending a couple of nights on the island paradise of Bocas del Tora, could not have been more pronounced. I don't think it is possible to encounter worse conditions in Central America. Not a village in sight after the first rolling hills leading away from the Caribbean coast. Heavy tropical rain, wind gusting in all directions, a slippery and badly maintained road surface, and impenetrable jungle to either side of the insanely steep road. Of course there was no shoulder. But we didn't have a choice because we needed to get back to the Pan-American Highway on the Pacific side because there was no road going south on the Atlantic side of Panama.

Now, Bocas del Toro, the gorgeous beaches and friendly Caribbean people seemed like a distant memory. Before us remained a stairway to heaven. Apparently, the color of heaven is emerald.

This was next level difficulty. Imagine you have to get up from your saddle because you need the extra strength to keep pushing your pedals. But instead of doing that every once in a while you do it for two days straight. Now add 60 pounds of gear.

It rained so hard the water bounced back from the ground and hit us in the face. An old Central America hand, who had a spread by the side of road, gave us coconuts while telling stories of tropical yetis. Tora disappeared. The usually car-bound Chilangos suffered, because the Mestres took the car and made them ride. We didn't really know how much more mountain there was. When we tried to ask, the locals looked at our bikes with consternation and said "Maybe about two more hours."

They meant driving, but was it a chicken bus, or a rice-cooker? Depending, it could be a day, or three for us. We stopped at a roadside restaurant with a straw roof, no walls, and a concrete floor. We ate a ton of chicken. It kept raining. We ate some more chicken. The proprietor of the place let us spend the night. Amber swapped a couple of tires that popped in the same pot hole down the street, first for two Nicaraguans and then two Dutch dudes.

Since the early days in Baja California she had started to feel more and more at home with her role in our group. Gone were the days of passing us without seeing us, or, completely forgetting how tired we were compared to her, and at the end of the day asking, "Alright, is everybody ready to train?"

Being the odd one out in a car was difficult, but like for most of us, B2B was a great learning experience. Of course, when she rode bicycle for the last three weeks with us she went back to passing us by.

When we woke up the next morning it was raining less. After a meager breakfast I pushed hard. I loved this. It was cool and moist, but my muscles burned. The road was quiet. After two hours I entered the clouds and the temperature dropped further. Cars appeared eerily out of the fog ahead, their headlights alerted me before I heard their sound.

For some reason Amber came to my mind. She and I had always had a tough time with each other. We have similar outspoken personalities. Under normal circumstances we would have bounced against each other and gone our separate ways. In a tribe, with a leader who is not willing to let go of anyone, we had to deal with each other.

B2B was a journey to paradigm shift all our lives, in Amber's case after her fiancé's violent death in Oakland.

Once, she had told me, "I visited the site of his death daily. Making mandalas, kissing them each night before I left. Talking to him. I know I wasn't fully in the real world. Capoeira was my only grip on myself. Loosing myself in the rhythm of the roda helped me find myself."

I said, "Reminds me of our friend at UCA who overcame PTSD after Iraq through Capoeira."

"Yeah, Capoeira does that. Fito and I had planned to move to Brazil. And that's what I wanted to do with B2B. But to tell you the truth, when we all left California, I wasn't really there. I was still in that other, the spirit world."

In Panama it seemed as though Amber was on her way to reconcile her two worlds. Surely, it was to be an amalgam since seldom do we live through traumatic experiences without gaining a larger understanding of ourselves. Either that, or we may break.

There is a lot of time to think when you are on a stairway to heaven. As I scaled higher the rain turned to cold mist and the further decreasing visibility reduced the size of my world. It reminded me of similarly exhausting but introspective moments in the Austrian Alps.

After three hours I made it to a ridge and used an ineffectual windbreak to wait in the freezing cold. First Juanjo, then Amber in her truck, then the rest came up one by one. Tora was still missing. Indi and Ken didn't make it.

We all knew what was happening. Tora was sulking somewhere. Indi was looking for a ride up the mountain because Amber finally refused to be his driver. Ken would take a long time since he hadn't ridden bike. We also knew that Mestres were coming up at some point in case help was needed and that we could not wait and freeze our butts off half way up this insane mountain.

So we bounced out of there. A bit later a big truck slowly passed Mariano and I, we saw two chains hanging on the back, punched pedal, caught up, and grabbed on. Riding up the hill like that is easy on the legs, but hard on the nerves and shoulder. Since it was a winding mountain road at this point, it also had downhill sections. But you can't hold on while the truck is going downhill because if it breaks you smash into it from behind. So you have to race along and time it perfectly to latch back on. If you overshoot to the side and lose balance, you'll get pulpified by the back wheel. Sorry mom.

We came upon a reservoir that covered an enormous valley. The vegetation was starting to turn alpine. On the other side of the valley-spanning dam the lonely road wound up further into the misty sky. It was pure Game of Thrones shit.

Here we waited for everyone to collect. Ken arrived (props) about an hour later and Indi followed in the bed of a pick-up truck, bitching about Amber. We giggled at all three of them and continued, our lungs bursting at 7000 feet, our legs on fire, our bellies hungry. We had been riding across the dragon's tail with little food (on days like that a lot of chicken is still a little food) for two days straight and the cold was getting to us. We laughed at Big Sur, and cursed Bocas del Toro.

And then, two hours later, we saw the perfect continental divide. Imperceptibly at first, the road turned into a small decline, then came a curve around a small rocky cone, and boom, there she was. A knife edged ridge that you would expect in the Strait of Magellan. And the road went right along the top of it. The wind roared from east to west, from cold to hot, wet to dry, ready to fling anyone who dared to cross down into an abyss, a bottomless cliff.

While Balão and I tried to record the sound of the gale force wind around us, a sound we imagined old earth to make, we watched Mariano nearly fly into the abyss. He and his bike were literally lifted and pushed towards the edge by the wind, but he managed to touch down just before the barbed wire next to the cliff.

After watching my mates being pushed to the right, I rode on the left side of the road, doubled over to the left of my handle bar, leaning so far into the wind that had it stopped for a split second I would fallen flat on my face.

Then we burned rubber on the western, bone dry side of the spine. Two days of uphill took twenty minutes to go down again. Totally. Worth. It.

It is these intensely challenging moments that inspire us to be our best, to live our highest truths and dreams, to know that we can do anything and that nobody can stop us.

We need to work for these moments, in our case 9000 miles and thousands of hours of bicycling. These moments don't just happen.

Apparently, you need to put in somewhere around ten thousand hours to be the next Mozart or Tiger Woods, but say for a moment that you commit to practice three hours a day for ten years, what would you do? No need to focus on riding bicycle around the world. Anything in the world is up for grabs to follow your dream.

Learn economics, knitting, or become the world's best fly fisher. Since you won't have time to watch TV you will want less material stuff. You will have more money, more space in your garage, and, most valuably, more time. Yes, it sounds a bit like a contradiction to do more stuff to be less busy, but it's quite the winning combination.

Walatowa Nation
Date: April 25th, 2014
Location: Panama City

B2B flew down a busy freeway. We were about to leave the North American continent across the Bridge of the Americas. Traffic got thicker and thicker approaching the Panama Canal.

On the other side was our goal, *Casco Viejo*, Panama City's ancient center, inhabited mostly by poor black folk and backpackers. The old town was a typically run-down assortment of three story Spanish New World style buildings in various states of repair, that's probably why they called it *Old Helmet*. It was strange to see perfectly renovated buildings right next to ruins.

But in order to get at the ceviche vendors in the old harbor we had to brave the shoulder free three-lane bridge across the Panama Canal.[18] Cars flew past an inch from me while I thought grand explorer and deep philosophical thoughts of continental drift and political silliness, because if continents eventually drift into each other or apart, why do borders matter? That seems like two mosquitoes fighting over who gets to sit on the left ass cheek of an elephant.

I won't lie, riding the bridge was big for me. This little kid from Vienna's Leopoldstadt was actually riding his bicycle across the Panama Canal from North to South America.

#NunkaPara

In Panama City the Walatowas from Jimez Pueblo joined us, and soon after figuring out that the best way around the Darien Gap between Panama and Colombia was a speed boat ride along the Atlantic coast, we were headed to the eastern side of Panama.

"EEEEEEÁÁÁÁÁÁÁÁ!"

The Walatowas' war cry crashed off the rocks and crags.

"EEEEEEÁÁÁÁÁÁÁÁ!"

Off the trees and the ferns.

"HOOOOOOEE!"

And there was Mestre, leading it with gusto and mouth wide open.

"HOOOOOOEE!"

The two Native Americans were slingshot shooting, weed smoking, and freaking hard riding road warriors. Their tribe still lived on (somewhat diminished) ancestral land above Albuquerque, New Mexico and was famous for their strong runners and rain dancers.

The two Walatowas, like all of us, started the journey out with way too much stuff and immediately began to donate hiking boots (really bro?), clothes, and jackets. They were also always picking up all kinds of natural materials to make things out of and soon slingshots, an atlatl, and a drum appeared on their bikes.

One of the fascinating things about a journey with a man like Mestre Acordeon, is to discover the different motivations that drive people to join. Yes, there is an overarching lust for adventure, but dig a little deeper, and you find hidden gems.

Whatever fires your passion, when it does hit you, you better grab on with all you've got or miss out on the ride of your life.

I asked *Gavião* (Falcon), skinny and light on his feet, a naturally quiet and introspective type, who often wrote into his journal during the journey, "Why did you join us now? You already missed out on two thirds."

Gavião pulled his black, long hair into a bun at the nape of his neck and said, "We tried to come earlier man, but we couldn't figure out the money thing. We had to raise funds from the tribes."

"Oh that's, cool, they gave you cash?"

---

[18] This sentence illustrates our digestive tract's comfort level with Montezuma's Revenge at that point of our journey.

"Yeah we bought our bikes and all the gear with it. Even the camera and computer shit that was stolen from us the first night in the hostel in Panama City."

"Hah, same shit happened to me and Bebum in San Francisco, first night out."

"No shit."

"Yeah, fuck it, at least we carry less. But so, why are you here?"

"You know on the Rez things can be pretty tough. There are a lot of people drinking, unemployment is high. Cam and I are the first ones to go through a college education in this program that was started."

We rode in silence for a bit, then Gavião said, "You know, I started Capoeira seven years ago. I loved it. I used to do flips and shit onto the couch. My grampa would holler at me to stop. But I never stopped, I just kept on training and training."

"I can just see little Gavião spreading his wings."

He laughed, "Yeah. But when I learned about the history of Capoeira, about slavery, and how they used Capoeira to overcome adversity I was amazed."

"Hmmm."

"I felt like my people's history is similar. And then this trip came up. I thought that it was perfect. I could inspire folks on the rez, show them what we can do. That we are still powerful."

That kind of gave me goosebumps.

He threw his hand angrily and continued, "We have no passion, no discipline. We don't achieve shit anymore. I want to show people that we can, that we just need to knuckle down and do it. Like everyone else."

"That's awesome bro."

We rode past some shanties, Gavião flashed his coal eyes at the poverty around us and said, "I studied anthropology. I've seen our past. I want a different future. Capoeira gives me a way to re-form communities and teach physical and mental self-confidence to the youth of the Pueblos."

What can I say about this inspiring young man other than that I will support his mission in any way that I can.

His cousin Cam was bulkier, sort of ponderous, and soon would cut his black, long hair into a Mohawk. Cam graduated in Visual Art, archery, and tomfoolery. He could at times be the rudest motherfucker on the planet, and yet, the most sensitive things would flow from him.

After our return to the USA, I visited Jimez Pueblo Feast Day for the Walatowa Batizado and saw Cam's art on the wall. He reminds me of the crude shape of Gustav Klimt, both so in contrast to their exquisite creations.

There is a near cliché First Nation, yet altogether real quiet strength in both their countenance. Maybe they teach that mile long Native American Stare in Rez schools. But they were also fun loving and silly. Cam would ride past a pretty girl and rip open his always asleep seeming eyes to yell, "Is that an ass I see?!?!"

We'd turn to look, and he'd continue, "No, that's an Açaiiii!!!"

And although he could easily pass for a native inhabitant of Brazil, his Portengol was hilariously redneckish, though better than Gavião's, who was just a little too perfectionist to make the necessary mistakes to learn a new language. The two were quite the comical soulful combo.

Once we left Panama City for Colombia via the San Blas island paradise the Walatowas immediately fit like a glove on a smoothly operating calloused fist. Mariano, Banano, and I rode and lived hard. Indi and Ken partied hard and rode Mestre's car harder. Unfortunately, for those two, Mestre sold the crew car in

Panama City. So Ken stayed back to mooch on someone else and Indi finally had to ride full-time.

The Walatowas were the true Hashimi of the new world, leaving aside that historically there seem to not actually have been any Hashimi, assassins or not. They would smoke and ride like devils. My personal problem was that after we rolled a fatty blunt I wanted to ride chill, take in the vibrant colors and smell the flowers while the rest of the crew just wanted to burn down the open road. But pain was not an option for me. We rode in a pack and nobody was leaving anyone behind.

I loved discovering these out of bounds characters. These haters of convention and implementers of new thought. We are the nomads in our people's eternal hunting grounds. We are the perpetually pubescent challengers of your convention. Minus the acne.

Today, the Walatowas are bringing Capoeira and their growing wisdom back to the Rez. The start is an after school program. After centuries of subjugation and death for the Indigenous Peoples of the Americas it is fantastic to watch these young men step up.

The Kuna – Or why Friday was Native American
Date: April 28th, 2014
Location: San Blas Islands, Panama

She wore traditional tribal clothing. A long tight skirt and a square-necked tight blouse, both with complex, mostly red and yellowish floral patterns and seemingly designed to un-flatter. Only once did she show her unfriendly eyes from behind a red bandana.

She was the first Kuna I had ever seen. Most of them would be equally unapproachable. They reminded me of those naturally ornery people in certain mountain valleys in Switzerland who hadn't spoken with their neighbors in the next valley in centuries and now couldn't even understand each other anymore. I respected her desire for privacy. If you've managed to remain unmolested from the occupiers for 500 years you've probably got something that I don't want to mess with.

The Kuna live on hundreds of islands strung out along the Atlantic side of Panama towards Colombia. Most of the islands are too small to sustain a community. Other than a home for Friday and the occasional Columbian drug runner they provide little entertainment and much untouched nature. Few pass by here, but for us the ride in the speed boat, which consisted of two monster engines with an attached wooden dingy, was the best way to get around the Darien Gap. The friendly people who agreed to take us to Columbia can only be described as a hippie outfit. You can find them in the local bar in Casco Viejo in Panama City.

A more welcome detour was seldom forced upon the weary traveler. Instead of schlepping our bikes through a tropical version of a melting permafrost, including leeches, deadly critters, and various folks with machine guns we island hopped from one paradise to the next for four days. Here *"läßt man die Seele baumeln"* – here you let the soul hang out.

Mestre had been enticing, or depending on your point of view, scaring the crap out of us, with plans of kayaking from Panama to Colombia, going as far as showing me YouTube videos of people who had done this. In the end cooler heads prevailed[19].

The San Blas island utopia is one of Central America's best kept secrets. The only reason why I can mention this hidden gem is because there are no resorts, no toilets, and certainly no air-condition, so most tourists won't make it there.

The tribe has freedom and autonomy to run their affairs. What they don't have is land. They use every last speck of the larger, habitable islands and extend the available acreage with stilts and decks into the ocean. If you go for a swim near their communities pay attention to the currents as their outhouses are perched right over the ocean. San Blas, as so many places, is paradise only if you don't have to live there.

> *Under a leaden sky we drown our joy*
> *Above a choppy sea we leave our earth*
> *Here an up-side-down boat floats by*
> *A palm tree grows on its sandy bank*

One evening, we were staying on one of the bigger islands, I was walking and playing my flute and chatting to kids. A gringo playing flute in a Central American village square is surely quite strange, but to the sheltered Kuna kids I must have been like a blond alien. Still, they also wanted to learn how to play. All through the Americas I loved seeing the surprise and excitement in kids' eyes if they could produce a sound from the flute after only a few minutes of trying.

"You know how to make a sound with a bottle? Just like that, blow over its rim," I'd coax them along, even though their friends were giggling at them.

Someone much smarter than I once said that the sound of a flute floats on your breath, and so comes infused with your soul. Apparently this attracts kids, who often want happy songs, and women, who always asked for melancholy songs. In fact, during the entire journey only one woman asked me for a happy song. Even today, I can not stop thinking about what that means.

Men, crude fuckers that they usually are, seem to be more into teasing flautists about playing the *skinflute*… sticks and stones, is all I am going to say, my no-sex having friends.

Soon Mestres strolled by and saw the local interest in the flute. Mestre asked me to fetch his Berimbau, and when I returned with it he started a Roda with a hundred Kuna. Mestre's white mane stood out amongst a sea of short, happily dancing Kuna.

> A maré 'tá cheia, ioió,
> A maré 'tá cheia, iaiá!
> A maré subiu
> Sobe mare!
> A maré desceu
> Desce maré!
>> The tide is up, yoyó
>> The tide is up, yayá!
>> The tide rose up
>> Rise up tide!
>> The tide came down
>> Come down tide!

---

[19] Mestra Suelly

Even in this remote place, hearts opened to Mestre's Berimbau. We mixed into the crowd and together we found that unwitting human sweet spot of music, community, and movement. Mestre bounced on the balls of his feet, wailing on the Berimbau, wearing his big Santa Claus grin, that he so often makes fun of by comparing it to his own Mestre's haughty public countenance.

With these seemingly simple, yet open-hearted gestures he draws in, organizes, and spiritualizes people around the magic of his instrument and leads us on a stroll to a shared rhythm of freedom.

The Kuna kids played in the Roda and the local leaders didn't get mad at us for this outsized interaction with their population. The drunken town fool got into it with Indi, which was also some kind of providence, because Indi loves the small folk as well as the patron saint of thieves.

The rhythm of *Sao Bento Grande de Regional* will get anyone head-nodding. Mestre's Berimbau cried and the world kept turning on her verga.

More seriously, later that night, we discussed if we'd need to amputate Sequestrado Contramestre Espanta's arm below the elbow because of a scorpion sting. We thought we might just have to do it civil war era style - give him a bottle of moonshine, tie him down, and saw the thing right off.

Alas, the next day, he was better and the angry welts becalmed. And so was our little intrepid group. We enjoyed getting away from the city of Panama and entering this time portal to a quasi-past.

Each morning, the monster engine with the wooden dingy attached bumped us for a few hours to the next palm tree paradise sand bank. There we would have a sandwich lunch that our hippie outfit brought along, and so, though there were no butlers and fancy tents, we felt like decadent safari tourists for a cherished small period.

During the breaks on the islands we practiced back-hand springs into the sand and learned how to hold our breath for a minute. We played music and met other wanderers on this happily but somewhat uneasily traveled road. In the afternoons we continued to our goal for the night.

Not just once I imagined being Robinson Crusoe, "Tell me Friday, why did you not come on Thursday?"

"Well Robinson, on Thursday, clearly, you were not ready for Friday."

A perfect parable for the story of my life; always thinking that whatever knowledge I had just gained, came at the perfect time, even though it was really just the first time I was smart enough to recognize what had been around all the while.

On the fourth and last day of our cyclo exile, we passed what was the most diligent yet silliest drug search of the entire trip - upon *entering* Colombia. We carried all our belongings from a rocky shore where our speedboat parked (and where I stashed my pipe) through torrential rain to a guardhouse where dogs sniffed all our things.

Of course it made no sense to search anyone *entering* Columbia, but in reality it is reciprocity. Just like Brazil fingerprinted tourists from the USA after 9/11, who then walked out of Brazilian airports with inked fingers. Makes me giggle. Brazil didn't have fancy electronic finger print machines. The Colombian reciprocity was somewhat dumber though, since bringing coke to Colombia would be like bringing sand to the beach, or a thong to Brazil.

Do I look like I carry any contraband?

Where the Colombian Gangsters are
Date: May 2ⁿᵈ, 2014
Location: San Onofre, Colombia

A week later, a brutally hot flat expanse of nothing much other than dry brush awaited us between the small Colombian town of San Onofre and Cartagena, jewel of the Caribbean. B2B was excited to visit the city through which the majority of Spanish South America's wealth absconded to Europe. We were mostly not excited to ride the 120km to get there. Mostly, because for an Austrian I have a strange affinity to heat.

B2B must thank Mestra Suelly for visiting divine places such as Cartagena or Bocas del Toro. If it had been up to Mestre Acordeon the journey would have consisted of Capoeira, riding, Capoeira, riding faster, more Capoeira, and probably some kayaking[20].

---

[20] O Mestre, can we go again soon, please?

Without Mestra's calming effect we also may have had more fights. Even in his old age (not compared to Mama Rosa, I know Mestre) Mestre has little patience for BS. Back in Honduras a guesthouse owner changed the price on us after we moved in. Unfortunately, for the guy Mestra Suelly wasn't around. Mariano and I saw Mestre ramp up, exchanged a grin, and sat back to watch the fireworks.

Because, really, if you sat next to Mestre Acordeon in Mazatlán when he set the air on fire for Tora's enlightenment, then you know that at that point you either wait to back Mestre up or you watch the other guy cower before the anvil and lighting temper.

People usually cower. It's like General Patton materializes under you, when you were just happily bouncing on Santa's knee a minute ago. You do not want to shit your pants on Santa Patton's knees.

I like both the testosterone driven rumbler from the mean streets of Salvador and the Grecian philosopher leader. At any point in time you may defend yourself against his *cabeçada* (head butt), learn how to play Bossa Nova on a flute, and discuss how to build a perfect snow cave or why disadvantaged kids do not make it out of the favela.

That intensity also carries unforeseen consequences. After we told that hotel guy to go fuck himself we rode thirty minutes in circles behind Mestre to find an equally expensive alternative. An entertaining spectacle to the rest of the B2B crew who saw us cross the central square multiple times from different directions. I wouldn't have said anything either. Watching us do a Charlie Chaplin on the square would have been too funny to interrupt rudely with an offer to show us their place.

That night Mariano cleaned Mestre's drive train, despite mosquito and ant attacks. Small actions like that went a long way to maintain a positive equilibrium. I only realized this a year later, which shows just how close to being on the spectrum I really am.

But all that was ancient B2B history, and here in Colombia, before hitting those 120km to Cartagena, we enjoyed a strangely calm family ride. Calm, because Mestre's favorites Tora, Ken, and Amber had been replaced by the Walatowas. Strange, because it doesn't seem possible to dredge anything but horrible civil war news and hyper violent drug cartel Hollywood fair out of the recesses of our minds when it comes to Colombia.

While traversing nine countries, we had learned to take with a grain of salt any warnings about how dangerous the next country south was. But we respected Colombia. You'd be a fool not to respect Colombia. We expected wise guys sent back from the jails of New York and dudes getting all Miami Vice on us.

Instead, after crossing the Gulf of Uraba from Panama to Colombia a donkey-drawn carriage transported our boxed bikes from the beach to a hostel. No wise guys, no Uzis.

B2B, and Mestre foremost, had spent substantial time figuring out how to ride through Colombia's dangerous north-west. In order not to become sequestrados ourselves we took the coastal way towards Cartagena instead of heading straight inland towards Medellin.

The coastal road was pristine and undulating through verdant fields and small forested hills. Plant life bursts from all surfaces, like the Cumbia tunes that pop from every corner and building.

We cruised past tranquil Caribbean seaside towns inhabited mostly by black people on scooters. The magic of three girls riding a scooter sideways is apparently not confined to Asia. In fact, it seems that nubile, sideways riding woman folk take it upon themselves to cause bicycle accidents the world over. I'm not suggesting that's what caused Indi to crack open his head on the asphalt a couple of weeks later. No, that was because he wasn't wearing a helmet when a motorcycle hit him. Ok, kids? Don't become organ donors because you think a helmet isn't cool.

He needed a ton of stitches and went ahead to Bogota to recover. Unfortunately, Indi's accident would bring about his early return to Mexico a few weeks later. It was heart-breaking.

Life along the coast felt old. As though nothing here had changed for a few hundred years. People here lead a quiet existence far away from the eyes of the world. They seemed unconcerned, happy. On scooters. The question whether to develop or not remains of Shakespearean size.

When we reached the small town of San Onofre a couple of days later, Mariano and I stayed back because I needed to work on my Greencard issue. The issue was, if you remember, that some asshole stole it on the first night of this trip.

I had received a new appointment to replace it - back in Seattle, because Greencards are only dealt with inside of the USA, three weeks hence, and luckily right during Candeias' Batizado. Stoked to combine necessary red tape meandering with playing some games with my Capoeira family back in the USA meant I had to organize a temporary visa. An entirely entertaining prospect if all you hear on the embassy tape is that they don't take phone calls, don't answer emails, and that it takes a least two weeks to get an appointment to initiate the issuance of a letter of transportation. Which also takes two weeks. And I still had to ride 1500 miles to Bogota via Cartagena. I was going to have to go to Bogota early.

San Onofre is one of those towns that make your alarm bells jangle just a tad too insistently. That morning, Mariano and I cooked vegetables, called girlfriend (Mariano), and listened to idiotic embassy tapes (Pirata). Then we went out to pick up some more veggies and a grilled chicken for lunch. We bought some sticky corn type snack from an old Mestizo lady. Reminded me of Burma.

We stood there taking in the life of the town, munching, and minding our own business when the hustler materialized.

"Hola amigos, everytiing okayyy," with an accent straight out of a Scorsese movie.

Finally, I thought.

"Tranquilo hermano. Nos gustamos los aperitivos de la Senora." (All good, we like the Lady's snacks.)

"Ah, habla espanol! Bien!" (Ah, you speak Spanish, great.)

I didn't trust him at all. Shitty, little shifty character, but about as tall as Mariano and I, in his white Bermuda shorts and cliché gold chain forming a demarcation line so that he would know where to stop shaving. Limbs moved all over the place in practiced street hustler manner that asked for trust in all the wrong places.

"My friends, over there, we want to invite you for a drink. Come with me."

I didn't need to look at Mariano to know that he enjoyed the prospect about as much as contracting genital herpes.

Mariano said, "Gracias Amigo. But we can't. We only wanted to eat a little and that's it."

Hustler ramped it up a bit, "Ohhh, hermanos, esta bien. It's beautiful here, we can all go down to the beach and drink some cervecas."

Mariano said, "That sounds great, but we can't."

He was getting more frantic, "Just ask the lady, you can trust me," he said as he looked at the lady. She shrugged a sort of agreement. A not inconsiderable act of valor and skill since she couldn't be obvious about it. She wouldn't be selling on the market much longer, if she were to tell us this guy is about to take us for all we had. Not that we needed convincing, but it was nice to have her opinion in the matter.

While Mariano had done most talking until then, I offered my hand to the guy and said, "Gracias hermano, pero estamos muy cansados y necesitamos ir!" (Thanks bro, we are tired, we gotta go.)

I was kinda proud of my Spanish when he slapped my hand away and yelled at me, "Su mano en su culo!"

Ah, stick it where the sun don't shine. Good to know that's what that means. I switched from innocent to ready-to-rumble in a millisecond, things you learn in a Yakuza bar in Ropongi, and stared him down hard as he continued, "If I say so, you will not leave this town alive."

"Well son, that really makes me want to come with you," I said.

I gave him another hard stare and started walking. Mariano did the same.

He yelled after us, "If I see you outside of town, I will have you killed!"

At least he didn't pull a gun on us like the guy three months later. We headed back to the hotel, triple locked it the fuck up, and left for Cartagena at 4.30 a.m. the next morning.

Sometimes, you have to know when to bail and so that you can live to tell the tale.

The misty morning promised a gorgeous day. A couple of hours into the ride Mariano and I bought five mangoes, like nectar from the gods, for 50 cents and made tracks.

While the bad thing about not riding in a group are streethustlers with gold chain demarcations, the good thing is that you can go as slow, or as fast as you like. 50 miles later, when we came to the left turn to Cartagena, the sun was hot in the sky and Mariano started to suffer. He should be the Austrian and I the Chilean. After some deep-fried delicacies (haha) we continued. We did not want to enter Cartagena at night so we rode through the blazing heat for another thirty miles until we came to a last little hill baby. I was starting to feel lightheaded and had goosebumps up and down my arms. We stopped under some trees. I guessed Mariano felt worse.

He huffed, "You get these shakes during late stage exhaustion and dehydration."

"Speak for yourself, bruh."

"Its cardiac drift. Your heart starts racing without any apparent reason. Basically, if you continue forcing your body, it will go into shock and you die of a stroke."

"Good to know, Bio Nerd. You're a hazard."

We dragged ourselves to a dry goods store a mile further, drank all their coke, and continued. An hour later we passed through the outskirts of Cartagena and followed an endless artery for another hour right to the magical old town.

I shot a video of us entering.

"Mariano, how many kilometers did we ride today?"

His answer, "I am dying."

I laughed at him, "How many bro?"

"120. I am dying."

The old town lived up to its image. Exquisite Spanish manor homes form the heart of a city with monster fortifications that haven't been taken, except by the Spanish themselves when they came to smash the first Latin American white people (As in, local Spandiards who wanted to stop paying taxes to the King) revolution in the mouth.

Following that early revolutionary mishap, Simon Bolivar, whose home you can visit here, freed the Spanish lands south and including of Panama to the north, so that the Colonials could keep more of the bounty for themselves rather than sharing it with the homeland. The tight, fancy streets were an oxymoronic pleasure to ride through with all our dirty hippie baggage. As always we headed to the center of town, that's where you find B2B at the end of a long day, and waited to hear from them.

A hustler, one that wanted to do business instead of larceny, found us first and offered to sell us some dirt cheap[21], pristine end-product of the sacred coca plant, which apparently you can go right to sleep on, even though you just snorted an ass-rail the size of the Grand Canyon. And if that's not a holy thing, I don't know what is. I imagined the trail of crap that the stuff gets cut with to arrive in Japan where fifteen years earlier I had experienced the most suicidal come-downs in mind-expansion history.

Because the hustler knew Cartagena like the back of his hand, I took the opportunity to gain some anthropologic/historical insights, "So what about Colombia. I remember reading about the FARC and the militias as a kid. Looking around Cartagena, it seems peaceful."

He looked at me like only a gringo would consider his shithole peaceful, "Well, it is better than before. Ten years ago you could not do any business here."

I said, "Even in this beautiful tourist-tranquilized town? I feel like I walked on a Spanish *Sound of Music* set."

He laughed, "Yes, especially here, and with all you cash cows around."

"When you say 'could not do business', what do you mean?"

"Every store, every restaurant, every business had to pay protection money."

"To the police?"

Now, he laughed outright at me, "No, the FARC. The police always take their cut, that goes without saying."

I was as shocked that the "people's" guerillas had resorted to mafia practices as much as by my own naïveté. I may have to agree with my friend Z, who is not sure if he would side with humanity against the AI (Except that we'll have built it, so it's going to be an asshole for sure). One would be remiss to not acknowledge that the drugs purchased from the hustler also supported the FARC.

Soon, we received an email that told us the location of our Pousada three blocks away, provided *muy barratissimo* (very cheaply) by the kind Capoeiristas of the Capoeira Nativos of Colombia.

The jewel of the Caribbean is a strange place. Maybe it seems less so if you just stepped off a plane from some air-conditioned country. But if you had an opportunity to tour San Onofre, to see the flies on the meat in the high-noon sun and the fish wives in meager shades, you might reconsider. You might call Cartagena a Potemkin Village.

---

[21] The weed he sold us was twice the price.

From one homeless (privileged) person to another in ritzy Cartagena

We spent three days in Cartagena after which there remained a ride of 600 miles and 20,000 feet over two mountain ridges to Bogota. I absolutely hated having to take a plane, but embassy red-tape awaited me.

In Bogota I had one friend: Shiado, my Grupo Candeias amigo. I had met him at a B2B event in San Diego. Twenty years ago, he was one of the first Capoeiristas in Colombia, he used to watch VHS tapes of Mestre Acordeon back in those days. He and his family welcomed me into their home like a son, despite the fact that Shiado had just suffered a horrible motorcycle accident in which his foot was crushed. They were so kind that even a nominally horrible city like Bogota became comfortable. I repaid them by making green smoothies and cooking vegetables every day, which Shiado hated with a passion.

"Não Pirata, quero não verduras. Preciso de carne para melhorar minha perna." (No veggies, I need meat to heal my leg.)

"Broder, se um Pirata come verduras, vc pode também." (If a Pirate eats veggies, so can you.)

"Porra Princessa! Voce precisa salchicha de burro." (<<*untranslatable*>> Princess, you need Donkey Sausage)

Their home was in *Casa Linda* (Beautiful House), an hour south of the Centro. The only thing further south was Ciudade Bolivar, slum of a bazillion internally displaced Colombians. The only thing Linda about Casa Linda was the veggie store and the fattest-ass banana leave tamales in the world.

Bogota is not a fun, touristy town. Because of this, Shiado's family was worried when I got home late on the first day.

"Pirata, aiii. Você não está morto!" (You are not dead.)

"Porqué irmao, tudo certo." (Of course not, why?)

"Eu postei no Facebook: Ajude me, gringo perdido em Bogotá." (I posted on FB, gringo lost in Bogota, help.)

"But it's ok. After your dad took me to the US Embassy on the little Busetta, I just walked all over town. I had to fix the cracked screen on my phone."

"Where did you go?"

I showed him on a map. They stared at me like I lost my mind, and sat me down with some Tinto (sugar with a couple of drops of black coffee), an Arepa (delicious fat Bogota corn tortilla) with a donkey's sausage, and spoke some plain truth to me. About how many people get robbed every day, and how juicy a target a gringo is. They also pointed out that I was a generally naïve white boy who is lucky to be alive.

Three weeks later, Tuchegas and Balão were mugged at knife point in broad daylight on the way to Montserrat, the mountain top monastery three thousand feet above the city and ten thousand feet above sea level. They probably didn't get a warning from their hosts like I did.

I spent a month dealing with the punks at the US Embassy and training Capoeira. My favorite thing was teaching kids at night in the square of Casa Linda with Shiado on his crutches. It reminded me that Capoeira doesn't need a roof, a stereo, or mats.

I played flute in most of Bogota's churches, visited a bunch of museums, as well as a hospital in Ciudad Bolivar for Shiado's checkup with a surgeon.

Going to the hospital gave me an opportunity to ask, "How does the Colombian Healthcare System work?"

Shiado said, "We have five groups, split up according to income. The bottom two, the poorest groups, do not need to pay anything. The top pays nearly in full for their healthcare."

"Oh!" I said, "You mean Colombia uses means tests to determine how much people can afford? I will need to bring this novel concept back to the so-called developed world."

Before we could continue, the surgeon called Shiado in and told him, "Your leg will have to be amputated."

Shiado said, "No," walked out, and continued his Vaseline and zero painkillers treatment. A year later he visited Grupo Candeias in Seattle. Without crutches, though his ankle was stiff. Played games with (now) Contramestre Fenix, too. I have never met anyone with more testicular fortitude. Forget riding bicycle for a year. You want to learn absolute determination? Do yourself a favor and take some Capoeira classes with Instrutor Shiado.

While getting to know Bogota I tried to lay some ground work for Mestre's documentary. Many Capoeira groups had charitable projects in the Comunidades (hillside slums of Bogota).

I had immense admiration for Gardel, who worked on top of *Montserrat del Sur* - Montserrat of the South, our tongue in cheek name for the Comunidade way up on the mountain, far away from the real tourist magnet. He taught Capoeira in schools to help kids overcome traumatizing lives. His pay was shit, the commute long, and the neighborhood dangerous. The honor of spending a day with this inspiring young man and teaching classes to his kids was a highlight of my entire year on a bike.

With Gardel and his kids at Montserrat del Sur in Bogota

When the rest of B2B arrived in Bogota, Mestre called a meeting with the Bogota Capoeiristas to set up his schedule while in town. The groups all wanted Mestre to teach workshops. Quickly the schedule filled up. But it was getting late, and so, after taking obligatory Mestre photos, Shiado, on his crutches, and I had to catch the two-hour bus ride back to Portal Tunal.

Two stops from Casa Linda, people getting of the bus started to sprint away. I asked Shiado, "Why are they running?"

"It's so that they don't get robbed."

I will always remember Bogota. For the warmth that Shiado and Instrutor Batata showed a lost gringo. For flying back to Seattle to get my Greencard and a new Capoeira Belt. For the literally breathtaking first Roda on the real Montserrat, where Instrutor Perico played Cavalaria with a smile when the police came - the police always come, even though you might just be dancing.

For men like Gardel who have little comforts in their own lives, yet still go into the Comunidades every day to make small differences.

Part III

The Mighty Amazon
Date: April 28ᵗʰ, 2014
Location: Rio Negro, Hella Upstream in the Amazon Basin

When I stepped on the tarmac the air punched me in the gut like a
sledgehammer. We had flown from always chilly Bogota at an altitude of 8300
feet to the border between Colombia and Brazil in the always steaming upper
Amazon. You live in Miami. You think you know humid. You don't. It's like
thinking you know diarrhea before you go to India.

Most of that morning past me by like a dream. The early cab ride to the
airport, my bike in a box, airport security trying to confiscate my new
yellow/orange belt.

All I could think of was the river. Pink Dolphins! Anacondas and crocs the
size of small submarines. Naked natives and small fishes that boldly follow your
pee stream where no one has gone before. I was headed to the real-life, frikkin'
largest river in the known universe.

All my life it hung like a black hole right in the center of my geographical
need-to-go list. It had only been a matter of time before this Pirate ended up
swimming with the Piranhas. You want stats? I give you stats.

- 20 % of the world's river flow
- Larger than the next seven rivers *combined* (kind of like the Offensive
  Budget of the USA)
- When it rains the river swells to 70 miles and rises 50 feet

Did I mention pink dolphins?

The actual border was a small intersection in the middle of the towns of
Leticia (Colombia) and Tapatinga (Brazil). No guards, no military, nobody
asking for passports. Didn't even have a stop light. A tacit admission that
nobody can control the movement of pretty much anything at the confluence of
these three jungle borders (Peru was on the third side) and many more rivers.
Struck me as strange considering the near cavity search level harassment we
endured entering Colombia.

We stayed at generous Capoeirista Papagaio's pension in Tapatinga and
organized a boat passage to Manaus. I also bought a mosquito net. Best five
dollars I've ever spent, a gift that kept on giving every night when I heard the
bloodsuckers angrily buzzing *outside* my net.

The World Cup had just started, and charmingly a Colombian parade
invaded Brazilian Tapatinga on motorcycles, pickup trucks, and bicycles
celebrating a win good-naturedly. If Scots did this in England, it would cause
WWIII.

B2B was giddy. We had reached the promised land. Despite all the people
who called Mestre *a fool trying to live the dream of a youngster,* and because of all
the positivity and support shown us we had done the impossible. We had ridden
12,000 km on bicycles, played and trained Capoeira everywhere, and shot a
documentary while at it. Here in this sleepy corner of Brazil we allowed
ourselves a small measure of pride. Then Mestre yelled at us to clean our room to
make sure we stayed firmly rooted in the swamps of the Amazon.

Mariano and I took the Mestres in a local TukTuk to a remote location to
shoot a Facebook video to tell the world that Mestre Acordeon had arrived in his
homeland. Mariano set up the beautiful shot on a high bank above the mile-wide
Rio Solimões. Mestre stood in Brazil, looked at Colombia and Peru, and was at

his charming yet understated best. After we took the shot, I shook Mestre's hand, looked him in the eye, and told him "Thank you Mestre. I would not be here without you. This is the best moment of my life."

And if I said it too many times I still didn't say it often enough. And if I said it in São Luís after watching Mestres from all over Maranhão come to Mestre Nelsinho's Friday Roda to ask about Mestre Bimba and Capoeira, in Teotihuacan and on Lago Atitlan, in Granada and in Cartagena, on the Bridge of the Americas and here in the Amazon, I always meant it from the bottom of my heart.

Mestre did a workshop for local Capoeiristas. Because it was our first Roda in Brazil we brought a lot of *Axé* (energy). Afterwards the crowd mobbed Mestre Acordeon. A preview for the rest of Brazil. The adoration in Tapatinga was getting a little overwhelming so we started singing, "MES ACORDEO-ON MES ACORDEO-ON," which had become sort of a mantra for bringing B2B back down to earth from up on high on top of our steel horses.

Three days later, we were on our way to Manaus on a dilapidated river cruiser. It had no cabins, chairs, benches, tables or any other amenities you'd expect on a boat. Instead, it had ceiling railings along the length of it to hang your hammocks on. There were also some reasonably horrible toilets and showers, nothing you wouldn't expect in a two-dollar Guesthouse in any of the more interesting places around the world.

B2B and three hundred locals gently swayed down the mother of all rivers. Crying babies, three Football Worldcup games per day, and work on Mestre's documentary filled our days. Whenever the boat's direction changed the satellite dish on the roof had to be adjusted with a hand winch and appropriate curses directed at the captain for messing with the picture, always when someone scored a goal, of course. We were so close to the equator that the dish pointed straight up. If you ever wonder which way is north, it's the opposite direction of your closest satellite dish. Unless you are in the southern hemisphere. This progressive direction change of the ever present satellite dishes was somehow very meaningful to me throughout the trip.

Mississippi sized rivers joined as tributaries every few miles and grey Dolphins surfaced. The vistas of sunsets lighting up towering thunder clouds above the Amazon will remain burned into our minds. At night the captain used a powerful search light to avoid sand banks and other un/known hazards. I could not help but be reminded of the Irrawaddy, giver of life to Burma, and not just because the boat was similarly lacking in confidence inducing technology.

It was the perfect time for Mestre and I to sit down and do some writing for the documentary, which was of course a huge honor for me. To be allowed to contribute to Mestre's project was so special to me that it took me quite some time (ten minutes) to start telling him what to do with the story.

I try to force myself to disregard people's stature so that intimidation doesn't freeze my brain. For example, imagining some highfalutin CEO on the shitter usually can have a rather equalizing effect on our psyche, though I refrained from that mental exercise with Mestre since I already enjoyed watching his daily nutbutter administration.

On the river I found myself in an introspective mood. A quiet life from former times seems to come naturally to us when we travel in the bosom of nature, at her own pulse's tranquil speed instead of humanity's more frantic pace. The rivers of the world bear primordial messages from faraway that all too soon will be lost amongst the walls of dams built to light homes behind other walls. Of course hydro-electric power is better than the coal fired type, so you can't really be mad at the Three Gorges dam unless you are mad at Florida or the Maldives.

We constantly alter natural beauty to something that may (hopefully) one day be a created landscape of a kind of artificial beauty. If this makes you want to vomit on my shoes, believe me, I understand. I just spent a year riding through nature. However, keep in mind that Europe has been an intensely managed landscape for 2000 years. Still, most tourists who go there think it is rather pretty.

The subjugation of the natural world has happened long before our time and we are too citified to be able to tell the difference. Europe used to be covered in a primordial forest before Homo Sapiens. What is left of it is Białowieża Forest, a national park as far away from humanity as it is difficult to pronounce, straddling the Belarus and Poland border. Border no-man's lands, such as between the Korea's are the last truly wild places in existence. We apparently inherited our bitching sense of irony directly from nature.

No message is more primordial then that of the Amazon. The constant rush of water underneath you takes you into a long forgotten embrace. Here you feel as though you returned to the cradle of life. In this dense, wet chaos the soup of creation is rife with life. It drips of leaves and dances in shadows. It attacks your senses with indifferent gusto. You feel it on your skin and taste it in the air.

This always dank and sometimes dark world lets demons inhabit our cultures' nooks and crannies. Imagine a blood moon rises above the river on a stormy night, and a virgin drowns just when the eclipse hits. If you had that sort of mind you'd think someone set the poor damsel up to gain some *justifying* power.

Jarringly, we hit Manaus five days later on a sunny hot morning. The city's port was abuzz. Brazil was still in the feverish grip of the *Copa do Mundo* (Soccer World Cup). The hostel outrageously set us each back 30 USD.

We met Mestre Cobra Mansa for an ice cream date. The two Mestres chatted for two hours, which was kind of like watching two presidents talk. You think they are discussing matters of geopolitical (Capoeira) import when really, they are probably commiserating about their bad backs and pubescent daughters.

The next day local Capoeiristas organized an 8x10 room for all ten of us in a sports complex next to the World Cup stadium. Thankfully, Mestres had their own digs. As impressive as it is for a septuagenarian to ride to Brazil, sleeping like a sardine would be pushing it. Unfortunately, we missed the USA game but Switzerland against Honduras was up the next day. We *mandinga'd* (we were sneaky) past the check points and I scanned the crowd for tickets. Unlikely, I thought, at the World Cup. I knew FIFA thought scalping was worse than the plague. They hated for someone other than Sepp Blatter to make money.

I whisper-asked people for tickets in German, English, Spanish, Portuguese, and a mix thereof as I walked through the milling crowd, "You have tix? Willst du verkaufen? Quero Billeti. Tem Ticketch?"

Finally, I saw a guy in red and white talking to a couple of girls, waving two tickets. Swiss people always seem so helpful with their color-inverted red cross. Until you try to get at the African Dictator's or Apple's cash, that is.

"Grützi," I called out the familiar Swiss-German hello.

"Servus. Von wo bist denn du?" (Hi, where you from?)

"From Austria. Are you selling these?"

"Yeah."

"Girls not buying?"

"I don't know, are you?"

"Ja!"

Ten minutes later Mariano and I drank a cold one on the main stand cheering for opposing teams. The Swiss won 3:1. A few weeks later the Germans opened up holes the size of a Rio Tinto mine in the interior defense of Brazil and a national depression set in, which is the obviously real cause for Brazil's current malaise. Lava Chato Balderdash. Pfffft.

We came out of the game - Check Bucket List - and looked for the rest of the gang who were at a roda on the river waterfront. From the cab we saw the circle in white. The energy was frantic, our guys wide-eyed. The Capoeira Contemporânea in Manaus is known to be fast and aggressive. Players didn't throw more than one or two kicks before they threw punches. I regretted the beers I had. I definitely didn't want to get into that roda tipsy. Where was Bebum when you needed him? Ah, right, fixing his visa back in Tapatinga.

His Capoeira group had bought him a ticket from Costa Rica to the border where he caught up with us. Still, he made the journey down the Amazon a few days behind us because he had to re-apply for his visa that had disappeared with his Passport and his phone in Costa Rica.

A day later B2B was back on the river on our way to Parintins, stoked to visit one of Brazil's most famous festivals. Every year tens of thousands of people come to the tiny village on an island in the Amazon to experience *Bumba meu Boi*. A mind-blowing rebirth, fertility ritual, end-of-harvest, large-as-fuck-party, which happened to be happening exactly when we came through.

Mariano and I called this phenomenon of perfect timing, for example hitting cool season in the Baja Desert, or dry season in Central America, or party season in the Amazon *Mestre Mandinga* (magic). In reality, a sufficiently advanced form of life is indistinguishable from magic. I don't care that Arthur C. Clarke referred to aliens and not to Mestre Acordeon. Wait a minute…

On our way down the spine of the Americas we had seen plenty of cultural and artisanal festivals so I was a bit blasé. *Boi* was I in for a surprise. The size of the thing should have become obvious on seeing the McMansion sized demons, birds, and dragons parked around town.

Parintins was fanatic about their annual festa. Blue for the Caprichosos, with a black bull that had a blue star on his forehead, and Red for the Garantidos, with a white Bull that had a red heart on his forehead.

For three nights from 9 p.m. until 2 a.m. all of Parintins was in the stadium. Either cheering in wild, choreographed pandemonium for their color or being absolutely stone-faced when the other side was on. Both performed ritualistic mythologies of the Amazon. It was the same story three days in a row with ever more awe inspiring choreographic displays.

We all needed to wear blue because we were in the Caprichoso stands with our host Professora Andorinha. The Garantidos were on, and I couldn't help shaking my booty until I noticed that that it was apparently entirely inappropriate to give in to the bone-rattling rhythm of the Garantido enemy because the stone faced Caprichoso fans shot daggers into my back(side). Except for the cute guys, they just stared.

Enormous fire breathing demons, hundreds of dancers and drummers, and thousands of fans stomping, clapping, and singing war songs made my head spin. No wonder people from as far as Rio pay top dollar to fly to this backwater.

We stayed for nearly a week and before we left I had to check one more thing of my bucket list – swimming in the Amazon. Anacondas, alligators, and little bold fishes be damned. Of course, it would have been better to jump into a main stream instead of into the brackish side arm in back of Parintins. But I only found out later that that's where the wild things are. Luckily, none of them came to investigate (drag our lifeless corpses to the bottom of the brownish, murky waters). Also, none of us peed while swimming.

Soon, we packed our bikes on another boat to Belem and the delta of the Amazon. The river became wider by the hour and the passengers spent slow and peaceful days contemplating the passage of time and life. Distances are measured somewhat relatively here. Upstream takes longer than down. It seemed that time, like everything else on the Amazon, also floated on pontoons.

I met charmingly named Maiby Glorize. I admit, we weren't doing much talking. It was more gesticulating and using my phone translator (Your mind out of the gutter). At the time I only had about three weeks of Portuguese under my belt. I was atrocious.

Cappuccino freckled, curly-haired, and green eyed Maiby hails from a small, small village, like a short, short skirt, along the sometimes banks of the Amazon two days downstream from Parintins.

She had just finished her degree in Biology and was reading a book on Limnology prepping for her Masters. That's a thing. Brainy beauty equals Kryptonite for my unbearable lightness of being. Especially, floating on a river of time. Maiby was on her way to visit home for the first time in two years. Things and people she touched seemed to vibrate just a little bit from the tension she was under.

She pointed down from the ship, "Usually there is land here."

I said, "Get out!"

She laughed, threw her hair, "Sim, during dry season the river is over there," she lifted her hand to a point half a mile away.

"How much higher is the water level now?"

"Uhm… fifteen meters."

A day later I felt like I was in an Amazonian *Out of Africa* as I unloaded her luggage. A hug and quick melancholy later I watched her stand on the dock in her flowing dress. A quiet oasis amidst porters, harried passengers, piles of luggage, furniture, and food stuffs.

Nearly a year later, Professora Andorinha would tell me the fable of a dolphin river spirit who takes the form of man to seduce the most beautiful girls of the Amazon with his… never mind.

Though I am reasonably sure that dolphin bro is quite capable of finding the most soulful girl along the banks of the biggest river in the world by himself, some would put Maiby right at the top of his short, short list.

Life is like Capoeira
Date: May 11ᵗʰ, 2014
Location: Somewhere on the Amazon

The Meia Lua came out of nowhere. I was playing a watchful beginning of a *jogo* (game), trying to find my opponent's measure when suddenly all I saw was a white shadow at my temple. As I twisted my head out of the way of his heel at the last possible moment the thought crossed my mind that this guy might be assuming that anyone who rides with Mestre Acordeon is a long time Capoeirista. Or he just wanted to crack me one.

About six inches shorter than I but bulky, he wasn't wearing adabas (tight white capoeira pants) and hadn't yet made any moves that obviously defined him. I was hoping to see that playful CDO jump back with arms wide open because if you know a player's group you know some of his moves.

Vivo no ninho de cobra

I live in a Cobra's Nest
I'm cobra that a cobra doesn't bite
If she bites me she is dead
If she doesn't bite she is gone

After my improvised *esquiva* to escape his kick I didn't counter kick but continued watching, rolling around him, side skipping, changing directions. I got long legs, I don't need to be all *jogo de dentro* (inside game) all the time.

This time Mestre could not help me because he was not around. In any case, he would just watch me get knocked on my ass because since the first time that I had asked him months ago, "Mestre, what do you think about my game," he had told me, "Piratata, you play too direct. You don't always have to hit right back, or take the first opening. Watch a little longer, let the game develop."

Which is a completely logical extension of my personality, and a perfect example why it's so hard for me, or anyone else, to change our games. Capoeira gives you the freedom to be yourself. Capoeira will teach you, if you let it, to master your weaknesses, your blind spots, your assumptions, and autopilots. Or it will continue putting a boot in your ass. If you are too afraid, it will make you braver. If you are too serious, it will relax you. If you are too cocky, it will humble you. If you always have a smile on your face it will grin right back atcha. And put a boot in your ass.

I continued to jinga with the anonymous Capoeirista, waiting for an opening and trying to have a conversation at the same time. This combination of playing with and against each other is what makes Capoeira a unique martial art. Soon we shook hands and I counted my blessings that all I had was a close call. Like I said many times before, "I am a Capoeira baby," and will remain one for a long time.

It took me the longest time to play freely in front of Mestre. He is so intense when he is in the *batteria* (row of musical instruments in a Capoeira roda) that it can constrict your game. I hoped he would be happy that I was trying to follow his advice to jinga and watch.

The point is not to get got
Contramestre Versatil

That's another way of putting it. A way that I personally understand better. Because if you get got once, you are probably dead. Of course, if you are an Angolero you might laugh, and think that all that matters is the ground, and the energy you receive from it.

None of this is even close to your horizon when you start Capoeira. Especially, we Westerners feel as if we entered an alternate platonic, and sometimes not so platonic, love reality. You feel like you ended up in some weird paradise of a human ego suppression zone. We adore this community that embraces us with open hearts and arms. It is so amazing that you forget it's a martial art. Go to Manaus if you want to remember.

When you start Capoeira you want to be like the advanced players - strong, smooth, and confident. You train and grow, and like a baby you take your first steps under the guidance of others.

Like a youngster you soon start revolting against the authority. You become aware that the somewhat unfair assumption that our Capoeira instructors are immortal and ethical beings, forged in the cauldron of a gigantic historic wrong, is incorrect. At that point most of us realize that Life is not like Capoeira. But, instead, that Capoeira very much is like Life. Life that will always be dominated by human ego. Egos that we fight more or less unsuccessfully.

We may call those who have let go of the eternal ego satisfaction race, wise. Of course the closer to kicking the bucket we get the easier it is to let go, so it might just be a result of giving up the charade instead of an actual wisdom accrual.

Regardless of our long term prospects in life, there will always be Capoeira. Capoeira that beckons you with its promise of knowing yourself, of growing into your true self. You may not see this for a long time. And if you do not humble yourself you might not ever. And that is why we never stop growing in Capoeira. We start in the dirt yet we reach for the stars.

And with us, so does Capoeira. The progression from a violent birth to Unesco World Heritage has been an arduous journey, but seems to continue.

Capoeira has always embraced the downtrodden, the physically and mentally handicapped. But we have done so from the goodness of our hearts and an understanding that love, respect, and a sense of accomplishment will go a long way. Inclusive actions were not based on a professional understanding of healing. Today, Capoeira's therapeutic aspect for the mentally troubled is being discovered by people like Contramestre Versatil, who applies scientific processes to therapy strategies.

The psychotherapy community is currently experiencing a growth development away from Sigmund Freud era couch-surfing patients towards various movement and music oriented therapies. Capoeira happens to hit a sweet-spot of rhythmic mental and physical expression. This is not to say we can all dance our way out of bipolarity. But it does acknowledge that combining traditional strategies with Capoeira has the potential for healing.

The application of Capoeira in novel areas is driven by Capoeiristas who seek to combine their professional background with the potential in their art. It seems Capoeira's evolution may yet bear unexpected fruit.

I know at least one Capoeirista who overcame PTSD, including hyper sensitivity and aggression, after returning from Iraq and Afghanistan through Capoeira. The most important aspect in his recovery was the music, the application of rhythm to his body. He thinks the metronome-like cadence of the Berimbau re-aligned his mind.

The roda, Capoeira's ritual circle, is also an appropriate expression of our species. As humans we evolved to simultaneously compete and cooperate in a socially highly complex pack. We forget this, our common past, in our hyper-individualized present.

But in the roda you must be fully present in front of your peers, or you are gone. You must co-operate and compete, for in order to create a beautiful jogo you must engage in a dialog. You can't lie. You can't fabricate. You are you. You will accept you, or you will run away. This simultaneous facing and exposing of oneself is much harder to overcome than not being able to do a move.

Thus we share our purest truth, the deepest expression of ourselves, with and simultaneously against one another. Accompanied by our voices, carrying chants to the sky above and down into our deepest being.

Thus we are human. Asking and answering. Demanding and pushing. Competing and cooperating. Fighting and dancing. Once your body realizes this, you can never stop it from seeking out a roda. You must let it find its balance.

My own balance is in the balanca itself. As you by now know, I am a fairly direct person. I try to be diplomatic and mostly fail dreadfully. That directness, as Mestre keeps pointing out, is also my first instinct in Capoeira.

But over time I noticed that the game of Capoeira made me less confrontational, more patient and accepting. If you LOL at this, I tell you, you should have met me ten years ago. Mestre certainly helped this process along with his question, "So Piratata, how is Pirata working out for you?"

And thus, for the first time, at least in my life, Capoeira is like life and life is like Capoeira.

Nordestinios
Date: May 14ᵗʰ, 2014
Location: Belem, Amazon Delta

That day though, when Mariano and I semi-purposely abetted Mestre in leaving us behind in Belem. We arrived early on the boat from Parintins, rolled out of our hammocks onto our bikes and rode straight to the Mercado to eat a strange bowl of savory Açai with smallish black beans in it. I can now say, that I found a not very tasty way of eating Açai.

The group tried to decide what to do: ride immediately or stick around one night. Belem, gateway to mysterious riches and Fitzcarraldo-like adventures, Mariano and I weren't about to not explore it, and so, after hanging about ineffectually for a couple of hours, like in the army B2B did this a lot, the two of us left to take a little ride around old town.

You know its ancient because they are calling their promenade a *Strand*; it's filled with malandros (rascals), drunks, and vendors selling *Guarana* - a local smoothie like heaven.

Whatever they call their seaside, you also know you are in a fucked up place when you see buzzards chilling on building roofs like it's an Ennio Morricone Western. I shot a Facebook video talking blithely about how cool it is to ride again after having been in Bogota and on the Amazon for weeks. Don't be fooled, we were hyper aware of our surroundings.

When we returned to the Strand ten minutes later Mestre was gone. Neither surprised, nor unhappy, we found a guesthouse and then walked in the direction of some really loud music. It was an afternoon block party, with too many people packed into a park to do much more than be squeezed in a sweaty Cachaça rich embrace.

Surely, Belem and Manaus are considered backwaters in Brazil, but to us cyclo nomads they were fine examples of civilizational advancement. This party even had *Punto Bebums*, which are really little more than a Brazilian selling homemade fifty Cent Caipirinhas out of a freezer box. And if that's not civilized, I don't know what is. The Punto Bebums made us miss our lost brother and we toasted one or three to his health and probable free ride down the Amazon.

After weeks in the jungle we finally felt that we were about to see the real Brazil. The Brazil of Samba and Sugar, Capoeira and Forró, Rio's Christo on a rock and epic levels of corruption. The Brazil in which priests leave one tower on their church unfinished because then they don't have to pay off Rome. Brazil, where people drive around in boomboxes called cars (including inbuilt generator), just in case they need to start a party in the middle of the street. We were ready to experience all the whack, conflicting, lazy, impatient, and sexy that Brazil had to offer.

At the start of our journey, Mariano used to shy away from risks. He even offered me access to a phone app that connected to some crazy Latino Navy Seal type special forces who'd drop from a helicopter when the shit hit the van. But I figured the first thing the bad guys would do is break your phone so nobody can GPS your kidnapped ass and so I politely, one hopes, declined Mariano's offer ("what a crock of shit, bruh").

By the time we reached Belem he was all about exploration. We got lost in the backstreets of old town Belem. It was quiet, lurking, and, like many equatorial cities, moldy. I don't know if it is the underlying sense of danger that attracts me to these places. Here I remain vigilant as a baseline, notice the smell of urine on corners and the faded shutter that moves just a tiny bit in the distance behind me. Here I find myself in a constant state of alertness and wonder if that means I am more alive or more full of shit.

But even after hanging around Punto Bebums all day, quasi calling our third bro spiritually, he didn't show up at the harbor. The next day Mariano and I rode. Mestre exerted this magical pull. Maybe the difference between Bebum and I was that I had become tied to the tribe, while he had spent six months alone.

The industrialized south of the city elevated motorists not giving a shit to a whole new level. I watched a truck barrel past Mariano by an inch as we passed a parked car. He turned around and looked at me like someone just pulled the magic carpet out from under him. No more shenanigans.

We rode hard, barely stopping to eat. The heat was tropical and the wind started blowing. In the wrong direction. Windmills on the horizon pointed the same way as my handlebars. On a bicycle you know that you are headed for a shitty creek when you see windmills. If they point in the direction of your travel, then you are riding up the shitty creek. If they spin crazily, you should go with the flow, or take the bus.

Not B2B though, we made like Don Quichote and waded up that creek for two thousand miles all the way to Recife. If the trade winds had been kind in Baja California, now they repaid us with a vengeance.

Back in Mexico's Chiapas, Mariano said to me, "Shit, side wind is blowing me off the road. All these bags are like a sail. Makes the side wind worse than actual head wind."

He was wrong. Dead wrong.

We fought through the sparsely populated and completely flat Amazonas Basin. The land is poor, and the soil must be too because the only thing growing around here was brush and crazy. Reminded me of Baja California, though that landscape is more varied.

Brazil's North felt like a fourth world nation. Even the churches had fallen into disrepair. There were no clinics or medicines, schools were an afterthought, and the tiny stores sold Coca-Cola, cookies, and crackers. Sometimes they carried rotten tomatoes, carrots, cucumbers, or onions. I ate a lot of canned sardines with those.

One medicine that there is plenty of in Brazil's Northeast is Cachaça. The cheapest 0.75-liter bottle of the local cane liquor is 51 for five Reals, cheaper than water. In 2014, after international capital had been leaving Brazil for a couple of years, driving the Brazilian currency into the cellar to make more room for the Chicago Boys' cavalry, that was about a buck twenty. It tastes as bad as it is cheap. You take a sip of the infernal thing, then you cough, and say in a smoky Motown voice, "*AHHHH, Como um golpe na cara.*" (like a punch in the face)

Sugar makes Brazil's Northeast go round. Except it looks a little wobbly on its feet, like the countless drunks we saw.

This one time, Bebum, who had finally caught up a few days south of Belem, the Walatowas, and I were way ahead and needed to wait. We stopped at a roadside eatery consisting of a roof and tables but no customers. Only the middle-aged proprietress, whose cheap bleach job suggested a sort of desperately insistent sexiness and one blind-drunk friend of hers were around. His rice cooker was parked right in front of the place.

My Walatowa brothers were a little melancholy because back on the Rez it was feast day, their annual rain dance celebration, a time when anyone who visits any home is fed copious amounts of delicious Walatowa food varieties: green chili, red chili, and really spicy chili.

The Brazilians immediately asked us, "Where are you from?"

We were a geographically confusing bunch. The Walatowas easily passed for Brazilian natives, and Bebum and I were at that point, to put it kindly, truly gypsy-fied hippies. We explained that Austria does not have Kangaroos and that the Walatowas are not Indios from Amazonas but actually gringos from the USA. Which is when Cam, as usual, pulled out his hilarious Walatowa redneck accent.

"*Nooo, ehstou de Tribo… Tribo del Novu Meschico.*" (No, I'm a tribe… Tribe of New Mexico)

The startled Brazilian timidly asked, "*De Meschico?*" (Mexico?)

"*Naooo! Nova Meschico. No, no, no, Estados Unidos! INDIGINA!*" (NO! New Mexico, USA, Indiginous)

The Brazilians shrugged, realizing that this conversation wouldn't progress much further.

"*Nao ehestou* Mexico! Fuuuuck, I ain't no Mexicaint!" (I am not Mexico)

Then they wanted to know about the bikes.

Bebum told them, "Pedalando de California." (We rode from California)

Pack mode in Brazil's Northeast

He might as well have said we dropped in from the dark side of the moon. We counted to three until their jaws fell to the floor in unison. At which point we politely commenced helping them pick up their shocked mandibles by explaining that, "It took a long time," "It's not such a big deal," and, "doesn't everyone around here ride their bicycles all the time?"

Maybe what made the statement so extraordinary to them was not the geographical distance, but rather an inability to imagine such a journey. If one has no options to leave, the mind must stay rooted, also.

After calming everyone's nerves a little bit, especially the desperately sexy ones, we asked, *"O Senhora, voce tem baneiro?"* (Do you have showers?)

In Brazil's Northeast water is considered to be an inalienable right. People always offered frozen water bottles in exchange for empty ones and wherever we stopped, there was usually a shower or a bucket available. In the south of Brazil they don't give a shit if you are dying of thirst, they still charge you a buck per bottle.

After the bucket, we sat down and asked for everything she had left in the kitchen. The Walatowas explained that it was feast day and that they were missing home:

Cam, "Esta dia del fiesta." (Its party day)

Desperate Sexiness, "Huh?"

"Muito comida na casa." (Lots of food in the house)

"Ah, você está com fome?" (You are hungry?)

"No, in mia casa." (No, in my house)

"Huh?"

"Affff, fuck it."

Of course, as one does in Brazil, we poured liberal amounts of *Farofa* (manioc flour, also known as nutrient-free filler, eaten with everything in Brazil) over our food.

They asked us about our trip and the proprietress kept checking out the Walatowas' gluteus maximus and Bebum's dreads (shit, it's my book, I can say she checked out whatever I want). It's oxymoronically entertaining what an impression a man's shirtless upper body will make in a country where it seems to be against the law to wear more than dental floss for bikinis. A side note to European girls though; don't even think about taking your tops off on the beach.

The blind-drunk guy didn't like this at all. It's tough to compete for attention with four semi-naked aliens if all you've got is stale alcohol breath. He got up and wobbled to his car. We were still eating, so I only looked at him sideways when he came back. A mistake I am not happy about because I was used to keeping random cats in constant field of vision.

He sat down across from us, smacked a gun down on the table, pointed the business end at us, and looked us in the eye. No wobble this time. We took a look at the gun, another at each other, asked for the check, mounted our bikes, and GTFO. A drunk and a gun are not generally a health-promoting combination.

#*Pé Quente, Cabeça Fria*
Hot feet, cool head – Capoeira expression,
play with a lot of energy but calmly

This sort of random violent threat is obviously possible anywhere in Brazil, or in any country with large wealth inequality. Four months later I visited São Paulo and saw beautiful art galleries, fancy stores, and tons of advertisement for educational opportunities. Every day, I used a local bus terminal the size of a small Northeastern Brazilian village that seemed to have been designed by Oscar Niemeyer's heirs. It was an amazing piece of modern architecture. There are plenty of poor areas in Sao Paulo, but just the money for this one bus terminal could have built a hundred schools and a thousand clinics up north.

For a country that prides itself on being a BRIC member this inequality is damning. But then again, all those nations don't care much about their poor. Maybe it's actually in the BRIC membership booklet:

Article 2: Zero Fucks given about poverty.

Right after Article 1: Follow previous overlords into feudal/capitalist oblivion.

It makes me sad to hear well-off Brazilians complain that the Bolsa Familia child support payment of 90 Realis a month paid to families who keep their children in school instead of forcing them to work is merely a vote getter.

Not just out of a quasi-christian sense of duty, but also because it is practical. Worldwide, the best way to alleviate poverty is to educate women and girls. Bolsa Familia is a small step in the right direction.

Yes, Dilma Rousseff was probably corrupt. But, so is the rest of the gang. When her last presidential opponent, Aécio Neves, was governor of *Minas Gerais* (Rich mining state in Brazil) teachers' salaries in that state became the lowest in Brazil. Lower than Amazonia. In the US this would like be Silicon Valley teachers earning less than their colleagues in Mississippi.

Personally, I'd rather have a corrupt president spending money on the poor than on the rich. The rich don't need any help with that.

And lest you think that we in the West are somehow above banana republic type politics, let us clear up a couple of facts, about the so-called developed West, the United States, for example. Each Congresswo/man spends three million dollars on their election campaign every two years, which means they need to raise 4100 USD per day for two years straight, including on Independence Day and Thanksgiving. The only people who earn this sort of wage in an honest fashion are Wall Street employees and high-end prostitutes servicing Arab Oil Princes.

You figure out what your politicians are selling.

Like Brazilians, US citizens could vote for change, it just never seems to happen. So before anyone complains about small government this or rampant capitalism that, check which part of the US Government apparatus gets the biggest slice of your budget pie. I'll give you a hint: it's not education or healthcare.

If you are then still ok with the way the USA spends her money, as confirmed by your vote, then you are part of the military-industrial complex, also known as the largest, so as not to say fattest, welfare mom in the world. A welfare mom with a billion dollar a week kill-brown people habit, whose offensive budget is the only bill that gets passed in a bipartisan way, every single year.

> *A jángada me leva*
> *Pra outro lugar*
> *Eu não sei onde eu vou*
> *Nas ondas do mar*
>> The raft, it takes me
>> To another place
>> I don't know where
>> On the waves of the sea

It is easy to blame the increase in poverty from the poles to the equator on the heat or the laziness of the locals. But in reality these areas, both north and south of the equator are where millions of enslaved Africans were sent because mines and equatorial cash crops require intense labor. Don't ask me why precious metals seem to congregate at the waist of the earth as it would obviously have been much easier on everyone if there had been a gold rush in Madrid instead of in Guanajuato.

Seville, Lisbon, Amsterdam, Brussels, Paris, and London rest on the shoulders of tens (hundreds?) millions of dead enslaved Africans. Apparently, instead of realizing this awful privilege, some people today are still caught in a kind of Hitlerian Darwinism, thinking that the frigid cold of Europe made white people more evolved than the Africans, and therefor claim some kind of inevitability of evolutionary process and global domination. Are we saying that it took billions of years to evolve humans, yet in the last 5000 years, white people grew bigger frontal cortices? Seems far-fetched.

O chicote me corta
Me faz chorar
Eu não quero mais issó
E vou-la pro mar

> The whip cuts me
> It makes me cry
> I don't want any more of this
> I'll go to the ocean

Today's imploding Middle East is nothing but a modern oil version of the centuries old, Western resource grab. Again, we believe the stories that the justifying castes spin, and think that the heathens with their towels on their heads deserve everything they have coming to them. They are not like you and I, with children and parents, and hopes and dreams. They are not victims; they are perps, terrorists, sub-humans - the lot of them. All 220 million.

Eu vou me embora da terra
Eu vou pro mar
No navio negreiro
Rezo a ienamjáh

> I will leave this earth
> I will go to the sea
> On the slave ship
> Praying to Lemanja

While every trigger-happy conservative in the world tells you that a healthy home is the most important thing for a healthy life they seem to forget to ask one thing: How healthy is it for a child to grow up as a slave, watching her parents being treated like animals, her brother whipped in the Pelourinho, and knowing that her future is to be a breeding mare to the same oppressor who has been brutalizing her family? Can we in good conscience say that hundreds of years of this horror won't leave scars until today? We easily trace other populations' cultural artefacts back to thousands of years. The ten commandments come to mind, which are cemented into most Western folks, whether they are raging christians or atheists, such as myself.

It is in fact surprising that the heirs to these enslaved populations are not completely insane pathological psychopaths. But it is not surprising that we, who are supposed to do unto others as we would have them do unto us, we, who have profited from this insanity for five hundred years, are not willing to spend the same amount of wealth for at least the next five hundred years, to make things right. In my opinion, the catholic church should be first in line to drop her billions of Vatican bank dollars on health insurance and education instead of bible classes in the developing world. Especially, since the current pope is so eager for a changed economic system.

There are still people in Brazil who don't want to give the slave's descendants those 90 Reals a month, giving a kid a tiny chance to help himself out of this misery by learning a little bit of math and writing. There are still people in the USA who refuse to acknowledge the impact this history has had on today's descendants of enslaved Africans. Why do we not see the fairness and wisdom in spending serious time and money on babying the African American population for a few generations with free education, free health care, free daily hugs, and last but never least, free respect. We did the opposite before, so this seems rather logical in order to turn things around.

If one half of you wouldn't call me a lily-livered, bleeding-heart liberal and the other half a condescending, privileged white boy, I'd make my birthday a global Hug-a-POC day.

> *Eu pérdi a raçao*
> *Meu sófrimento*
> *Por que a escravidão*
> *No tem fundamento*
> > I forgot the reason
> > For my suffering
> > Because Slavery
> > Has no basis

If you think that I am being harsh, that this is not your fault, that neither you, nor your family ever profited from this evil, please visit Mel Fisher's museum in Key West, Florida. Why do I send you to a treasure hunter's self-aggrandizing gift to the world?

In 1622, when the Mayflower cats were mistakenly rescued by the real North Americans, a treasure fleet set sail from Cartagena, Colombia to King Philip VI's lair in Seville. The fleet followed a well-established system. Between 1561 and 1748, two fleets per year were stacked to the roof with more money than god and sent on their merry way to the old world. That would be 254 treasure FLEETS, not individual boats.

That year, the most valuable ship was the Antocha. She carried 500 million Dollar and capsized in a hurricane - hook, line, and rich folk on board. You can't actually imagine that much money, considering it was the 16th century. It's like Jeff Bezos took all his 120 Billion, put them on one of his penile spaceships to send to the moon so that the Pope could fight the Pastafarians up there, but unfortunately the thing blew its wad before reaching orbit, in a sort of cosmically fair coitus interruptus.

Since most of these riches financed European religious wars for peasants to die in and palaces for the rich and the church to live in, I'd say Karma, the fickle manwhore, apparently gets it right everyone once in a while.

To say that European societies didn't profit from the accumulation of stolen wealth to be invested in science, healthcare, and education is like saying that I don't profit from buying cheap Nike sneakers produced with child labor in Vietnam.

A maré, a maré, me leva ao céu
A maré, a maré, me leva ao céu
Tide, oh tide, take me to heaven

It's a good thing that I had 3000 miles of riding through sugar plantations ahead of me, giving me ample time to contemplate opportunities to rectify some of the injustices this world has seen in the name of my own ancestors.

The Power of Capoeira
Date: May 27ᵗʰ, 2014
Location: Outside of São Luís, Maranhão

What if Slavery did not exist? No Enslaved Africans in the Americas. No Arabic eunuchs in ancient China. No sex-slaves in today's Asia, Central Europe, or anywhere else. No child slave labor. No slave-like work conditions. No slavery. Period.

A beautiful thought. Someone should write an alternative history novel about it. Since I already talked your ear off how today's Western dominance is due to the milking of slave labor and plunder of foreign lands, I won't, for now.

But what about the "somewhat" less controversial connection of slavery to Capoeira. In this context only one simple, yet powerful, question remains.

Would there be Capoeira?

You may believe that Africans already played Capoeira, or that enslaved Afro-Brazilians fought their oppressors using Capoeira, or that Capoeira developed much later in the harbor towns of Bahia. This complicated history is shrouded in undocumented mysteries. We mostly just don't know. In the end what matters is that Capoeira's seeds came from Mae Afrika and merged with global elements in Brazil.

When you ask a Capoeirista why they dedicate their life to the art they soon mention community and love. They talk about the group that supports them, and the roda. Because of this community forming power and because many Capoeiristas discover new approaches to life through their practice we speak of Capoeira's ability to transform lives.

In Capoeira we travel to other groups' events. We treat each other like family. We don't put our visitors up in hotels. We pick them up from the airport and drive them around, they sleep in our beds, and we cook for them. We also beat the shit out of each other in Capoeira workshops eight hours a day.

Do this for a few years, and suddenly your Capoeira family extends across the continent. Do it for a decade and your Capoeira family extends across the globe.

B2B in particular was blessed. There are no words that can describe the hospitality we received on our journey. "Mi casa es tu casa" simply does not do the constant generosity justice.

Yet, still, the most important transformation that Capoeira affects is not on these personal levels. No, it is that Capoeira transformed a great evil into a great force for love. Capoeira came into existence through slavery, yet today spreads joy, art, and community.

Born out of hatred, forged into love.

Even though Capoeira comes from the dangerous ghettos of Brazil, it arrives in the rest of the world carrying a message of community and love. Maybe the new environments force our Mestres to let the more martial aspects of Capoeira go, still, we can't ignore the communities that these leaders create.

If you dedicate your life to this art you will end up spreading the good word. If you are from Brazil you will pack your bags, move to Russia and bemoan your freezing bones. You will follow your dream to the USA or Asia, and wonder at the distant nature of the people around you.

You will BBQ and make Caipirinhas with your students. You'll help each other move, you will be bride's maids and best men at weddings. You will raise your children together. Every day you will kick each other and feel the power of focused human energy in the roda. Your group will become your tribe.

Capoeira has room for all. There are as many styles of jingas as there are Capoeiristas. Although your Mestre will try his best to teach you his correct version, in the end he'll tell you that your Capoeira is your Capoeira, and that the way you express yourself is your freedom.

It is a simple yet difficult to understand concept. The easiest way would be to watch a Roda and pay attention to the player's intentions. Their personalities emerge. Don't be distracted by the flashy moves and the backflips. For women, the beauty of Capoeira is that excellence is not based on strength or size. Speed, flexibility, and use of space are all important weapons.

Know a person's Capoeira and you will know them. And in that variety we find our own expression, our opportunity to be ourselves in a much too straight-jacketed world.

Whatever your race or your creed, if you entered one roda boa (a good roda) you can't let go. It addresses a basic human need to be part of a kin in a ritualistic and yet realistic manner. Realistic because you will get your ass kicked if you don't take it as real, and ritualistic, well it should be obvious from the content of this book.

Why? That is probably better answered by ancient knowledge, or simply through being human. The good thing is that you do not need to believe to experience. All you need to do is play.

Follow one of the Mestres eking out a living trying to get people in the barren barrios of Houston to sing a song in Portuguese, so that there may grow a small daisy of creativity and love in a concrete ghetto, in a soul-less school of drones, in a world that too easily forgets our tribal roots.

Maybe you trained in one of Mestre Xuxo's five different academias across four different states in Austria. Herr Xuxo drove hundreds of miles every week to teach. Many Austrians still did not appreciate the cultural treasure in their midst, so he moved to China. Maybe you are with Mestre Pelourinho who managed to convince the United States of America Immigration Agency, a notoriously inflexible bunch, to give this amazingly bendy Brasilero a visa that enables him to teach in Tijuana and San Diego on the same day.

Or you are inspired by Contra Mestre Aramé, a stringy beanstalk of a Mexican Capoeirista from Grupo Longe do Mar, and you move to Palestine and teach Capoeira to children, many of whom are battered and abused girls, in refugee camps across the Middle East.

What these Capoeiristas all have in common is an astonishing love for their students. As one they say, "I do this for my students. I love to see them grow, change their perspective, and become Capoeiristas. I don't need money; I don't need fame. What I need is my family. And my freedom."

Born in shackles, forged into freedom.

Capoeira – An Offer You Can't Refuse?
Date: Anytime
Location: Anywhere

> Nem tudo que reluz é ouro
> Nem tudo que balança cai
> Cai cai cai cai
> Capoeira balança mas não cai
> > Not everything that shines is gold
> > Not everything that sways, falls
> > Fall fall fall fall
> > A Capoeirista sways, but doesn't fall

The most important aspect of Capoeira is that it was developed by enslaved Africans in Brazil. This formed Capoeira's central aspect of personal liberty which is in a constant tug of war with the need to teach the responsibility and discipline required of anyone who uses their body as a weapon.

Despite this libertarian bent many Capoeira groups display a definite cultish adoration of their leaders. The Mestres eat first, they shower first, and they sleep in the good beds, sometimes with a couple of capoeira groupies. This kind of respect is usually reserved for wise elders and rock stars, not for back-flipping, face-kicking bros.

How does Capoeira as an expression of anti-authority and of anti-slavery mesh with this?

A true Master of anything will include in their mastery, the skill of humility. They will not expect, nor accept, the ill-fitting trappings of authoritarianism, and oxymoronically only at that point should we be willing to grant them special stature.

I am obviously not making a case for the groupie thing.

There is a tendency to hero worship in Capoeira. We Westerners are so amazed by the sheer force of physical and personal ability, that criticism happens mostly in the form of gossip instead of constructive conversations. When we witness errors, we excuse them as cultural, which certainly is demeaning and racist. As if Brazilians, martial artists, or men in general are incapable of controlling their urges.

Do we not want to admit that, because Capoeira is a human activity, it comes with all that our species has to offer, the good as well as the bad? Instead of attempting this deeper evaluation, only an inadequate examination of our voluntarily accepted leaders remains.

Is it because they can easily beat our ass anytime they want? Kind of a return to more basic animal kingdom behavior patterns. Or do we, in reality, happily soak in this inexpensive letting go of control?

We live in a world in which we are supposed to be individually responsible for everything: ourselves, our family, our career, our emotions, even for our country. In such a world, it may just be plain easier to give in to the comfort of not being accountable, if it is in a context that does not threaten our overall status. More positively, and maybe realistically, put: we like being part of something larger than ourselves, with someone around who tells us what to do.

But if it's so easy to adopt authoritarian behavior patterns, we need to acknowledge and examine the fact that those have mostly disappeared from the western world, at least outside of the dictatorship we call work. I ask if following leaders in a religion, politics, or a martial art is therefore an expression of needing a place in a pecking order? Are we all just pretend-free?

I have no answer to these questions because I have not spent enough time in the roda, neither the one of Capoeira, nor the roda of life.

Yet, it is fascinating for me to watch Capoeira Mestres exert influence over a group of people who don't usually follow anyone's orders unless it is within said context of work.

Mestres inhabit a unique space in our world. They are the living embodiment of an art form rooted in some mystery. An art that defies classification, constantly evolves, and bears little to no organization. Mestres carry responsibility for Capoeira's practice and development. They must ensure that Capoeira's inherent freedom does not lead to a dilution of the art, and vice versa, that a necessary conservation of traditions does not result in a curtailing of that central basic idea of individual expression and liberty.

This is not an easy edge to balance. On the journey of Capoeira, the opportunities to fail by far outnumber all those perfect, white grains of sand on Copacabana Beach.

That Japanese Shit
Date: May 28ᵗʰ,2014
Location: São Luís, Maranhão

I was sitting in our room cutting up veggies. If you think that I talk too much about cooking veggies, remember that the daily tasks of bike-touring are fairly monotonous. You ride, you eat, you sleep - rinse, repeat. If you are picky you'll do laundry every day.

No matter if you are a pasta, rice, or lentil aficionado, a good selection of spices is essential for any long-term expedition. Italian herbs for salads and stews. Cumin is great for meats and fish, helps disinfecting it, too. Use turmeric to help with infections. Curry – yum. Put chili no everything. Except when you are having an intense religious communion with Lord Montezuma. In that case, I suggest white rice, black tea, and bananas. Otherwise, that shit will burn twice as much.

The B2B kings of food were Diego and Balão. When they BBQ'd at Villa Mariposa in Costa Rica or grilled an entire Amazonas fish in Tapatinga there was a samba party in our mouths. I am eagerly awaiting their *B2B* cook book - *Please your inner foodie with a camping stove and a spork.*

Between their cooking and the always present delicious street food you could nearly call B2B a culinary expedition and make that famous reservation-free travel foodie on TV jealous. Tacos, Tlayudas, Pupusas, and Arepas are all tasty, but it becomes vitamin deficient not to eat any greens for a year. Hence, you read a lot about cooking veggies, because, screw you, I spent a lot of time cooking veggies.

Suddenly Cam yelled, "That Japanese shit tho," he was examining a multitude of slowly popping, yellowish pustules on his feet.

"Yummie, meu brother. Thanks for sharing," I said.

I know, it's gross. But don't never worry your little head over it. We had been sharing rooms for months, we knew everything, and some things we didn't want to know, about each other. Someone was always snoring, playing berimbau or pandero, typing emails, editing photos or videos, chatting, playing capoeira, cooking, sewing, playing flute or didgeridoo, or having a hissy-fit. Like Trotsky said, "You may not be interested in war, but war is certainly interested in you."

The upside is that these days I am able to sleep through anything. Though, I am kinda lonely, when I don't have five hairy dudes climbing all over each other in a ten by ten room while I am trying to get the latest social media thing out.

"Yooooh, That Japanese shit tho!"

I checked Cam's feet from across the room. It didn't at all look like the hundreds of infected mosquito bites all over Tora's body that Cam was referring to. Tora and I were probably the two juiciest targets for the *Mosquites*, as he called them. He dealt with them using his snake poison kit, a set of plastic syringes designed to suck out the venom by creating a vacuum. Made Tora look like Tom and Jerry with some kind of cartoon disease.

I developed a mantra to deal with my apparent attractiveness to the female bloodsuckers of the world. Both strategies are equally nuts to most people. My mantra, should you be silly enough to want to try it, was based on Muad'dib's litany against fear.

I don't itch
I don't even see the mosquito
It is too small for me to mind
It is too small to bother me
I don't even feel it
I will let the itch pass through me
As if it never existed

Crazy right? But if I made it through the first minutes it seemed to work.

Cam's malaise was something else, though, probably related to going swimming in the Amazon with open wounds. I needed to break it to him gently.

I said, "No bro, it's not that Japanese Shit."

"What's it then?"

"It's actually, and I am sorry to tell you this… Walla-foot!"

"Na su cullo Pirata!" (Stick it where the sun don't shine. I hear this a lot.)

"Hey man, you need to go to a pharmacy. Look how swollen your foot is. You need antibiotics."

Cam started laughing.

I asked, "What?"

"Na, it's just the way you say antibiotics bro. AaanteeBeeahtika!"

"Whatever Walla-foot."

"It's not a tuuumor."

Right then Tartaruga came into the room, lifted up his right arm, pointed at his armpit and said in his droll, high-pitched voice, "What THEEE fuuuck?!?!"

Cam and I saw the juicy pustule growing under Tartarugas arm and grinned at each other.

I said, "Oh shit!"

And together we yelled, "It's WALLA-PIT!"

"What the fuck is Walla-pit," asked Tartaruga desperately.

"That Japanese Shit!"

Most importantly, when speaking to the world of you - never speak too seriously.

Red Lantern
Date: May 31ˢᵗ, 2014
Location: Capoeira Group Laborarte, São Luís

This is another one of those moments when a writer asks how much of the truth is required.

Ten months into the journey, B2B truly was a well-oiled machine. We made it past the Colombian gangsters, the Amazonian alligators, and even survived each other. Everybody knew their responsibilities, and those without, knew theirs too. Here in São Luís the fantastic Laborarte Capoeira Angola group put us up in a pretty good sized room. Good sized, if you don't arrive with ten bicycles and forty panniers.

But no matter how professional we were at filming interviews and Capoeira, no matter how good or bad we were at figuring out dangerous cities, one embarrassing problem followed us around like a trail of brown, nasty sludge. Sludge that you just can't shake.

It took until São Luís before Tora found a solution. I am just glad that it was Tora, because it's way too easy to mistake correlation between my quasi German heritage and that stoic people's strange bend towards scatology with actual causation. You all would very quickly call me a *Schluchtenscheisser* (happily untranslatable. I mean it is, but I won't) in addition to Poocasso. One Scheiss-Nickname per epic journey with Mestre Acordeon, is enough, thank you very much.

What is instead important was the trail of love that B2B left behind - and that other trail. You laugh, but go on a long distance ride and you will see how much you eat. We stuffed at least four thousand calories into our bellies every day. And what goes in must apparently come out. Now, imagine ten such food fiends riding through E. coli infected parts unknown. Yeah. That's what happened.

It all began at Contramestre Chin's house in Santa Barbara. Though we tried our very bestest to be good guests, cleaning up after ourselves, volunteering to help out, do dishes (Mestre), sweep the floor and throw out the garbage (Mestra) there was one thing that we could not control: the brown sludge trail. In the interest of your mental hygiene I will cut the long-waiting-lines-in-front-of-the-shitter story short and just tell you that it started with Tora and ended with a rotor rooter.

There are no rotor rooters anywhere south of the border. You are supposed to toss your toilet paper in a trash bin because the pipes there can only take so much, well, shit. They don't even have toilet seats. After a day of riding, it was always a race to sit first because you knew if you were sixth to shit you'd be stuck with this shit: figuring out how to unclog a toilet without a plunger.

And you absolutely had to, because you knew somebody was in line behind you. Obviously, the toilet always clogged on you in the middle of the night, in a room full of sleeping beasts who will throw things at you if you wake them up with your improvisational attempts at fuckery, I mean, plumbery.

In Central America B2B considered buying a plunger. I suggested that if you clog you carry, until someone else proves worthy to take up the scepter of dubious honor. Kind of like the Red Lantern in the Tour de France, except that one shows that you are last, not that you are full of shit. But since Diego already carried a toilet brush, to clean his bicycle bottles[22] with, we thought a plunger would have gone a little far. Wouldn't want people to think that we are a bunch of Germans joyriding through Brazil. Especially not after that 1:7 in the World Cup. Oh, Snap!

So here I offer this wee bit of life changing advice to you who is planning your epic bicycle adventure to hopefully everywhere.

1. Cut off the bottom of a plastic two-liter water bottle. Size matters.
2. Carefully insert now open bottom of bottle in toilet.
3. Commence vigorous plungery.
4. I suggest you keep the cap on the bottle while using.

Thus, in São Luís the legend grew. And it shall not cause me any wonderment that it started there. Amidst that Japanese Shit, Walla-Foot, and impromptu plumbery it was a legend full of mirth. A legend of the common man. The one who likes booze and women in the dark backroom of a Guatemalan house of pleasure.

Here Brazil finally took shape with violent, sultry power, and a cunning, yet laughing embrace. We watched our backs when we went out, played slow but sneaky jogos, and ate Mama Rita's night-time street BBQ. We met the wiliest old mandingero, Mestre Patinho, who told drunken stories from the olden days. Tora gave Mestre a conniption playing in the welcoming roda in short-short, skin-tight bike shorts

Mestre got red in the face and gulped a quiet, "PORRA!"

And such are our impressions of this tranquil, yet overdriven country, that's been lurking on the horizons of our Capoeira minds. The one we forget when we think only of marvelous Rio, Pélé, and Carnaval.

In São Luís we saw the past meet the future and we heard drums in the dark distance. Their beat swirled around me like the dress of the Tambourine de Creole dancer. Here I found weeping buildings, precariously leaning against each other. Their pretty paint, like makeup after a good night on the town, draining down tired cheeks. The decay and faded classical colors reminded me of that ancient thing that Kampot's abandoned French robber baron villas in Cambodia have.

> Maranhão Maranhão ô ô
> que saudades do meu Maranhão ô ô
> Maranhão Maranhão oh, oh
> How I miss my Maranhão oh, oh

Old town São Luís continues its colorful, chaotic cadence. She stays dirty, and lively. But leave the center behind, take one of the narrow, cobblestoned streets past patient concrete, down towards the river, and turn right. And there, just on the other side of the white bridge next to the sea, there on the horizon you can find that curse: Glitzy, though glassy, eyes stretching to the sky like greedy children of doom. There strives the quest of the formerly ruled to imitate that which is so unworthy of the best of compliments. There the beaches are white and people bleach their hair. Even on their arms and legs.

---

[22] Also a futile battle. Better to use liter bottles.

So instead, follow me through these tired streets. Come along into those ancient churches, still offering some of the best acoustics in the world. You may find yourself skipping along to drumming emerging from a dark doorway. But only if you take your time and some lazy days. Amongst the museums and the tacky stores, close by the guaranas and the central market, there, you will find the syncopated melodies of a flute and a didge, and a floating drum, or three, of tradition, filling you with sound. An alley of love straight to your heart.

Back in Nicaragua, in the cathedral of Leon, Mariano had dared me to play my flute in the middle of the church. And so I did, because Pirata is always down for a truth or dare. Before, I had often laid the sun to rest in the Pacific or played for kids on central plazas, but never in a church. The amplified sound of my soft Thai bamboo flute inside the church seemed to float into some kind of spiritual realm. I was hooked. There was also that lady shedding a tear. From then on I searched out the best church acoustics in each town that we passed.

So walk with me along late afternoon, sun-warmed alleys as the notes float on my breath and suspend the very time between here and there. Let go of yourself, of this time. Human magic lives in those wet, old walls. In the shadows out back we find our rhythm in communion with our song. In a small dilapidated church of sound, a sound so full, as to fill your soul.

Forró
Date: July 20th, 2014
Location: Fortaleza

Sorry, no, this chapter is not about gyrating madly on the beach with pretty girls in thongs (either you or them). And the traditional dance of Forró, is much less naughty anyway. By the time B2B arrived in Fortaleza, Forró's home, we had been riding into the wind for four weeks. How much wind? Well, just north of

Fortaleza is some of the world's best Kitesurfing. You could say by the time we arrived in its home, we were a little too winded for Forró.

Just outside of Fortaleza I had my first collision of the journey. It was a motorcycle – the most dangerous of traffic participants. One had already taken out Indi in Colombia. I was making a left to get to a beach with Mariano. I saw a motorcycle turn left behind me as well and so I walked my bike between my legs across the street in front of it, looking to my right for oncoming traffic. Suddenly, I heard the motorcycle gun its engine. Whipping my head around I saw him come right at me. The rider was looking back over his shoulder instead of to his front at me.

I have no idea how, but I did a *Queixada* (sideways scissor kick) over my handle bar, tossed my bike squarely at the motorcycle accelerating at me and jumped back. The motorcycle's front punched into my back wheel close to the saddle, and fell over with the rider on top.

He would have hit my left leg straight on. Mariano called it amazing, though this miraculous escape was just instinct taking over. Ask my parents someday about the flip I executed over my handlebar when I was ten years old. Like an Olympic gymnast, or rather a circus clown, conveniently parking my bike's front wheel between the slats of the bench that I had just run into, while ending up seated on the other end of the same bench.

After the motorcyclist and I checked ourselves for injuries I helped him pick up his heavy Enduro and sent him on his way. Mestre came back to help fix my bike. We did not speak, but I knew we were thinking the same thing.

On top of my bike I had been in complete control of my environment, except for falling over all the time, of course. But ten months into the trip exhaustion had caught up with me. We tried to bend my wheel somewhat straight but in the end I just disengaged my back breaks so that the wheel could egg along freely.

We entered Fortaleza and were met by Mestre Ratto and his group. He put all of B2B up in his two room apartment two blocks from the beach and went and stayed somewhere else. The things people did for Mestre Acordeon and B2B were astonishing. While I often expressed my thanks, one can never really compensate for the constant mana falling from the sky other than paying it forward.

When B2B was over, and I traveled around Brazil to train with as many Mestres as I could, I ran into Mestre Ratto at CM Pingo's Aruandé event in Brasilia. If you are a Capoeirista, you know that I was lucky to have him monitor my games at Mestre Kall's roda by Braslia's TV Tower.

On the first night in Fortaleza, Mestre Acordeon, held a meeting.

He said, "From now, I want us all to ride together. We are close to our goal and we must focus. There will be a lot of Capoeira and dangerous areas. We need to represent and be safe. Everybody should stay within eyesight from now on."

We would have to ride at speeds we were not comfortable with. No longer, could Mariano and I wait for two hours in the morning and then catch up.

Mestre continued, "You know I don't like smoking or too much partying. But I never forbade it. To me every person is free to do what they want. But now I am asking you to stop. In Brazil these things are different. Here drugs of any kind are associated with gangs and extreme violence. People don't make a distinction between pot and harder drugs."

Since banging on a hotel door in El Salvador late one night I had calmed my piratical ways down a lot, so this was not a problem for me. I kind of liked the idea of getting additional focus.

Mariano shook Mestre's hand and said, "Ok Mestre, I can't speak for all of us, but I promise I will do what you ask."

A little theatrical, but in an adorable way Mariano is prone to these grand gestures. It was understood that we would all follow Mestre's order. After the meeting the extended Brotherhood went to the beach and had one last communal joint and a good bonding session.

On the day we left Fortaleza, Mariano's dad joined to ride with us for three weeks. Bebum and I rode with Mariano to the airport and picked up old man Wechsler. He had silver hair, laconic eyes, and huge calves. That apple sticks close to those trunks. We used to joke that if we ran out of food all of B2B could live of Mariano's calves for at least a week. Also, you ladies should count yourself lucky that Mariano inherited the calves and not those piercing blue eyes.

One week later, we met a middle-aged and rather attractive wannabe hippie lady. She told Mariano about an Ayahuasca Ceremony in the hippie enclave of *Canoa Quebrado* (Broken Canoe) two days south of us. Mariano and I had planned to expand our minds (thanks for that line, POTUS) with the psychedelic vine from the Amazon from the beginning, and he seemed interested in going to Canoa. I was not a fan of the idea because Mestre told us to stick together and to stop getting high.

Two days later, I rode past the turnoff to Canoa with the Wallatowas and Bebum. When we caught up with Mestre we saw that Mariano, his dad, Banano, and Juanjo weren't there. They had taken a left towards Lucy in the Sky with Diamonds land. We continued south with Mestre. A day later, Mariano shot me a message on Whatsapp.

"Yo, Pirata, why aren't you here?"

"What do you mean?"

"I left you a cairn at the exit to Canoa."

"Oh, I didn't see it, but I wouldn't have gone anyway mate."

"Well the ceremony is on bro, you should come back."

"Na man, I don't want to leave Mestre. I know you are with your dad, do your thing," I wasn't happy that he bailed like that, but in a way I understood because of his dad's visit.

What really blew my stack was that Bebum and Cam decided to return the eighty kilometers to Canoa Quebrado. Though all of us were mad at people bailing just after the meeting in in Fortaleza, we now entered the most tranquil time in Brazil. Mestre seemed to adjust his persona depending on how many cats he needed to herd. Now, with only eight remaining, he reverted to the Grampa Santa Claus we remembered from Baja California.

In Central America, when we were twelve he was a Lieutenant, concerned for your life and kind of a badass that will fight for you. Since Fortaleza, he had been a slightly harsh, if fair Army Capitan. When Team Ayahuasca returned to the B2B fold in Natal, he became a motherfucking General who aimed to tear you a new one every chance he got. I completely understood.

This only got worse when the guys decided to bail again to a Jazz Festival right after Natal, where we stayed with Mestre Indio. We passed João Pessoa without them, and started turning south towards Recife. The dry brush land of the northeast had been replaced with oceans of sugar cane and field workers in hazmat suits.

A couple of weeks later, we were on our way into Recife on an early morning ride. Bebum had caught up from the festival with Juanjo by catching a ride on a truck. Cam and Banano had gotten a ride all the way to Mestre Mago's academia. Only Mariano and his dad were man enough to ride.

The situations was strained. But before Mestre laid down the general law, Bebum and I had to have it out. It had been brewing for some time. At least in me.

That morning we rode 40 miles in a two-hour mad dash (how do Mestres do it?) towards Recife. We stopped on the outskirts to rest and eat. When we were nearly done Bebum left. While he was gone Mestre saddled up. Mestre doesn't do such a thing without purpose. Bebum, it seems, had made one too many wrong decisions.

It was my turn to make a decision. Ride with Mestre or wait for Bebum. I did not know where Mestre Mago's academia was located, because I knew I was going to ride into town in a pack and so I had not bothered looking at a map. I left Bebum's bike behind and took off with the rest. Apparently, I had reached my limit as well. I am not proud of this moment at all. No excuses.

Bebum let me know about it as soon as he caught up with a bunch of alibi bananas[23] that he had bought for the crew.

"Fuck you Pirata, why didn't you wait for me? I would never leave your bike like that."

"Bro, I am tired of having to deal with your bad decision making."

We were standing on the side of the freeway with Diego, Tuchegas, and Balão and yelled at each other at the top of our lungs.

"What the fuck do you mean?"

"Think. You keep disappearing, you never communicate, Mestre just asked us a month ago to stick together, and you bounce for half of that time to go to festivals and shit."

"So what's it got to do with today?"

"Once again you made the wrong call and left when you shouldn't have."

"And you just leave my bike."

Of course I felt shitty about that's, so I yelled, "Fuck you man. I don't know where the school is. This traffic is nuts. Mestre asked us to stick together. I am sticking together."

Recife was nuts to ride bicycle into from the north. We were on a freeway with pot holes the size of beetles, the Volkswagen kind, and traffic out of your mother's perfect third world nightmare.

"We could just ride into the center of town, like we always do, and find these guys. You know we always catch up."

"No bro, I am done with this shit."

Then we had to start riding again. We rode for ten minutes and it helped us to quiet down some.

Bebum came riding up to me, "OK, honey, let's not do this passive aggressive shit, what's really going on. Why did you leave me behind?"

"Bro, your sarcasm is not gonna do shit. I am pissed, you think your tone is gonna make me any happier?"

While we both swerved all over a freeway populated with most of Ayrton Senna's nephews, to avoid the water filled potholes, I swallowed my pride and said, "Bro, I am sorry about that. That was shitty of me."

"Ok, so what's happening?"

"Remember how I sent you a bunch of money to Guadalajara to help you stay there and fix your knee? I even asked everyone on B2B to donate for your ass. You never said a word of thanks. That's one thing."

---

[23] You buy Alibi bananas for five cents for everyone every once in a while because you don't have any money to buy your own food for months.

It seemed like I was getting through to him a little bit, just when he hit a foot-deep pothole hiding under a puddle.

"And then when you left us again in Leon, in Nica. When Mariano and I tried to talk you out of leaving because you were getting disengaged from the project too much, remember what you said there?"

"No."

"You said that I don't need to worry about you, because people just like to give you shit all the time. That really hurt. That was sort of it for me. I often thought about sending you money for bus tickets to catch up after that, but I never did. I was over helping you."

"Shit bro, I am an asshole."

"Yeah, you are. But I am too."

We stopped and hugged. Nothing like a good yelling match between bros to clear the air. Unfortunately, at the time he didn't learn anything other than doing a better job of saying thank you for getting free shit.

Bebum practices a sort of drunken, falling down pay-it-forward philosophy that is difficult to maintain in a world in which not everyone does the same. I don't know how well it would work anyway, if nobody has shit, whose shit will everyone share? However, my old leftie soul is still intensely attracted to this more Sacred Economy that Bebum is trying to build and while I am writing this book I am certainly relying on the kindness of my friends when I come back to the developed world for a few months out of each year.

An hour later, we arrived at Mestre Mago's Centro de Capoeira São Salomão close to the Universidade Federal de Pernambuco (Federal University of Pernambuco). Even with the stale taste in my mouth from fighting with Bebum and riding without Mariano I had a huge grin on my face.

Mestre Mago had been with us for a month in California. We all remembered the sad day when we left our other brothers and sisters in San Diego. I told Mestre Mago that arriving at his Academia was, "Our first homecoming".

It was an amazing feeling. In my mind Salvador was next.

Still, there was a lot of conflict between the B2B members and when all the mind expanded fools showed up, it seemed like the B2B brotherhood was finally coming apart at the seams.

It was Mestre's 71ˢ birthday during the week of our stay. Can you believe it? This crazy, old man actually rode all the way to Brazil. I got him a cake. After he forced me to have a piece with him, I bounced out of there again to stay at my Couchsurfing hosts pad to which I had been escaping. Mestre was in a black mood most of the time now. I knew it wasn't directed at me, but it's too powerful to ignore even then.

Mestra's influence was immensely important then. You could always rely on her telling it straight to you, whether you deserved a hug or a kick in the pants. Which is why the following was so surprising.

One typically tropical and mosquito rich Pernambuco night, after another Capoeira Regional class with Mestre Mago, I sat with her on the front porch of the guesthouse amongst the chirping cicadas and muffled university street noise from beyond the compound wall, and asked her the question that B2B gets asked the most, "How has this trip changed you, Mestra?"

She thought and said, "I don't know Pirata."

You always had to force Mestres Acordeon and Suelly to speak about themselves and their own experiences, a most welcome difference to most of the rest of the world. So I tried again, "Now that we made it all the way to Recife and we are nearly at our goal, how do you feel?"

"I am really amazed to see how strong Mestre is. I was so worried about him trying to do this insane journey, but he showed over and over again that he is much stronger than I ever imagined."

I said, "Mestra, seeing his straight back leading in the distance always kept me going. But what about you?"

Mestra said, "You know Pirata, I am by nature a timid person. I get nervous and scared easily. I am a worrier."

Here it is appropriate to insert that on hearing her words my jaw fairly rested on the floor of Mestre Mago's fine front porch. This is Mestra Suelly, first female Capoeira Master in North America, takes on anyone in the Roda, rides her bike across two continents. She had even overcome her fear of downhill rides and enjoyed flying.

And despite that she is not much taller than four feet (sorry Mestra, you *are* short) she usually comes out on top. She is an example of how women can excel in a martial art through agility, spatial understanding, and speed, while remaining graceful in a feminine expression of power. Did I mention she is in her late 50s? She had climbed every mountain and ridden through every nasty situation that I had been in, and now she told me that she was scared.

It made no sense.

Mestra Suelly continued, "I don't know if I will worry less about things in the future, but on this trip I definitely learned that I don't need to worry about Mestre, and that I was able to do this thing, too."

After we spoke, I walked back through the quiet University that was run-down in that sweaty equatorial way. It's a lot harder to maintain a building when it's 100% humidity and 95 degrees all the time. If you stood still for too long, things would probably start growing up around your feet.

I was thinking about Mestra, realizing again how complex we all are, how much is hidden in all of us. What she told me made sense after all. I had seen her trying to hide in many rodas, sort of fading into the background, so that Mestre would not call on her to say a few words in front of a crowd. He usually did, and she'd come digging out behind a chair, a potted plant, or around thirty formados. Even after thirty years, the two haven't stopped trying to improve each other and their craft. What a great relationship.

I had also seen her worry for her husband, yelling after Mestre at the top of her lung "Mestreeeee be careful," as he executed (this word suggests somewhat too much control) another hair-raising maneuver in Central American city traffic to find a Pousada (guesthouse) that eventually seemed to have been located in the other direction after all.

Of course he wouldn't listen and she'd stand up in her saddle to race after him and scream, "Biiiraaaaaa!"

While it was often amusing to the rest of us to watch our Mestres interact in their familiar way we also appreciated how difficult it must be for them to separate these roles. You could always tell by the way they addressed each other, "Baby" for informal sweetness, "Mestre" for Capoeira and authority situations, "Bira" for cold fear or hot fire.

A few days later we left Recife. The end of B2B was near. Following the Linea Verde (Green Line, name of gorgeously picturesque coastal road) for the last few 600 miles to Salvador seemed like an easy proposition. But Mestre also planned to get there in eighteen days and shoot a bunch of material with the newly arrived Instrutora Ursa from Projéto Kirimuré. Ursa had been with Projéto Kirumuré her entire childhood, and she was going to ride with us for the last month of the journey.

I asked him, "Mestre, I know you want to get this over with, but how can we ride 1000km and shoot a bunch of conversations in eighteen days?"

"Hmmm"

"Plus Ursa hasn't ridden bike in her life, let alone all those kilometers. She is really gonna hurt."

"Hmmm"

He was set on maintaining that schedule, probably in order to avoid any more shenanigans.

Neither Ursa nor Amber, who had also joined us to ride bicycle for the last leg to Salvador would have an easy time. The physical part wasn't going to be the only challenge for the two. Ursa was struggling with her role at Kirimuré and Amber had finally rid herself of the truck, the last physical link to her past with her fiancé. Like the rest of us, she owned what she carried. On a bicycle you can't carry little treasures and mandalas to keep you safe from the demons of your night. Your world becomes as small and as real as it gets. Peninha, as her Capoeira name suggests the littlest amongst us, was about to take a giant last step to becoming whole again. Whole and new.

A Beautiful Lie
Date: August, 28ᵗʰ, 2014
Location: Recife

Nobody likes a liar. If you go on a dating web site you won't find anyone saying, "I love lying, and I want to be with a person like me." Yet, it would be difficult to find someone who has never lied. We all do it. Small lies, big lies, white lies, oil company reports on Climate Change. There are painful truths, and truths that will set you free. Sometimes, we want to be lied to and often the biggest lies are the easiest to believe.

For a writer, the truth is like a weightless yoke around our necks. It only becomes Plutonium heavy when we mince our words. Nobody wastes their time reading lies. Nobody, that is, who doesn't want to be lied to.

Or course, there may be plenty of those. The internet has democratized lying just like everything else it touches. Now, it isn't just the province of various power structures to spread a thick layer of bullshit over every surface of our pristine planet. Everybody can get in on the shit shoveling.

But a reader knows Solzhenitsyn spoke from his heart in *Gulag Archipelago*, and that makes you turn the page, that makes you trust him. Paolo Coelho… not so much.

A writer may want to bend your mind to his idea. But the truth can not be bent.

What follows is the story of a beautiful lie. And although we continued south along a gorgeous coast filled with gorgeous people, this one is not entirely pretty.

It goes something like this:

Many, many years ago in a land far, far away there lived a King of Gold. 't was a promised land, of riches untold, where mysteries unfold…

yaddayaddayadda, bullshitbullshit, and so on and so forth.

Like in most tall tales there are swashbuckling pirates, unimaginable wealth, and gorgeous mermaids. Golden cities grow out of mud and ancient forests give way to sugar factories. In this tale the sexiest yet saddest dance is not an oxymoron. In this tale, like in so many, wealth is filthy and poverty wears many faces.

Yet, the only thing more difficult to understand than Brazil's inequality is her ambiguity. Let me state it as explicitly as I can. I have been learning Portuguese for a few years, and *agreement* is not a word in Brazilian Portuguese. Unless people bitch about corrupt politicians and FIFA. In fact, the corruption and inefficiency plaguing Brazil may nest in the nooks and crannies of her ambiguity.

But linguistic escapism is only the tip of the cultural iceberg. Personal communication is not direct either. In order to understand a social interaction one must read between the lines. Even gringos from North America, who are a fairly polite bunch, are not as subtle as Brazilians. It's sort of incongruous, because on her beaches the asses are always so in your face, that you think all of Brazil must be fairly direct and to the point. Finally, I get why I didn't understand my Brazilian boss until he smacked me in the head (figuratively, you can't smack people at Microsoft).

Forget Germans or Austrians, we are club wielding barbarians in a room full of porcelain compared to these communication tap dancers, who, without wanting to belabor the truthiness point, always leave room to negotiate. When it comes to comparing interpersonal styles I am your Conan, I know it's not really a challenge to imagine, and Brazilians are goo-covered ballerinas, slippery from a mud wrestling match.

A year ago I thought this flexibility of spirit was a Capoeira, rather than a Brazilian thing, but now that I've spent some time in Brazil it seems that it may be the other way around. This could explain why Capoeira, with its constant evasive maneuvers and hidden *malandrage* (sneakiness), an essentially ambiguous way of life, did not come to be in other slave economies.

I have learned a small thing or two about this indirectness – mostly by sticking my foot right into my own mouth – yet, like I told Mestre in Nicaragua, I am not sure I want to retain these lessons. After my cyclo-centric journey, I already have to deal with my newfound, quasi conservative regard for churches and small towns. Not being disturbingly direct might actually kill me.

It seems that this ambiguity, the same way a certain basic stoicism is good for Asia, works great for Brazilians. But there is one problem – on a clock there are no lines to read between. No ambiguity there. And interesting side-effect of this is to see these most impatient of people constantly make each other wait, because everyone is always late.

Not only are they mostly late, and always ready to party, but these inheritors of a rich and dark history are gorgeous. Both men and women. Chiseled chins, ripped abdominals, bountiful boobs and *bundas* (butts), green eyes in dark faces overcoming their recessive obligations. You could not possibly design a sexier human by today's standard than you often see dancing the night away in a samba de rua (street samba).

Warren Beatty's line as *Bullworth*, a suddenly honest politician, about wanting "to deconstruct racial boundaries" not only is a great strategy against racism, but also for creating beauty. Lest you want to book your ticket to Brazil like Mike right away, you should know that we also saw some real ugly motherfuckers.

It took me four months to understand that all that perfect, somewhat light-colored straight hair is ironed and bleached, and that the roundest asses are the result of blood, sweat, and tears in the gym or on the plastic surgeon's gurney. Though I was aware that Brazil is the global epicenter of plastic surgery, it is nevertheless jarring to see it so on display. This naked desperation of people trying to white-y-fy their skin, their hair, their bodies, even themselves, disturbs me. Stockholm Syndrome apparently works on a societal level. In Mexico everyone still crosses themselves in front of churches, trying to get into the white man's heaven. And in Brazil they cut themselves up, because what, waiting for heaven to finally be white takes too long?

The saddest thing about this adulteration of a perfect, racially deconstructed body is that it is not necessary. The beauty image in Central and Latin America has always been centered around a big bunda, which is entirely more friendly to the natural tendencies of the female body. Women in the south have it easy compared to the USA. You got some natural chunk in your trunk? Perfect. And if you want to work out and make it a little firmer it is fine that the first thing that goes are the fat pockets in your upper body. Dudes are looking at your ass anyway. Compare that to the West: Everybody wants to be skinny and have a little perky behind, but once they have trained and starved themselves to the appropriate proportions they have to get a boob job in order to fulfill a completely ludicrous top-heavy beauty image. To round out this human insanity let's not forget that in Asia it is all about the double eyelid and butt enhancement operations.

That even in Brazil people succumb to the lust for image via the plastic surgeon's scalpel, just goes to show that no matter where you live you will always be manipulated into buying things that you don't have and probably don't need.

But even after finding out that the beauty is skin-deep while the inequality reaches to the bone, the death knell to my infatuation with Brazil only came when I learned that most lyrics of Samba, symbol extraordinaire for Brazilian laize-faire sexiness, are completely triste. Are in fact so sad, that you would cry your eyes out were you not so busy trying to control the tent in your pants.

I kid though, I still love you Brazil. My love is tough, what can I say.

Is the fakeness a result of the ambiguity, or is it the other way around? Is it just another nook and cranny to be filled with seeming perfection or is it an expression of a deep level of sadness at how much better life could be? What happens when you marry someone with blond, straight hair and a big bunda, and your kids have flat butts and afros?

When I was at CM Pingo's event in Brasilia, I stayed with my Capoeira friend in one of the newer satellite neighborhoods at the edge of town. Since Brasilia has the highest income per person in all of Latin America, I stupidly assumed that newer and rich means cleaner and gleaming.

I was wrong. We navigated black hole type potholes, horrifyingly ugly streets, and household trash stacked sky high. We sat for hours in traffic trying to get to the center of town and I wondered what the hell people had been talking about, calling this city gorgeous. It looked just like the dirt poor joints that I rode through on my bicycle up north.

When I finally visited the center of Brasilia, quod erat demonstrandum, the center of Brazilian power, it hit me. The retro-chic, airplane shaped Niemeyer-designed streets and buildings, the cool sixties style, the effective shape and efficient planning of open spaces were Gataca and the Jetsons made real. It was gorgeous. And it was a lie.

A beautiful lie.

Like sexy yet sad samba, like the straight blond hair, like the perfect asses. Walk to the back of the shiny government buildings and you see trash floating in the alleys. Drive through the poor neighborhoods on the other side of the lake and see the millions who came to build this town. See the dull eyes of the north and northeast, resigned to a life of serfdom and cachaça.

Suddenly, the constant party that is part and parcel of Brazil seems so necessary, so beautiful, and yet so tragic. And everyone knows it.

Here, in the one city that is the least, yet at the same time, the most Brazilian, I finally understood why Brazilians are so angry at their inability to affect change in their nominal democracy. I resolved to stop asking them to be more patient with their country. They know it's bullshit. They live a beautiful lie. And who would want to exchange that for an ugly truth?

Bebum bebums it one more Time
Date: September 06th, 2014
Location: Maceió

To say that Maceió in the state of Sergipe is dangerous is somewhat of an understatement. Google the city and the auto populator offers "Maceió *Brazil Violence*" as the first option. Go ahead, hit search. At the time of writing the top result from Pravda[24] was "*The Most Violent City in the World.*" Not that Pravda has gotten any more reliable since it's not run by the KGB any longer, right? Wait, it still is.

Crack cocaine fuels this violent epidemic that is so in contrast with Sergipe's gorgeous emerald, tropical setting. Picturesque bays, islands, and inlets dot the coast. Quaint little palm tree hamlets abound.

B2B didn't care. We hustled through Maceió as if the devil herself, probably using Lance Armstrong's doping regime, was on our heels. We, as they say, got the fuck outa Dodge.

The group spread out to film during the quiet early hours of the day. We needed to shoot but we also needed to ride hard. Mestres, Diego, Tuchegas, Juanjo, Balão and I rode together, but once we were nearly out of town I volunteered to wait for the rest along the ocean road. While I waited, Tora suddenly showed up, head held high, beatific expression on his face in his I-am-obviously-harmless-please-don't-bother-me mode. I rode with him a little to make sure he got out of town alive.

After we caught up with the Mestre gang, I waited with Juanjo, using the time to try to figure out what to do about his tire problems. They were bald as an eagle and he had run out of tubes. Just that morning I watched him embed a screw in his front wheel. No fun to fix a screw sized hole in a tube if you know you don't have backups and you have different sized wheels than all your boys. Once the Walatowas caught up, Juanjo, Cam, Gavião and I kept on riding. I knew Mariano was with whoever was left.

As we made our way out of town, Juanjo caught another flat. We spotted a Borracharia (no, it's not a Mexican place to get drunk. In Brazil it's a tire place) and stopped to have his tubes fixed industrially. Bebum, Banano, and Mariano passed us on their way to catch up with Mestre. We waived them through.

The Walatowas and I practiced our Portuguese with the malandros of the Borracharia, which was on the side of the road leading back to Maceió.

Thirty minutes later, a car pulled up with Bebum on the passenger side. He leaned out the window looking a little white faced, and said, "This guy hit me. He came out of a side street onto the freeway and ran right into me. Alls I could do was punch it to get out ahead of him, but he hit my back wheel and my guitar."

Later, I saw Banano's heartbreaking photo of Bebum standing there on the side of the road with his busted guitar. His shoulders slope and his eyes are full

---

[24] I wonder why Russia reports random violence in other countries.

of all the lonely times of the previous seven months. All he had left on this earth was B2B and his instruments.

I asked him, "You hurt man?"

"No bro, I am ok. But I have to go back to Maceió to force this guy to buy me new wheels."

"Ok, do you want me to come along? The Walatowas and Juanjo don't need me here with them. They can wait."

"Na, its ok bro."

Unbeknownst to us, Mestre had caught a ride to return from up ahead a couple of hours before, to check on Bebum. Can you imagine this bug-eyed, wild-haired, sweaty, and red-faced Santa Claus waving you down, actually, probably jumping in front of your car, *demanding* a lift? "Wait, where is Rudolf?" would have been the wrong thing to say. Once Mestre had found out that Bebum was ok he had gone back to riding on. I thought this was mighty big of Mestre, considering the inconsideration that Bebum had shown at times.

Judging by the sun it got pretty late and I knew we weren't going to catch up to Mestre that day. Three hours later, I heard "Pirataaaaaaa!" from a passing bus, and we breathed a sigh of relief[25]. We rode the couple of miles to where the accident had happened. When we caught up Bebum's bike was already functional again.

I looked up to check daylight and saw a storm as black as the night brewing. We barely made it to a rudimentary gas station with a roof and spent the next two hours waiting out the tropical deluge. When night fell, the rain remained unrelenting. We waited. After the accident, the screw-sized flats and all the other bad omens we felt that riding into this biblical storm on an unlit, potholed freeway leading to the crack capital of the world, would be tempting fate to some extent.

Sitting there listlessly, we were ready to camp in the back of the gas station, when at 8 p.m. the proprietor asked us to leave his premises. Nobody had ever done that before. Of course, if you live twenty miles south of Maceió you might want to shutter your place up once night falls, too. Especially, during a storm with a bunch of smelly hippies of dubious nationality on your door step.

So we took out our few working lights (it had been a long year), stripped down to our shorts, because it would take exactly less than one second to be drenched to the bone, and rode out into the cold, dark rain.

I asked everyone to ride against traffic on the side of the road we were on. No matter how freaky it is to look at cars speeding right at you, and you know they can't see you at all, it is better to see them coming than not. At least you could try to throw yourself into the ditch if you saw one aiming for you.

We rode for a mile. It was an endless, brutal, water needles in our faces mile. We found every water-camouflaged pot hole on the way, because are you going to swerve around in front of that oncoming truck or are you going to take your chances and see if you drop through to the other side of the world? At that point the Great Wall of China sounded kinda nice, modern day Nazi State and all.

We pulled in under an overpass. Not the best spot for this part of the world, but we simply could not continue in the rain. We were shaking from the cold, scared for our lives, and had nothing to eat all afternoon. We needed shelter.

---

[25] Try finding the right bus in the crack capital of the world in a foreign language within hours. It is easy to take this kind of skill for granted, but like everything in life, it takes practice.

After trying to warm up with some semi-dry clothes, and dealing with a hustler who tried to lure us into a gringo digesting trap, the rain relented somewhat and we rode again. Over the next mile we stopped at every restaurant, palapa, and hotel. Most of them were already closed for the night and nobody would take us in. Entirely unusual for our trip, but like I said, quite understandable considering the violent nature of this part of Brazil.

Finally, Bebum came through. He had wandered off down a sandy side street, returning just before I started to worry, and found a guesthouse run by an Italian who offered his palapa to us for free. We put up our Hammocks and slept a wet, hungry night.

The next morning, the sun greeted us with a smile so brilliant it made us think the day before was just a bad dream. We hit the road and started catching up the thirty odd miles we thought the rest was ahead of us. Riding southwards from Maceió, past gorgeous jungles, pretty turquoise bays, and over emerald rivers lifted out spirits considerably.

But although the day started out well enough, it soon seemed that it was my turn to get screwed by my gear. I was cruising behind Cam when I heard a wrenching sound from my back, and as my legs spun without resistance on my front crank I saw the chain loosely dangling on the cassette on my back wheel, and the back derailleur[26] and attendant screws merrily bouncing along behind my wheel and finally disappearing into the grass next to the road.

Let me explain this to you: The back derailleur falling off your bicycle while you are riding is like your transmission dropping out the bottom of your car while you cruise down the highway. Not something I'd recommend you try at home. Especially not with the next bike store either 200 miles ahead or 30 miles back, in the aforementioned crack capital of the world.

At first we kind of all stood around scratching our heads. The screw that held the derailleur to my frame had threaded into the metal and loosened it so that it fell off.

I said, "You think we can turn it into a Fixie?" (single speed)

Bebum said, "Don't think so, chain too long, though we could take out links. Angle is too weird. And without the derailleur…"

"Wire is definitely not going to work. You are going to have to pull me."

"Shit bro, my bike has fewer gears than yours."

"But she is prettier! In a circus sort of way."

We scratched our heads some more.

Then it came to me, "Oh, shit, I have that bag of random screws and things that I have been carrying for Mestre for 10,000 miles."

By some kind of crazy miracle one of the screws was just the right size to fit into the thread that the old screw had worked into the metal.

We jerry-rigged my bike and continued, though only at about 60% power. I did not want to move the derailleur back and forth more than I had to, but at the same time I had to manage how much pressure I put on the pedals, because, probably not independently of my break-away derailleur, my gears were slipping.

The problem had started on only two gears a few hundred miles north of Recife. I went to a quite professional bike store where they wanted 300 USD for a new drive train. Not an expense I wanted to incur three weeks from the finish. I hoped I would be able to baby my bike through the flats to Salvador. Now that seemed like a big mistake.

---

[26] Arm thingy attached to back gears that shifts those gears for you.

Still, we were happy to be riding in the sun. Especially Bebum, because he finally had a right-sized front wheel again. He still didn't have a front break, and now the tube was an inch too short for his new wheel, but in typical Bebum fashion he was all positive about the future that surely was going be smiling up ahead, just around the corner.

Of course, up ahead, just around the corner, Future, the fickle bitch, was smirking in our faces. I say this without rancor. The Walatowas, Bebum, and I were halfway through a gorgeous coconut hamlet, when I heard a loud BANG from Bebum's bike. I saw his front tube explode out to the side and rip the tire off the wheel. The ten miles since morning had done the inch-too-short tube in.

We stopped to see if Bebum could fix his problem and started harvesting Coconuts. That day I learned how to crack open coconuts using nothing more than the ancient, yet effective, industrially deconstructed method of banging coconut on ground. It's an Arnold thing.

Finally, Bebum was, if not confident of his fix, good to go. We started riding, and faced the first uphill of the day. We assumed that Juanjo was waiting at the top of the gentle incline of maybe 400 feet, a hill we usually wouldn't even notice. Except if your front tube is an inch short and your gears are worn to the bone.

What did I learn from all this? It really sucks when you bite into your handlebar because the chain slips when you put any pressure on your pedals. The hill reduced my available gears from nine to four. About halfway up I stopped trying to ride, got off, and started running my bike. Bebum was behind me.

Thirty seconds later, I heard a loud BANG! Yep, tube went again. We walked out bikes to the rest stop at the top of the hill.

I said, "First let's eat some over-priced food."

Juanjo showed us were we could get some grub. Then we talked about what to do.

I asked, "Any news from anyone up ahead?"

Juanjo said, "Just Tora on Whatsapp says how it serves you right that your gears are falling apart because you are mean."

"Wow, that's a little harsh."

"He tells you good luck with the rolling hills up ahead."

Later I found out it was Mariano playing one of his more inappropriate childish pranks via Tora's Whatsapp. However shitty the group vibe was, the pertinent info in the communication was *rolling hills*. My gears were definitely not going to carry me up and down those.

Bebum said, "Well, I have to stay here and try to catch a ride to the next town. My tubes just won't hold."

I said, "Ok that works, we can go fix our bikes together there."

I knew Bebum didn't have the 20 Reals to buy a new tube. I figured I would get myself a new chain and a cassette and a tube for Bebum. In these moments you would be an asshole if you got mad at your bro for not having any resources to take care of his business.

Bebum asked me, "Do you want to stay back and catch the ride with me, Pirata?"

The Walatowas and Juanjo looked at me as I pondered this option. I hadn't ridden in a car since the Shuking-all-Night-Long incident in Baja California. The idea was still as asinine as then.

"No, there is no way in hell that I am getting into a car 500 kilometers from Salvador."

"But bro, you are not going to be able to ride."

"I don't give a shit, if I have to run up every hill between here and Salvador, I am not driving. I am finishing this the way I started it. With my ass in the saddle!" Also somewhat theatrical, if you ask me, but it seems I must own the sometimes melodramatic Siegfried within.

And so I ran. The next forty kilometers led through endless sugar cane plantation. Tora/Mariano did not lie. It was one hill after the other. Two hundred feet up and two hundred feet down followed by, well, two hundred feet up and two hundred feet down. Since I had no gears to pedal with, I coasted downhill, making my 6'1" frame on a large bike with bags strapped to every possible surface as small as I could (not very), and then rolled up the next hill, also without pedaling. When the bike stopped rolling I jumped off and ran it to the top.

When your gears slide you try to glide

The Walatowas and Juanjo gave me a head start and overtook me about twenty hills later. Surprisingly, I was not running up those hills much slower than they were riding. Just goes to show you that riding uphill with an eighty-pound bike is more of a long-term proposition.

I never saw Bebum pass me in a car, because a) it's easy to miss a pickup speeding past, and b) I was busy running.

Four hours later I caught up with Mestre. I did not punch Tora/Mariano. Bebum never showed up.

Bahia
Date: September 10th, 2014
Location: Bahia

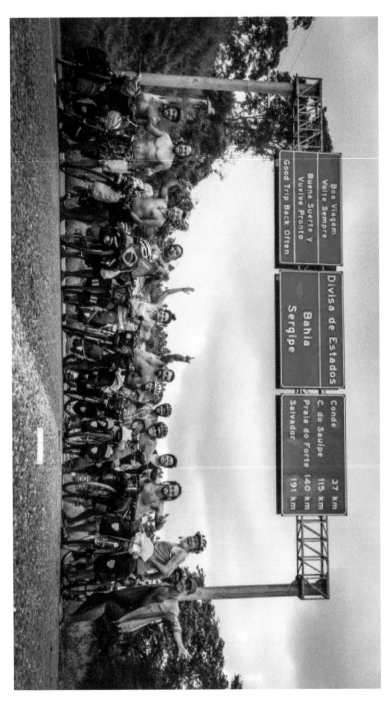

On this day in September, one year after leaving Berkeley, B2B stood at the *Divisaó* (state border) to Bahia. We had arrived in Capoeira's and Mestre Acordeon's homeland. After riding for nearly thirteen months we were about to traverse the hallowed ground that all Capoeiristas dream of visiting.

Strange, how the timing worked out. In Cali we went so slow that Bebum and I thought the journey would take at least two years. Instead Bebum wasn't around and the journey turned out to be exactly the year that Mestre had planned. It felt good to think back to Baja California, the brutal mountain rides past the volcanoes of Central America, the Colombian gangsters, and the Amazon.

We took the picture above lined up across the road right on the border to Bahia under the sign that said 191 kilometers to Salvador. I think most of us still have that picture as our computer background. We look happy, accomplished, and boisterous.

In reality those were the toughest days of the entire journey. All of us suffered under a year of continuous riding, training capoeira, and shooting film. Not having a home, sleeping on concrete, tiles or dirt for a year, and never eating right while doing some of the toughest things a human can do, took its toll.

To this day, it amazes me that eight of us made it all the way from Berkeley to Bahia, and that Mestre and Mestra found the willpower to push themselves on and on, despite their ailing bodies and many stressful moments as leaders of a regular ragtag bunch of whackos.

Of course, Mestre would not have it any other way. Both the challenge and the whackos. He loves those on the margins, those who have been dealt a tough hand - Capoeira does, too. And of course only a ragtag bunch of whackos is, well, whack enough to ride halfway around the world, even in the name of a good cause. There is no time like now to eat some crickets and ride bike for a few thousand miles.

Bebum and Tora are missing in the picture and that weighed heavy on our minds. Tora was riding by himself because he felt too stressed to be around people, and Bebum was still gone since Maceió a week earlier. I quieted my worried mind by telling myself he was going to be ok, that he had been missing for much of the trip, and that he had never communicated much.

Back in Mexico, when Bebum stayed behind in Guadalajara, Mestre had asked me nearly every other day, "Pirata, my friend, have you heard anything from Bebum?"

Your heart just does a little blissful flip-flop when you get to sit next to Poseidon and he is in old man, scratchy voice, comfortable attention mode, "No Mestre, I am sorry. I'll try to reach him again."

"Okay," Mestre had managed to sigh.

Bebum had always popped up again on my FB Messenger with some insane story like surviving by harvesting and selling coconuts on the beach, riding a bareback horse that he borrowed from a girl in northern Nicaragua.

But when Bebum continued disappearing without communicating, Mestre stopped asking.

However much Bebum was gone throughout the trip, I did not understand why he would bail now. I certainly wanted to ride into Salvador side by side with my brothers and sisters. My friends told me it's because he really didn't give a shit, but I didn't believe it. I thought something had happened to him.

Bebum's Mestre, Jamaika was also worried. He had already been calling police stations and hospitals around Maceió for a few days to no avail. He knew

Bebum best and he was putting pressure on me to get Mestre Acordeon to do something.

After a week of waiting I told Mestre Acordeon that I thought we should take action. He agreed, and we cast the net by writing a letter to the Capoeira Mestres we had visited along the coast in recent weeks, asking them to have their people look out for a dreadlocked white boy hippie on a circus bicycle. We had contacts to some special force and asked them for help, too. We hoped that Mestre's reputation would help us turn up any kind of news.

Tora, on the other hand, had been acting up the entirety of the trip. Picking fights with Capoeira Professors, B2B members, and random people all along the trip. I remember when he told Professor Mata Mosquito, "you are stupid," when Mata was working on Mestre's bike in Mexico City. He is lucky to be alive after that, is all I am going say. Since Tora had also been OK during his numerous disappearances, we decided to count our blessings and enjoyed the peace.

This was our situation when we took that picture at the border to Bahia. After Mestre asked us in Fortaleza to stick together and stop partying, first his lieutenant and half the group goes to get sky-high for a couple of weeks, and then the two biggest sources of worry on the journey simply go poof into thin air and disappear, yet again. You can imagine the black mood the old man was in on most of those days.

Rightfully so, in my opinion, it's ridiculous to put him through this considering that we got to go because of him. Most of us were aware of this and so we tried to deal with the situation as best we could. But Mestre's moods are powerful and they affected all of us. As a result, the conflicts amongst team members grew more pronounced because we fed of his more acerbic mood just as much as of his comfy gramper energies.

Even his kids, who helped us organize our arrival in Salvador felt the heat a bit. In Brazil, but especially closer to Salvador, I was the link between Mestre and his daughter Paulinha and his son Sanfona in Salvador, probably because I had the most reliable cell service. My WhatsApp conversations with Paulinha often went something like this.

Paulinha, "*Oi Pirata, como vai meu bem?*" (how is it going?)

Pirata "*Ugh, tudo tranquilo. Estou cansado irmã!*"

"Oh, you are tired? Did Mestre make you ride again at 4.30 a.m. in the morning?" (she calls her father Mestre)

"Yep, it's really difficult right now. We ride all day, at his lightning speed (haha) then we find some shitty pousada, eat, sleep, and ride again at 4.30 a.m."

"Can I talk to him?"

"Sure you can talk to him, but he just yelled at us for not cleaning up after ourselves and not giving enough of a tip."

"Uh, he's in a bad mood?"

"You know…"

"OK, I'll try later."

"*Beijos*"

If his own daughter doesn't want to talk to him on a bad day, you can imagine that Mestre's vibes felt a little bit like taking an acid bath to those who were actually beside him.

Mestre Acordeon's passion was always Capoeira itself. He was never interested in having a large Capoeira group and thereby making a lot of money. He sleeps, eats, and dreams Capoeira. For this reason, the Capoeira world recognizes his leadership. An unfortunate event on B2B would have made him feel responsible for the mishap, even though he often told us that we were responsible for our own actions and security, and it would have overshadowed the legacy of the journey. The only thing the world of Capoeira would have remembered about B2B was the white boy who got fed to the fishes in Maceió or the Japanese Meteorologist still howling at the moon somewhere in Bahia.

Neither Bebum nor Tora granted Mestre his due respect. In Costa Rica that was fine, even though somewhat rude, but in the dangerous Northeast of Brazil their actions went beyond inconsiderate. Mestre was livid about the situation. Everybody else got to ride at 4.30 a.m.

Sic Transit Gloria Mundi
Date: September 15th, 2014
Location: Arembepe, Bahia

B2B did not pass gloriously from this world. You can't say that we cratered, but fizzled out doesn't work either. Maybe a slow descending, a continuous submerging into the earth, which also nicely sums up the state of our equipment, bodies, and minds is an appropriate way of describing it.

I don't know if my fragile equipment affected me, or my mood, but in the last days of the journey I became a complete weight control freak. I got rid of everything that I did not absolutely need. When I could no longer exert pressure, I got rid of my moldy, torn, 17,000 km bike shoes. No point carrying them if I could not pull hard on the clips anyway.

My bags were tied down as tightly as possible, as opposed to earlier, when I often rode with bags open, not caring about the additional wind resistance. I felt good about riding this way, but maybe that was just my mind taking me home in some kind of fata morgana.

As we spent less than a month following the Linea Verde from Recife on southwards through Brazil's verdant sugar bowl, we did not play a single game of Capoeira. Eight Capoeiristas ride all the way through the Americas to Bahia, and then that happens? This certainly qualifies as some kind of epic coitus interruptus in the history of the world, like flying to the Moon and then not taking a giant leap.

While I was upset that we didn't play capoeira, that we didn't sit around campfires singing songs, reciting poems, and reminiscing about all the crazy things that happened it must have been heartbreaking for Mestre to feel like he couldn't allow himself this just reward. He is quite the sentimental man, but his sentimentality goes out the door when the shit hits the fan.

It even affected one of our more stoic members, Balão. Though, in a most unexpected manner. When you travel either in diarrhea infected lands and/or long distances on a bicycle there is one thing you pay a lot of attention to: your ass.

During the final stretches of our journey we paid a lot of attention to Balão's.

It started one day, when I was riding behind him on the gently undulating Linea Verde and noticed that he was riding rather gingerly, kind of trying to stand up or sitting sideways.

I asked, "Yo Balão, you doing ok? Why are you riding funky like that?"

Balão looked away, "Uhm, yeah, I am ok. Just a little pain."

"In your ass?"

I may have enjoyed asking that question.

"Yeah man, I have this weird thing. I can't sit on it or rub against it all day long. It feels like a huge pimple."

Because I knew that Balão is more reticent than most people about his private life, I figured he would be intensely embarrassed by this. I needed to be delicate.

"You can't rub against it all day?"

"Fuck you, Pirata!"

Mariano must have heard some of this because he came riding past and asked: "What's that? Your ass is boiling over? Damn diarrhea."

Humor may not fix intractably impolite situations, but it sure makes it easier to tolerate pain. If humans didn't evolve a sense of humor, Gobi and the Gipper might have blown the world to smithereens. But with humor, they could instead laugh about that prominent birthmark on the one hand, and the inability to do basic math[27] on the other.

It was the same for B2B. When a mountain just absolutely killed all of our legs, Mestra was sure to cackle, "Well, a good thing it's all downhill to Brazil from here!" or Diego would ask for the five thousandth time if there was going to be churrasco at the end of the day.

My Spanish and Portuguese gyrations must also have been rather entertaining. Portuguese has a lot of sounds that a Central European tongue isn't built for. All those *ninhos*, *beijos*, and *Xburgers* are a bitch to properly let slide of your tongue. What's an Xburger you ask? Well, of course it's a *ScheesseBurrgér*. Now, say X-Men.

Whatever scheet we were in, didn't look half as bad once we laughed at it. Of course, Balão's Boil was to be a different story. As we rode towards Salvador we accepted his wish to not publicly discuss it. We all had a number of ailments but there is only so much sharing people want to do about their backs, knees, wrists, digestive tracts, and nightly cramps.

It was the third last day of riding. After tomorrow's 60 miles short ride to Mestre Orelha in Arembepe, only twenty miles to Salvador remained.

I was trying to keep up with the group while running. The only one slower than I was Balão, and Mariano, who stayed with him.

At lunch, we were eating at a roadside when Mestre and Balão arrived in the back of a pickup truck. It's never good when one of us is in a car instead of on their bikes. If Mestre is in the truck with someone, it's really not good.

Mestre said to Mestra, "Balão passed out on the side of the road, and…"

Mestra interrupted him, "Woah, why is Balão passing out? What's wrong with him?"

Mestre said, "Mariano was riding with him for a long time, was actually pulling Balão up and down some hills with some rope. But at some point, Balão couldn't go anymore."

Mestra, "But why the hell is he passing out?"

Mestre, "Well, apparently he has a boil."

Mestra made like a question mark and Mestre continued, "Meninho de Rua[28] here, offered to take us to a hospital. You guys go to the next town and wait there for us."

It speaks to our experience level that we just went back to eating and cracking jokes about Balão's Boil as soon as they were gone. What else are you going to do, cry about it? We needed calories.

---

[27] Though "Tear down this wall Mr. Gorbatchov" still gives me the chills. You had to have been growing up 50 miles from the Iron Curtain to feel that. Thank you.

[28] Only in Brazil will an adult with a house in Salvador and one on the Linea Verde be called Streetboy.

A few hours later, Balão and Mestre came back to the small seaside town with Meninho who had generously offered us shelter.

That night we had a meeting to discuss our arrival in Salvador. As few times as we formally met at the beginning of the trip this had now flopped to the flipping opposite. We seemingly had a meeting every other day and Mestre usually found something to yell at us for.

We weren't clean enough, we took over too much space, he already knew that we weren't going to reimburse our host appropriately for all the water, gas, and internet we use (and toilets we clog), and finally, Mestre yelled at Balão, "Balão, when you have a boil on your butt you have to tell us. You can't keep it to yourself. You have to tell us."

Mariano giggled.

"Your boil affects us all."

We giggled.

Still, the circumstances weighed heavy on us. That same night, Mestre and I stood on the roof top of Meninho's house trying to make phone calls to organize some help for Bebum. We were frustrated, because I did not have enough credit on my phone to make calls. In Brazil long-distance phone calls are very expensive and my chip was from São Luís. I had just loaded ten Reals and it was gone three seconds after connecting. Ten Reals lasts for a week if all you do is WhatsApp and Facebook, but not for a long-distance call.

In the end there were no news. Neither the Special Forces nor anyone else had found anything. Bebum was gone.

The next day, I felt melancholy. This magical year was about to end. Even if I would go on another bicycle journey in the future it would not be in a group, or with Mestre Acordeon.

Of course, no matter how sad I felt about the end of the journey, my drive train still sucked the living daylight out of every quasi-push on the pedal.

Now Tora's perfectionism paid dividends, as his bicycle was riding just like on the first day. Mine, not so much. But he didn't laugh at me for not having replacement parts, the same way I had words of encouragement for him when his knee started giving out under all the weight he carried. We might want to fight about stupid raisins and hill-babies, but we still tried to have each other's backs in the end.

Still, no matter how tough the last days were, I always remembered how glad I was that I had had the courage to quit my job. I remembered the joys, the love, and the friendship as well as the dangers and the tribulations, which probably held more lessons than all the good parts.

We had to face that this amazing journey was coming to an end. Thinking about what to do after this endless summer was strange and scary for us. For a year we planned nothing. We got up every morning, rode south, and waited to see what would happen that day. Now, this had to change.

One night, I had a conversation with Mestre in a small seaside palm grove in Bahia. If you came across our camp you'd see ten hammocks strung between palm trees, a bunch of bikes locked together in a pile and Mestre and I contemplating the end of the road. The gang had gone to scrounge up some food in the sleepy village.

Now, that I think back to those days, it amazes me how little rest we took. We never just kicked back at the end of a day of riding. Tuchegas logged videos, Mariano, Banano, and Balão shot scenes. Diego edited film, Tora unpacked and repacked. I collected material from the group to post on Facebook or use in articles and looked for internet. And we still had to make dinner, fix bikes, and prepare for sleep.

Mestre sat in the hammock next to me and said, "Piratata, how are you doing?"

"I'm good Mestre. Better than Balão's boil."

"Hah, Balão!"

We giggled. I like those self-reflective moments with Mestre.

"I can't believe you yelled at him for that."

Mestre smiled sheepishly.

"Piratata, I don't know what I am going to do the next few weeks. I am so tired and I have so many things to work on."

"Yeah Mestre, we've been riding for a long time. Remember how happy we were when we left the USA in Tijuana?"

Mestre sighed, "Seems like a lifetime ago."

"It is for me Mestre. You know how much this trip has impacted me and I am sure the more time I have to think about things the more I will learn. In fact, I am thinking of writing a book, make something out of those silly blog posts."

"That's great Piratata!"

"I might finally get a couple of lessons into that thick head of mine."

Mestre chuckled, "You know you are one of my favorite writers. I am sure the book is going to be fantastic."

Wow. I mean WOW. Did Mestre just say that to me?

"Thank you Mestre, I hope you will like it, especially after you help me to not sound like an asshole half the time. But what's bugging you?"

"Ah, you know Piratata. I am just an old man with too many problems and a sore behind. If my body wouldn't hurt so much, I'd just keep on riding."

"Let's do B2A. Mariano and I have been talking from day one to keep going in Asia. Or maybe B2E. There is tons of Capoeira in Europe."

We paused, looking at our bikes. It was a beautiful thought. Instead of having to face the real world we would just ride into our respective sunsets.

"That would be nice. But I can't do that. You know, the school back home is not doing so well. Fewer students are returning and we are having some other problems, too. Projéto Kirimuré needs a lot of my attention. But the real problem is without UCA there is no Projéto Kirimuré. We fund all those kids through what we make in the academia."

"Sounds like a ton more than I ever would want to take on."

"Hah, Piratata, I feel the same way. I think Suelly and I will need to get a roommate when we get back to Berkeley."

Wtf? The biggest Mestre in the world of Capoeira, the Socrates of our art, needs to get a roommate to pay rent. While at the same time there are people who have their adaba in a bunch because their Mestre followed his dream of understanding Capoeira better.

Mestre said, "And then there is B2B. I finally have to actually make something out of all the film we shot."

"How much do we have Mestre?"

"Too much, Piratata," he said laughing ruefully, "Maybe ten Terabytes. I made many mistakes along the way." (it was 15 TB)

"Well, I am assuming this is your first time directing a documentary from the back of your saddle riding across half the world. I think people will forgive you the occasional error. Plus, you are rolling with a bunch of amateurs."

"You guys have been doing a great job. But now I have all those investors who want to see results."

"Hmmm, that's true, but they understand the monumental task you've set yourself."

"Piratata, you have helped me a lot with the script and trying to establish a narrative. So you know how difficult it is to find the story line and combine that with the footage that we have."

It is always strange but also gratifying when someone who you consider to be a mentor asks for advice or simply empties their heart. This is one of the attributes that make Mestre Acordeon a special leader. He is not afraid to humanize himself.

Yet the real world was closing in. It came with, unaccustomed for us, schedules and bank accounts. Mestre leads a simple life in a small house. But after a year-long absence, UCA, Projéto Kirimuré, and the B2B documentary seemed on the verge of imploding.

There was nothing to do but to keep on riding. You can imagine that Mestre Orelha's tranquil beach-front Bed & Breakfast in deceptively relaxed Arembepe was more than welcome. We nevertheless continued our acerbic ways and fought over who slept where, who would donate how much for their specific sleeping privilege, while holding Banano back from punching Tora. It made me want to go back to war room meetings at Microsoft. At least there I got paid to watch egos dance.

Like in Recife, I stayed away from people the following days other than to shoot film with Mariano and Mestre Beiramar, who had come to help us finish the documentary. We slept and trained in Mestre Orelha's academia and generally tried to not rip each other's heads off.

One night we took a class with tall and powerfully muscled (like someone tossed clay at him and it stuck) Mestre Orelha, a wonderfully warm and intimidating man with a rumble of a voice. You are always afraid of his hugs because you don't know if you will emerge again.

Towards the end of the class, Mestre Acordeon climbed up the tight stairs to the beautiful dark wood-floored academia. Mestre Orelha immediately stopped the class to offer the more senior Mestre the opportunity to teach or speak some words. Mestre waived off with his smiling show of unimportance.

During our stay, not a second would go by without Mestre Orelha and Mestre Acordeon matching each other with gratitude and humility. It was beautiful to see these two accomplished and respected men treat each other this way. The lesson was that you are never too old, smart, or powerful not to profit from humility towards your fellow humans. It is the wise man that learns from the fool. I'll need a lot more time to try to be a bit more like that.

At the end of class Mestre Orelha said, "*Agora, todo mundo vai jogar comigo!*"

He wanted to play all of us. Mariano asked, "*O Senhor, ão mesmo tempo?*"

Mestre nodded his head, grinning devilishly, he really did want to play everyone at the same time. We wondered if he actually meant for us to try and hit him or if it was supposed to be like one of those wannabe Kung-Fu master videos of a guy blowing on thirty dudes and they all fly away like leaves, except they are kind of running backwards.

Then Mestre Acordeon said, "*Eu vou jogar!*" (I will play)

He had this strange fire in his eye.

Mestre Orelha, looked at him, stood back and said, "*Com certeza, o Senhor!*" (Of course)

Now I kinda crapped my pants. We played, everybody jinga'd in that little place and Mestre flowed amongst all of us.

He punched, kicked, or leg-swept every single one of us within seconds. I had never seen anything like it in my life. The seventy-year-old Santa Claus hit me in the nose with the flat of his hand before I could even think to laugh at Tora getting kicked five times on the other side of the room just a moment before. The whole thing lasted seconds and when we were done Mestre was the happiest in months. The rest of us nursed bruises. Mestre Orelha stood with a thoughtful smile on his face.

Two days later Bebum sent us an email. He had been on an island at a Music Festival and wanted to join us again. In response, Mestre informed Bebum that he was no longer a part of B2B, and that was the end of that.

Last, but never Least
Date: September, 20th, 2014
Location: Salvador, Bahia

We rode into Salvador, Bahia on a glorious Saturday, September 20th 2014. 385 days after we left Berkeley. The sun smiled upon us and the sea breeze cooled us. The kids from Projéto Kirimuré, Paulinha, and Sanfona welcomed us with a grand party. Many of the old and old-school Régional Capoeiristas that Mestre came up with awaited us and even Ailton, from the Capoeira movie Besouro was there. We sang songs, danced in a big circle, listened to speechifying, and watched the kids ride our bikes around the park. We were in a daze.

Soon we made our way to Projéto Kirimuré in Itapuã, a sprawling, sometimes lethal, neighborhood of Salvador. We were part of a large procession including a fantastically loud Batucada (Brazilian drum line). You can't have a party in Brazil without a bunch of dudes beating on their drums.

Kids from Projéto Kirimuré welcome B2B.

Most of us had a Kirimuré kid riding on our saddles, on our handlebars or both while we pushed our bikes through the streets.

Why we rode

The festivities continued at Projéto Kirimuré with honors being made and given to the Mestres. We had a roda with Mestre Acordeon, Mestra Suelly, Mestre Boa Gente, and Mestre Balão. The kids played all of us. Grand donations to Projéto Kirimuré were made and accepted. Mariano cried when he said a few words. I cried all the time. And then we went to sleep.

It seems anti-climactic. After a year of none-stop physical exertion all we wanted to do was lie down. The crew around Tuchegas and Diego was bunking with some UCA folks who had flown down from Berkeley for the event. A couple of days after arriving, Tuchegas told me, "These guys always want to do something. But if I don't have to ride I just want to sleep."

We spent the next two weeks doing various functions at Projéto Kirimuré. The schedule wasn't grueling, except for Mariano, who constantly seemed to have to film something. I felt bad for him, but I stayed away. Mestre was still in a black mood most of the time.

I didn't mind lying down a lot myself and sort of fell into a kind of post-grand-toil syndrome. I didn't want to leave the house and spent the days sleeping in hammocks, cooking, eating, smoking, drinking, and writing. All of it therapeutic. Strangely, I did the same over the next three months in Brazil. The longer I kept moving from city to city the less energy I seemed to have for the usual joys of traveling. I'd go into town once, and out at night another time, but that was it. No more exploration for me. It seems, I had my fill of it.

After arriving in Itapuã, we had split into the usual three groups. Mestres stayed at Projéto Kirimuré. Mariano, the Chilangos, Walatowas, and I stayed at Meninho de Rua's house ten minutes from PK, which funnily yet logically, had exactly the same floor plan as his other house.

Amber, started staying with my group (Juanjo) a lot. Soon after the journey they moved to Rio together and made an actual B2B-Baby. Doesn't get any better than that as an affirmation of B2B and Amber's healing, which, while not conducted in public certainly progressed throughout the last few months of B2B. The two were to make their lives in Rio de Janeiro after the trip and apart from myself were the only ones who continued a life away from home.

One night, Bebum showed up at the house. We were in a quandary because Mestre had forbidden Bebum to benefit from tagging along with B2B, which is what staying at the house was. But Bebum was still our brother and we weren't about to kick him out on the night street of one of the most dangerous hoods north of Rio. He may have counted on that.

The next day he insisted on going to PK, despite Mariano and I pleading with him not to force the issue. But he didn't listen and made Mestre shake his hand in front of the kids and the news cameras that were present to film Mestre that day.

These seemingly trivial events cast a pall over the end of a journey of a life time. I still do not enjoy thinking about the end, but now, after writing this somewhat cathartic book, the amazingly positive parts overwhelm any negative memories.

Other than hanging out with the kids from Kirimuré and teaching them how to play flute we did two amazing things in Salvador. Firstly, we trained at Filhos de Bimba, Mestre Bimba's son's academia in the Pelourinho in Salvador.

Pelourinho, Salvador

Secondly, we made true on a promise that we had given each other at the beginning of the journey. We bought some cachaça, found the dingiest tattoo parlor in the ghetto, and got B2B tattoos.

B2B Tattoos, made in Itapoâ

Post Scriptum: Privilege Requires Responsibility
Date: September 20ᵗʰ, 2015
Location: Phoenix, Arizona

Here follow the things I learned while I spent a year riding bicycle with Mestre Acordeon. I attribute these lessons of life, love, and luta (fight) to Mestre's generosity of spirit and audacious vision.

The world is a beautiful place and every human in it is beautiful. Nature made us perfect to be happy. Yet our societies are far from perfect. One can not but notice this while riding bicycle for 12,000 miles.

Our lives could unfold a little happier were we to follow a few small strategies that connect us to our communal heritage:

Be kind, open, and honest. Respect your elders because they teach you. Be helpful to them and all others. Eat the food that nature evolved you to eat. Just because you can eat like a trashcan, doesn't mean you have to. Walk everywhere. Ok, you don't need to walk. Ride your bicycle though.

Never stop learning and never hate feeling stupid. Embrace stupid. This will enable you to expand in all directions until your very last beautiful day. Being

OK with being stupid also helps you check your ego. Which itself is made easiest by living in a tribe instead of an ego-bliss bunker. In a tribe you can't hide.

Play Capoeira.

Do all of this in moderation. Except the kindness. There can never be enough love in this world.

Some of us hit the geographic jackpot and were born in a developed country. A white man from Austria grows up with much more opportunity than a person of color, or a woman anywhere. Be kinder to those less fortunate than you.

For generations these geo-birth-lottery winners have taken resources from the losers. The winners promoted their own societies through investments in education, industry, healthcare, and science. This has led to great advances, and great imbalances.

While today's wealthy societies are not to be blamed for the misdeeds of previous generations, we now know that might, makes not right. It is as unacceptable to kill and steal on an individual level as it is on a nation-state level. We bear this responsibility for our nations' actions. Because our understanding of economics and morals are of higher quality than in the past, we know that if we lift one boat the whole fleet rises.

We also do not believe in a Darwinian competition of races anymore because we know that as small as the genetic difference between a chimpanzee and a human is, the genetic difference between human races is smaller than your chances of flying to Alpha Centauri. Instead we recognize what Darwin would have told us, "We are a species elevated above other animals by a small amount of self-awareness, yet we remain unaware of our position as part of an immutable system."

This forces us to recognize our shared human nature and the moral obligation to help the children of those whom our forefathers condemned to a life of serfdom.

While all humans do well to promote love of each other and life in general, our single most important responsibility is to fight against our own inner demons. We must fight our fears. We must overcome our egos.

Our egos make us fear that there is not enough. Our egos are never satisfied. One TV is not enough. One roof is not enough. One car is not enough. It is a never ending spiral, unless we snap out of it and control that voice in our head that screams, "More, more, more! Just in case we need it one day."

For what? One day that fourth TV is going to make me coffee in the morning? That third roof will cure my cancer? That second car will enable me to love my children better?

Our forefathers thought we must take the wealth of the Americas and use it for our own, ostensibly holier purposes. Our grandparents thought we must keep our gene pool clean for our own, ostensibly more evolved purposes. Today we think we must take the oil from the Middle East for our own, ostensibly more civilizational purposes.

Instead, a sharing of knowledge and resources will enable all humans to profit from each other. Even though we may not be born equal in our opportunities, all human beings are born equal in our rights. To give all humanity access to these rights requires a reversing of historical injustices.

Riding bicycle for a year affords ample time to consider the things that are important: Time or money? Friendship or possessions? Being right or loving right?

You may think that this year must have changed us, that obvious proof must be visible. But there is none. Today we live in the real world, like everyone else. We teach, we study, we repair, we cook, we write.

To see the change, you'd have to look inside our hearts and minds. There now resides a simple knowledge of our own happiness, and an eternal yearning for the freedom of the open road.

It is the greatest cause for gratitude to Mestre Acordeon that he enabled us to be free for one year. Free of our world and free of our selves.

Now go ride your bicycle. Don't even go anywhere. Just ride.